Common Dilemmas
in Couple Therapy

Common Dilemmas in Couple Therapy

JUDITH P. LEAVITT

Routledge
Taylor & Francis Group
New York   London

Routledge   Routledge
Taylor & Francis Group   Taylor & Francis Group
270 Madison Avenue   27 Church Road
New York, NY 10016   Hove, East Sussex BN3 2FA

© 2010 by Taylor and Francis Group, LLC
Routledge is an imprint of Taylor & Francis Group, an Informa business

Printed in the United States of America on acid-free paper
10 9 8 7 6 5 4 3 2 1

International Standard Book Number: 978-0-415-99990-8 (Hardback) 978-0-415-80001-3 (Paperback)

Library of Congress Cataloging-in-Publication Data

Leavitt, Judith P.
    Common dilemmas in couple therapy / by Judith P. Leavitt.
        p. ; cm.
    Includes bibliographical references and index.
    ISBN 978-0-415-99990-8 (hardback : alk. paper) -- ISBN 978-0-415-80001-3
    (pbk. : alk. paper)
    1. Couples therapy. I. Title.
    [DNLM: 1. Couples Therapy--methods. 2. Patient Compliance. 3. Treatment
    Refusal. WM 430.5.M3 L439c 2009]
    RC488.5.L42 2009
    616.89'1562--dc22   2009007489

Visit the Taylor & Francis Web site at
http://www.taylorandfrancis.com

and the Routledge Web site at
http://www.routledgementalhealth.com

To my dear father, Hart Day Leavitt,
who taught me the importance of humanism,
human character, and good writing.

Acknowledgments

A primary acknowledgment goes to Dean Abby, director of Continuing Education at the Massachusetts School of Professional Psychology, for his immeasurable support of my basic concepts for this book and for giving me the opportunity to develop my ideas through my teaching. This book would not have happened without the opportunities he gave me.

I also want to acknowledge the great support of my partner, George Hecker, through this writing and publishing process. He helped me with his input, support, patience, and insights.

Many thanks to my brother, Ned Leavitt, for his help in the contracting process.

My gratitude to Gina Ogden and Erlene Rosowsky for helping me find a publisher.

There are some special colleagues I wish to acknowledge, including Carol Cole, Lance Fiore, Aurelie Goodwin, and Starr Potts. I have shared clients over the years with each of them. Thanks to all of them for their amazing insights and their support during our work with difficult and exciting couples. They helped me in the development of the ideas and strategies that make up this book. I also want to acknowledge the important support and sharing of ideas and clients with the following colleagues: Marjorie Green, Paul Karofsky, Raquel Perlis, and Wendy Sobel.

Special thanks to my trusty local librarians, especially Andy Moore, who always seemed to find a way to get me the resources I needed.

I am indeed indebted to my editors, Dawn Moot, Marta Moldvai, George Zimmar, and Iris Fahrer for their support and their belief in my book. Thanks for seeing me through this process.

Author

Judith P. Leavitt, Ed.D. is a senior clinician, licensed psychologist, and diplomate-certified sex therapist with more than 30 years of clinical experience. She teaches Couples Therapy and Human Sexuality at the Massachusetts School of Professional Psychology in Boston, Massachusetts. For over a decade, she taught at the Smith School of Social Work. Dr. Leavitt frequently speaks at mental health centers, hospitals, and professional conferences. In addition to her therapy work, for more than ten years Dr. Leavitt served as a senior consultant to family businesses throughout the world with Transition Consulting Group. She taught family business at the Boston University School of Management. Dr. Leavitt is also a trained diversity consultant and was a trainer at Bell Atlantic.

Contents

SECTION IV   The Breakup of a Couple Relationship

Introduction

How am I going to help this couple get through this betrayal, this pain?
Can I help this couple navigate through this chaos to a place of connection and forgiveness?
What do I do when a couple is so entrenched and stuck?
How do I stop myself from just screaming at this partner who is so impossible?

I have left certain couple therapy sessions exhausted, drained, challenged, alive, racing, on edge. Why? The issues were complex and convoluted. Deep feelings of anger, hurt, and fear were rippling through my office. The clients' hearts were torn and my heart was heavy. My capacity to hold troubling relationships and the deepest level of my skills were challenged. My couples and I were wrestling with dark perplexing issues that go to the heart of the conundrum of intimacy: how to be attached and yet remain separate people.

I would lie awake going over the session again and again, sorting, reworking, planning, grieving, pushed to my edge. The next day, I would grab the phone to pour out my concerns to my colleagues. They knew and understood. They had been there—probably even that day. With 36 years of experience I could, in fact, handle these issues using the maximum level of my skills, wisdom, and compassion. What had I done when I had had only 5 or 10 years of experience? How do young and experienced therapists alike handle the stress and challenge of this demanding work?

I decided to put together seminars for professionals on how to work with these intense and difficult issues. For the Massachusetts School of Professional Psychology I designed a series of classes on the most common and challenging of these dilemmas. Therapists came, listened, and shared their own stories. As I taught about the dynamics of each dilemma, as I discussed strategies and focused on the therapist's roles and experiences in working with these dilemmas, there was a palpable exhale throughout the room. Couple therapists were hungry for help. Participants raved about the sessions. Participants came to more seminars. They learned from me and I learned from them. Together we recognized and struggled with these most difficult topics. My guidance sparked them and refreshed their energy and creativity.

Throughout this time, I wrote and then I wrote more. After some couple sessions I raced home and pounded out my experiences and my insights on my computer. I was on fire. I went deeper and deeper into the nature of each issue and my experiences as the therapist. My sessions were a live laboratory. I was consumed by what was happening, how it was happening, the patterns that were developing, how I found direction, how I helped people get to deep places of forgiveness, acceptance, and resolution. I was also reading everything I could get my hands on. I scoured the literature with the help of my ingenious local librarian, who had a way to find books in East Oshkosh. I found helpful related books, but I also discovered that no one had written what I was writing. This spurred me on.

My book developed from this journey. This book is about four common dilemmas that couple therapists face every day in their offices: (1) dealing with a difficult partner; (2) secrets; (3) dealing with a partner who won't/can't change; and (4) the breakup of a couple relationship. There is a clear void of material on how couple therapists can work effectively with these topics. This book is unique in addressing these four issues that are not often explored in depth in couple therapy books and trainings. Out of each dilemma poured the snakes, the passions, and the profound disappointments of human intimate partnerships. The purpose of this book is to (1) deeply explore the dynamics of each dilemma and give case illustrations; (2) give therapists the lifelines of many strategies to use in working with these difficulties; and (3) help couple therapists understand and handle their own profound experiences while doing this work.

The dilemmas are four disturbing, confounding, and complex issues that penetrate the dark and often ugly side of human intimate partnerships. They are about betrayal, resistance, and deep loss. Yet they are also about breakthroughs, transformation, and healing. In this book, I rip open the hurt, the meanness, and the helplessness that come with these experiences. I describe couples who are desperate, who hurt each other, and who give up on each other. I also discuss couples who, against all odds, probe into themselves, learn from each other, and grow closer. The road to healing is daunting to the couple and the therapist. The intricacy and nuances of working with the steps to healing are presented through the various therapy strategies laid out for each dilemma. Many case vignettes are presented. The vignettes and case studies illustrate couples caught in the middle of the dilemmas struggling with the pain, anger, and helplessness that these predicaments bring. They also show strategies that help the couples move to new places of understanding, growth, and forgiveness.

I show the crucial professional role that couple therapists can play in guiding a couple to healing, hope, and renewal. As the therapist, you need to play many roles in working with these dilemmas: supporter, confronter, witness, navigator, referee, container, leader, guide, director. You need to give your clients limits, direction, warnings, meaning, deep wisdom, and reassurance. Thus, you need to be versatile and flexible, often changing roles a number of times in a session. The dilemmas presented demand a high level of skill, balance, patience, compassion, wisdom, and stamina. Most of all, you need to provide balance at a time when couples are usually very out of balance. This requires you to hold the couple and to see the larger picture of their relationship beyond the issue or crisis that is present in the room.

Throughout this work the therapist's feelings and experiences must be recognized and addressed. As the therapist, you must often operate on all cylinders and at full attention. Your own emotions as well as the clients' can be raw and draining. The book explores the therapist's feelings as a way to validate and normalize what you are going through and alert you to experiences that, if left unattended, may interfere with the couples work. For example, if a couple is breaking up, you may have an investment in their staying together, particularly if you have worked with them for a long time. If a couple is stuck, you may take on too much responsibility for their work and not address their responsibility. Recognizing these experiences can help you move beyond them.

Although this work is very difficult, it is also potentially very rewarding. For example, helping a couple find their way through a betrayal to a place of healing, openness, and trust is a deeply touching and fulfilling experience. When the couple you thought could not possibly get beyond blaming and attacking finds understanding and caring through the therapy sessions, your faith in your work and in relationships is restored. This work can bring out the best and most knowledgeable parts of our professional (and personal) selves. We need help getting there. Going to colleagues is necessary for survival and success. Finding resources to give you direction and ideas is essential. I wrote this book to help couple therapists with this demanding and deeply moving work.

The theoretical approach of this book is phenomenological. There are two main branches of phenomenology: transcendental phenomenology, developed primarily by Edmund Husserl (1859–1938) and existential phenomenology, influenced primarily by the writings of Martin Heidegger (1889–1976). Transcendental phenomenology focuses on perception.

In his book *The interpreted world: An introduction to phenomenological psychology*, Spinelli (1989) writes, "… the objects which we perceive (including, of course, the people we interact with, as well as ourselves) exist in the way that they exist, through the meaning that each of us gives them" (p. 3). Our reality develops from the processing of the meaning and the interpretation that we give to something. Existential phenomenology is primarily concerned with existence as experienced by humans as individuals and with key themes of existence such as freedom, authenticity, aloneness, and nothingness.

Spinelli (1989) draws from both branches of phenomenology in his description of phenomenological psychology. Concerning the integration of the two branches Spinelli (1989) writes, "… in the end, your conclusions as to the meaning of the painting would be dependent on which interpretations were satisfactory enough to reduce the tension you experienced as a result of your confrontation of meaninglessness" (p. 6). (Here "the painting" represents any object we perceive.)

Spinelli (1989) describes phenomenological psychology as the study of an individual's conscious experience of the world: "Phenomenological psychology places the analysis of our conscious experience of the world as its primary goal" (p. 31). Personal subjective experience free of biases is its central concern. Each person is unique and sees the world in his or her own way. Awareness is central and grows from contact with the environment, sensing with all senses and integrating perception into meanings according to Kirchner (2000). Fulfilling one's potential, a goal of phenomenological therapy, happens through not adapting to one's social norms, but by expanding one's perceptions and possibilities. It is through experience that we learn.

Since phenomenology holds that there is no way to know exactly what is true, the goal is to understand the relativity of each person's (or culture's) perceptions and meanings (Brazier, 1993). For example, if a group of us is in a room and someone comes in and throws a snowball at each of us, one of us may be amused, one of us may be angry, and one of us may be afraid. How each of us feels is based on what we perceive. The person who is angry may perceive the snowball thrower to be challenging and aggressive. This angry person could then attach to this perception the intention that the snowball thrower meant to hurt him or her. This is how he or she creates meaning in the situation.

Fuller (1990) writes, "Phenomenology requires the meanings ... be taken just as they present themselves in everyday life" (p. 24). Fuller continues, "... without the blinding intervention of conventional presuppositions" (p. 28). Phenomenology also involves the study of how something occurs and the bringing forth of its hidden character or being. We tend not to notice the structure of the meaning of events. Phenomenology searches for the structural patterns that run through the meaning of events.

Spinelli (1989) describes phenomenological therapy as bringing together concepts from both branches of phenomenology. The goal of the phenomenological therapist is to help individuals examine, clarify, and reassess their understanding of life and thereby gain more mastery and control over their lives. The therapist's job is to "... enter into the client's inner world in order to best clarify and expose the client's **world views** and reflectively mirror them back for consideration" (p. 128). To do this, the therapist must put aside his or her own beliefs and assumptions as much as possible in order to see the client clearly.

The therapist's work is to understand where the client begins, to help him or her become aware of his or her perceptions, and to learn how these perceptions are formed into concepts and meaning. The therapist helps the client see that what the client presents is his or her perception rather than fact. The focus of therapy is on what is revealed in the situation at that moment. The basis of psychology is the study of immediate experience and awareness. "... the therapy places strong emphasis on the immediate, here-and-now experience of both the client and the therapist" (Spinelli, 1989, p. 130). The work of therapy is to help the client's perspective shift in such a way as to open to new possibilities, discoveries, and experimentations.

Gestalt psychology was initiated by several German psychologists in the 1930s and 1940s. Gestalt psychologists studied the relationship between an object and its context or background. Zinker (1994) writes about one of the central tenants of Gestalt psychology, "... the way an object is perceived *is related to the total configuration in which it is embedded*" (p. 47). Thus, perception is determined by the relationship between components as well as by the experience of each component. Gestalt therapy was deeply influenced by phenomenology. Wheeler (1994), a Gestalt therapist, writes, "... dynamic phenomenology ... is at the heart of all Gestalt work" (p. 49). "Psychotherapeutic phenomenon (Spinelli, 1980) working close to the patient's own experience, is one of the most beautiful aspects of Gestalt work" (Beaumont, 1994, p. 85). Wheeler (1994) further describes phenomenology as "... the study of the organization of experience ... how a person's living is organized, from her or his point of view, as he or she understands it and makes sense of it" (p. 4).

Fritz Perls with his wife Laura Perls developed Gestalt therapy. Perls was influenced by many thinkers and philosophies of his time including phenomenology, Zen Buddhism, and Gestalt psychology. Perls extended principles of perception to psychology and emphasized the notion of context in human relationships. His therapy work involved focusing on immediate experience through clients' sensations and feelings in the moment. Subsequent Gestalt therapists (Zinker, 1994; Wheeler & Backman, 1994) incorporated working with couples and families into Gestalt therapy. They focused on the experiences and boundaries of relationships. Zinker (1994) writes, "The therapist validates the experience of each while encouraging both to respect the other's way of seeing a situation" (p. 184).

Thus phenomenological therapy is well geared for couple therapy. The therapist's choice of interventions is governed by what is going to elucidate the clients' perceptions and allow greater understanding of how these perceptions lead to their conceptions of reality. Further, the therapist's choice of interventions is guided by what will help the partners expand their experience.

Cognitive behavioral therapy shares many core beliefs with phenomenological therapy. They both put primacy importance on the perceptions, the process of creation of meaning, and the importance of experience in creating new meanings. Each stresses the importance of understanding the client's view of reality and the impact of the environment in the formation of the client's reality. The therapist's role in each therapy is an active one, designed to help bring about the discovery of new understandings and meanings (Baucom, Epstein, & LaTaillade, 2002; Keim & Lapin, 2002). Spinelli (1989) discusses the similarities between behaviorism and phenomenological psychology, "... both ... focus upon observation and description. ... Both phenomenology and behaviourism stress the importance of environmental stimuli as catalysts to action" (p. 173). About cognitive psychology he writes, "A great deal of what phenomenological psychology has concluded about perception, for instance, would find little dispute among cognitive psychologists" (p. 175). Various strategies presented in this book derive from cognitive behavioral therapies.

Interventions presented in this book are influenced by Gestalt therapy as developed by Fritz Perls (1969) and later by Gestalt couple and family therapists such as Sonia Nevis and Joseph Zinker. One of Perls' gifts was his work on what is happening right now. He worked with clients to focus on their sensations and feelings in that moment. The interventions in this book are also influenced by family systems therapy. Joseph Zinker (1994), a Gestalt therapist who extended Gestalt therapy work into couple and family therapy, describes the intertwining of the development of Gestalt therapy and systems work. He writes, "... the reader should be aware of the interconnectedness of systems theory, field theory and Gestalt psychology" (p. 47). Zinker was greatly influenced by such family systems therapists as Carl Whitaker and Virginia Satir.

Therapists also need to understand where they start from and what their perceptions and meaning are in order not to impose them on the clients. It is vital that the therapists be able to look beyond their own values and culture in order to separate these preconceptions and to see the clients in their own realities. Thus, the therapists are an integral part of the couple therapy and need to be aware of their experience and impact.

My approach to couple therapy also has been influenced by the work of R.D. Laing. His work was exceptional in probing through the layers upon layers of meaning in the dynamics happening in front of us. He dug into the maze of behavior and consciousness that underlies the present phenomenon. "Laing saw his task as that of deciphering the hidden meanings behind the behavior of the mentally disturbed individual ... (pp. 140–141). Laing observed and provided his presence, empathy and reassurance so that he could eventually reconstruct the individual's situation and understand the fears being defended against" (Spinelli, 1989, p. 141). The depth of Laing's search into the patterns and intricacies of the human experience taught me to appreciate the complexity of intimate relationships. The reader is referred to Laing's (1969) rich book *The divided self* as well as to Perl's (1969) intriguing book *Gestalt therapy verbatim*.

My work with couples often involves dealing with what the couple is experiencing in the room and discovering the dynamics playing out between them in the current moment. Throughout this book the influences of my training in phenomenological therapy, Gestalt therapy, family systems therapy, and cognitive behavioral therapy are evident. Each of the dilemmas I address requires an approach that probes into the essence of the issues and discovers concrete ways of working with them. The dilemmas involve multilevel dynamics, high emotions, possible betrayal, possible fragmentation of the relationship, guilt, denial, and avoidance. Central issues in each dilemma include responsibility, accountability, being stuck, resistance, and high stress. Some of these issues have been written about as issues in themselves. For example, there are books on secrets and betrayal. Yet relatively little has been written about how to deal with these particular issues in couple therapy. At the same time, secrets and betrayal are very common in couple therapy. This book is written to help couple therapists who are searching both for ways of handling these dilemmas and for support for themselves as therapists. I have written about these dilemmas because they are difficult, they are pervasive, and they require so much from the couple therapist.

The book consists of four sections: Dealing With a Difficult Partner, Secrets in Couple Therapy, Dealing With a Partner Who Won't/Can't Change, and The Breakup of a Couple Relationship. Each section has a number of chapters.

Each of the four sections of the book contains three main themes. First, the issue itself is defined. Examples, subcategories, and stages are included. Subtleties and nuances of the issues are explored. References to other writings about the dilemma are discussed. Second, extensive strategies and their application are described. These strategies are drawn from my experiences and from the above-mentioned therapeutic approaches. These strategies are often subgrouped according to the goal for the intervention. Third, the depth of feelings and challenges that the therapist experiences doing couple therapy are exposed. Cases are interwoven throughout the chapters.

Cases presented in this book are composites of case histories and do not represent any given person or couple. Further, any possible identifying information has been removed or disguised to safeguard the privacy and confidentiality of any individual or couple.

Section I is about dealing with a difficult partner. As I express in Chapter 2, "Working with difficult partners should come with a warning label: This work may be hazardous to your health. You will probably experience heart palpitations, hot flashes, twitching, uncontrollable urges to scream, aggressive tendencies, feelings of total incompetence, helplessness, and a desire to leave your profession." A difficult partner is defined as someone who obstructs the couple therapy process. How does a couple therapist survive resistance, manipulation, and blaming? How does he or she help a couple with a difficult partner become more open and more intimate? Chapter 1 explores the dynamics of the difficult partner and explores six types of difficult partners. Also included is a description of Hanna's Precursors Model of Working With Difficult Partners. The chapter concludes with examining the essence of the difficult partner's behavior. Chapter 2 is an overview of how to work with the difficult partner in couple therapy. Included are an exploration of the therapist's experience, building a connection and alliance with the difficult partner and the couple, keeping balance through a systems approach, an overview of techniques to follow, and a description of working with the essence of the difficult partner's behavior. Chapter 3 presents specific and comprehensive strategies for dealing with the three greatest challenges in working with a difficult partner in couple therapy: control issues, taking responsibility for oneself, and coming out of hiding. Many strategies in each category are described. Chapter 4 presents further strategies for working with other specific types of difficult partners in couple therapy, other therapy options, issues for the therapist, and a case study.

Section II is about secrets in couple therapy. Imagine the tortuous path of maintaining or unraveling a secret and its effect. This section about secrets dares to wrestle with one of the most intricate and loaded issues in couple relationships. I define a secret as information that is knowingly or unknowingly withheld or denied and that would be hurtful, harmful, or upsetting to one's partner. Chapter 5 explores background material on secrets including Sissela Bok's important work on secrets, issues such as privacy versus secrecy, and privacy and secrecy in an intimate relationship. The theoretical approach of this book is discussed with regard to working with secrets. Types of secrets, consequences of secrets, why couples keep secrets, and maintaining secrets are tackled in Chapter 6. Secrets are hot potatoes for couple therapists. Do we want to know them or not? What do we do with them? Chapter 7 explores dilemmas for the therapist in working with secrets in couple therapy. The therapist's experiences, who knows what about the secret in the therapy, and why therapists hold secrets are explored. Guidelines, strategies, and case illustrations are given to allow therapists to navigate through these emotional and ethical minefields in Chapter 8. Three principal strategies are given for the therapist: holding a secret, helping a secret to emerge, and confronting the lying and the secrecy. In addition, issues about revealing secrets are explored. The chapter closes with a case study.

Section III is entitled "Dealing With a Partner Who Won't/Can't Change." Is the partner in a couple not changing because he or she can't or because he or she won't? Is the cause of his or her difficulty and lack of change biological or psychological? Chapter 9 introduces a new conceptualization of issues in which there are both biological and psychological elements. They are "crossover" issues. Crossover issues share common features such as confusion about the source of responsibility and ever changing available information about their nature. This chapter grapples with how distressing and immobilizing these crossover issues can be in a couples relationship. Dynamics of crossover issues such as how the issue is seen, how the couple views the issue, how they have addressed it, and the outcome of their efforts are explored. Couple and partner issues that contribute to the couple's difficulties are discussed. Chapter 10 addresses two central dilemmas in working with a couple with a crossover issue: Does the couple therapist challenge the person with the issue or work for acceptance by the partner? How does the therapist handle his or her own feelings of helplessness and frustration? Another focus of the chapter examines what the therapist can do when the couple and the partner with the COI become stuck. Many approaches and strategies are presented. The therapist's experience is probed, case vignettes are given, and a final case study is presented.

Section IV is entitled "The Breakup of a Couple Relationship." Dealing with a couple breaking up can be one of the most difficult and draining challenges of doing couple therapy. The sessions are usually quite emotional and demanding for the couple and the therapist. The couple's world is breaking apart and turning upside down. You, as the therapist, are there to keep chaos from erupting and to guide the couple forward through a thick and overwhelming forest. Chapter 11 discusses the dynamics of a breakup. Included are the following topics: previous loss, four types of breakups, factors that contribute to a breakup, how the breakup happens, and when in the therapy it happens. For 15 years, I ran a full-day workshop for people going through a breakup of a relationship. From this work and my clinical practice, I have developed six stages that couples go through during the breakup of their relationship (plus six more stages of healing afterward). Chapter 12 delves into the six stages of breaking up and explores how the four types of breakup unfold at each stage. The therapist's experiences of grieving, holding the caldron, and bringing healing are discussed at each stage. Specific therapist roles and strategies plus case examples are emphasized. Therapists are often navigators, referees, and limit setters. Further stages of healing beyond the breakup are described. The chapter concludes with a case study.

Bibliography for Introduction

Baucom, D.H., Epstein, N., & LaTaillade, J.L. (2002). Cognitive-behavioral couple therapy. In A.S. Gurman & N.S. Jacobson (Eds.), *The clinical handbook of couple therapy* (pp. 26–58). New York: Guilford Press.

Beaumont, H. (1994) *Self-organization and dialogue*. In G. Wheeler & S. Backman (Eds.), *On intimate ground: A gestalt approach to working with couples* (pp. 83–108). San Francisco: Jossey-Bass.

Brazier, D.D. (1993). *Key concepts of phenomenological therapy*. Retrieved October 2, 2008 from http://www.amidatrust.com/article_phen.html

Fuller, A.R. (1990). *Insight into value: An exploration of the premises of a phenomenological psychology*. Albany, NY: State University of New York Press.

Keim, J. & Lappin, J. (2002). Structural/strategic marital therapy. In A.S. Gurman & N.S. Jacobson (Eds.), *The clinical handbook of couples therapy* (3rd. ed., pp. 86–117). New York: Guilford Press.

Kirchner, M. (2000). Gestalt therapy theory: An overview. *Gestalt!, 4*. 1–16.

Perls, F. (1969). *Gestalt therapy verbatim*. Lafayette, CA: Real People Press.

Perls, F. (1973). *The gestalt approach and eye witness to therapy*. Ben Lomond, CA: Science and Behavioral Books.

Spinelli, E. (1989). *The interpreted world: An introduction to phenomenological psychology*. London: Sage Publications.

Wheeler, G. (1994). The tasks of intimacy: Reflections on a gestalt approach to working with couples. In G. Wheeler & S. Backman (Eds.), *On intimate ground: A gestalt approach to working with couples* (pp. 31–59). San Francisco: Jossey-Bass.

Wheeler, G. & Backman, S. (1994) (Eds.). *On intimate ground: A gestalt approach to working with couples*. San Francisco: Jossey-Bass.

Zinker, J.C. (1994) *In search of good form: Gestalt therapy with couples and families*. San Francisco: Jossey-Bass.

Section I

Dealing With a Difficult Partner

1

Types of Difficult Partners

Introduction

As couple therapists dealing with certain partners, we often want to pull our hair out, or scream—or ask them to leave. We are helpers and healers and don't like admitting that some clients are difficult to work with—very difficult. There is the wife who relentlessly blames her husband and regularly lectures him on what a good husband really is. There is the husband who thinks he is entitled to sex and says angrily that he is being cheated because his wife, who has been sexually abused, is not giving him what he is due. There is the client who argues with you and her partner at every turn. There is the client who wants to control the session and won't let you do your job. How do you stay calm? How do you direct the session? How do you find something that will get through to the partner? How do you build an alliance with a client whose behavior is repelling? How do you maintain objectivity? How do you address the couple system when one member of the relationship stands out as the problem?

Section I, Dealing With a Difficult Partner, is comprised of four chapters about therapy with a couple with a difficult partner and about the couple therapist. It is a section meant for the therapist to read, recognize, and better understand his or her experience and discover new strategies. It is also a section to validate the couple therapist's experiences, dilemmas, confusions, and feelings of helplessness. As therapists, we need to see our mistakes, learn how to handle situations differently, and recognize when there is not much that we can do.

Chapter 1 begins with looking at various types of difficult partners. Then it gives a description of Hanna's (2002) Precursors Model of Working With Difficult Clients and concludes with examining the essence of the difficult partner's behavior. Chapters 2, 3, and 4 explore different aspects of how to deal with a difficult partner in couple therapy. Chapter 2 is an overview of the primary issues in this work, including the therapist's experiences, building a connection and alliance, keeping a systemic balance, and an overview of the strategies to follow. Chapter 3 presents a model and specific therapy strategies for working with a couple with an offensive difficult partner. Chapter 4 applies these and additional strategies to working with other various types of difficult partners, looks at other therapy options, delves into the therapist's experience in this work, and presents a case study.

I am not addressing the client who may have serious issues but wants to work, is open to learning, and uses feedback. Working with this client can also be difficult, but for very different reasons. I am addressing working with people whose behavior in some way *obstructs* the therapeutic process. As the therapist, you are not only dealing with their issues, but also with all the roadblocks they actively throw against addressing the issues. One of the client's goals may be, in fact, to prevent you from getting to the real issues.

I focus here on behavioral interactions rather than diagnoses. I refer to the work of therapists who write about Narcissistic Personality Disorder, Borderline Personality Disorder, and Passive-Aggressive Personality Disorder because clients with these disorders exhibit many difficult and obstructive behaviors that pose great challenges for couple therapists. Yet partners can be difficult and obstructive without having one of these disorders. Their obstructing may derive from other sources such as anxiety, depression, illness, relationship issues, or attachment disorders.

In this book, my approach to working with difficult partners is from phenomenological psychology and Gestalt therapy (see Introduction for expanded description) in that it is based on each partner's immediate experience of the relationship. It is critical for the therapist to understand each partner's perceptions and the meanings he or she assigns to those perceptions. The work of the therapist is based on observation and sensing of the dynamics within each partner and the relationship. Zinker (1994) writes, "In Gestalt couple therapy, *awareness of process* is the foundation for meaningful change" (p. 167). In his book *Therapy With Difficult Clients*, Hanna (2002) references the importance of phenomenology in psychology in fostering awareness by seeing and observing. Working with difficult clients particularly demands acute attention and observation by the therapist. It is like learning the steps of a salsa: the movement is quick, challenging, and demanding. Missing any part can throw off the whole dance.

The goal of therapy is awareness and growth individually and together. Zinker (1994) describes the therapy process with couples:

We watch the couple … We allow something to become figural in the process, then we tell the couple about it. We call this sharing an *intervention*. The intervention widens the couple's awareness, drawing something from the background to make it figural. (p. 168)

Integrated with this approach are other therapies that work well with this orientation, specifically systemic, structural, and cognitive behavioral therapies. The application of these techniques is further explored in Chapter 2 in the section titled, "Overview of Techniques."

Because of the complexity of working with difficult partners in couple therapy, therapists often advocate a multifaceted approach. For example, Linehan and Dexter-Mazza (2008) describe Dialectical Behavioral Therapy (DBT) for working with borderline personality disorder, "The theoretical orientation to treatment is a blend of three theoretical positions: behavioral science, dialectical philosophy, and Zen practice" (p. 369). They write of the efficacy of DBT; "… DBT has the most empirical support at present and is generally considered the frontline treatment for the disorder" (p. 369).

As another example, Snyder, Schneider, and Castellani (2003) posit a pluralistic approach to working with difficult partners. They write:

Working with difficult couples requires thinking and practicing "outside the box." No single treatment or theoretical approach fully addresses the full spectrum of individual and relationship dysfunction that difficult couples frequently present. Thus, the more difficult the couple, the greater the need for therapists to draw on increasingly diverse intervention strategies to address individual and relationship problems. (p. 27)

Snyder et al. (2003) advocate a model that is "… theoretical pluralistic … in that it asserts the validity of multiple theoretical approaches to couple therapy and draws on each of these as relatively intact units" (p. 41). They have developed a model of sequential steps for working with couples that is different from the approach of this book. However, the phenomenological, Gestalt therapy, cognitive behavioral, systems approach of this book as described in the Introduction meets their criterion of a theoretical pluralistic model particularly because these models are related to each other both historically and conceptually.

Underneath their difficult behavior, some clients are desperate inside, suffering from depression and a sense of powerlessness (despite their controlling behavior). Linehan and Dexter-Mazza (2008) write of the excruciating emotional pain that clients with a borderline personality disorder experience. Benjamin (1996) describes the borderline personality client as having a "morbid fear of abandonment" and "feelings of emptiness" (p. 123). Beck, Freeman, Davis, and Associates (2004) cite numerous studies showing that borderline personality clients struggle with "...themes of dependency, helplessness, distrust ... fears of rejection, abandonment and losing emotional control" (p. 192).

Some difficult partners want to get out of their relationship and can't find a way to leave. Others are too threatened to face their own issues, fearing they will lose face, or worse, fall apart. Some are avoiding deep emotional issues, projecting their own feelings onto their partners. Others grew up with the model of behavior that they exhibit and are thus repeating their parents' behavior. Some are caught in socio-cultural images of a relationship in a way that blocks them from accepting a real person as a partner. Others are facing real traumas in their current lives. Thus, there are intrapsychic, systemic, historical, and sociocultural reasons for their behaviors. It is important to look for these underlying forces. Often in the therapy, it is difficult to get much beyond the difficult behavior to address these issues.

It may seem that individual therapy solely is warranted for difficult partners because they are so challenging. Yet, research evidence shows that couple therapy can be an important and helpful addition to other forms of individual therapy for difficult clients. Miklowitz (2001) cites studies showing marital therapy to be helpful with clients with bipolar disorder. Couples therapy is an *in vivo* situation in which the difficult partner's issues (as well as the other partner's and the couple's issues) come up and can be addressed right there in the room. Millon and Grossman (2007) write:

> Couple and family therapy provide an opportunity for behavioral exercises such as role-plays that increase empathy and sharpen insight into the problem-perpetuating nature of cognitive and behavioral habits specific to the patient's personal life. (p. 150)

Difficult Partner Behavior

The Offensive Difficult Partner

Often the difficult partner acts in an accusing, blaming, and denigrating way. This behavior can come out in an intense and relentless manner. Some of the tactics the difficult partner often uses are:

Tactic	Example
Verbal attacks and criticism	"You are the worst parent."
Contempt	"You couldn't be caring if your life depended on it."
Lecturing	"Can't you see that you are supposed to …"
Barraging with details	"After the show, you walked 6 blocks in the wrong direction, you dialed the wrong …"
Repeating and hammering	"How many times do I have to tell you…"
Interrupting	Starting to talk while the other is talking.
Sweeping generalizations	"I can never count on you."
Lying	Saying something false.
Bringing in others' views	"Our son agreed with me on this one."

Benjamin (1996) describes the behaviors of control, blame, and attack that characterize clients with borderline personality and narcissistic personality: "The BPD [borderline personality disorder] is quick to perceive IGNORE. Once that happens, the BPD swings into CONTROL, BLAME, ATTACK …" (p. 124).

The apparent goal of the difficult partner is to get the other partner to admit to fault and to agree to change his or her ways to make life better and more tolerable. The difficult partner's goal is also victory. This includes being right and winning the battle, real or imagined. At times it appears that he or she wants to hurt his or her partner. Clearly, there are times when the difficult partner will do whatever it takes to be on top.

Some of the above strategies are clear, but several warrant more description. Lecturing can take several forms: telling a partner how to do things, giving generalizations about how people (and therefore the partner) should act, giving lessons on such things as history and human nature, or citing chapter and verse about previous partner errors. Barraging with details can involve giving specific accounts of supporting evidence for the difficult partner's position. Hammering involves intense nonstop repetition interlaced with accusations. The trademarks of sweeping generalizations are "never" and "always." In addition, they involve broad negative descriptions of the other partner's behavior and character, or broad positive descriptions of the difficult partner's own behavior and character. The difficult partner will use repetition believing that if he or she didn't get through the first time, repeating more forcefully will surely get the point across. Contempt is particularly damaging because it involves condescension and derision.

The above behaviors are obvious, overt, and directly challenging. They can be overwhelming to the other partner and to the therapist. Sometimes they are like a Mack truck bearing down on anyone nearby. The method of the difficult client can be to control with raw power. Frequently, the other partner tries to be nice in the face of the barrage, gives a weak defense, or gives up. Some partners fight back, which only spurs on the difficult partner.

Often the difficult partner reacts to situations and couple issues as if they are a crisis (Benjamin, 1996). Issues and disagreements become blown up emotionally. Anger and hurt come pouring out as if the situation were dire. Linehan and Dexter-Mazza (2008) describe the emotional dysregulation and crisis reactions of clients with a borderline personality disorder. They write:

> Emotional dysregulation is a product of the combination of emotional vulnerability and difficulties in modulating emotional reactions. Emotional vulnerability is conceptualized as high sensitivity to emotional stimuli, intense emotional responses, and a slow return to emotional baseline. (p. 372)

There are also more subtle and confusing manipulative behaviors that difficult clients use. They may twist around what the partner is saying so that it comes out meaning something different from what was intended. (Difficult partners may well use this strategy with you, the therapist, too.) They may lie in a way that sounds quite reasonable and convincing and therefore disguises the intent. Difficult partners may put in some genuine emotions that throw off their partners and draw sympathy. They may act in a way that gets their partner riled up and then make the partner look like the problem. Sometimes difficult clients will use sarcasm to make their partner (or therapist) look or feel stupid.

For example, Lisa was fixated on how poorly her husband's family had treated her over the years. In the therapy sessions, she would slip into a barrage of stories about Bob's father's horrible treatment of her whenever she could. She controlled Bob by her sarcasm, hammering, lecturing, interrupting, and verbal attacks. Bob tried to defend himself, but she would have none of it. In fact, Bob had agreed to not see or talk to his father, but this was not enough. Lisa wanted him to pay for the years of her mistreatment. It appeared to be true that Bob's father was difficult. Yet, it was also apparent that Lisa's behavior provoked Bob's father and that Lisa was not interested in moving beyond the past. It seemed that Lisa's focus on the "mistreatment" by Bob's father was a way for Lisa to avoid discussing the couple's current issues.

Lying is a particularly interesting strategy. Difficult partners who lie do not blatantly lie, or so they think. The lies are often quite crafted and camouflaged. They think that there is no way their partner could find out the truth. They know their partner wants to believe them and is not very devious, certainly not like them. It is almost as if the difficult partner can't conceive of the other partner finding out. Plus, it doesn't matter if the other partner does find out because there are always new lies to be constructed. The lies often take the form of explanations. It can be quite fascinating to understand the thinking that goes into the convoluted constructions difficult partners develop. What is particularly chilling is to realize that often difficult partners lie, know they are lying, and yet believe they are *not* lying. How is this possible? Difficult partners believe they can manipulate the truth, so whatever new twist they come up with is true—until they need a new one. Because difficult partners are very good at explanations and others often believe them, they believe themselves in the moment. Narcissistic personality clients believe that they are entitled to what they want and need without regard to the needs of others (Benjamin, 1996). Lies are the grease that moves the machines of life when needed. They slide things through the cracks and get difficult partners what they want.

For example, when Joshua asked Brianna if she was having an affair, she claimed that she was not. Brianna could have believed she was not having an affair for any number of reasons: she had not had intercourse with her outside relationship; she was about to break it off; it would not harm her marriage to Joshua. She was lying, but did not see what she was doing as lying.

The Defensive Difficult Partner

Some difficult partners are obstructive through defensive behaviors. When they feel attacked, cornered, misunderstood, maligned or just afraid, they may act defensively in the following ways:

1. Turning the other partner's needs and requests into extremes to focus away from one's own behavior ("All you think about is sex").
2. Justifying behavior in such a way that makes it the other partner's fault.
3. Twisting the story so that it comes out being the other partner's fault.
4. Bringing up history or other's views to explain or justify behavior.
5. Using his or her own frailties as an accusation ("You didn't protect me when I was depressed").

Thus, some difficult partners are primarily defensive rather than offensive. They appear to be more open and they get along better in the world. They don't become defensive and show their difficult behavior until pushed or until asked to deal with certain very sensitive issues. Then they become more aggressive. Thus, they often show passive-aggressive personality characteristics. Benjamin (1996) writes of such clients, "These individuals are seemingly compliant and agreeable, but ultimately oppositional and judgmental" (p. 262). This behavior may catch the other partner or the therapist off guard. If the other partner brings up a challenging issue, things may turn upside down quickly. The other partner may refer to the difficult client's "good" side and "bad" side. The defensive partner's anger is often based on tremendous fear and insecurity. He or she would rather do most anything than deal with certain issues.

For example, Kay had a history of drug addition. Being sexual brought up all the out-of-control feelings of being high on drugs and of working through several phobias with which she had struggled. In the couple's therapy with her partner Joan, she was cooperative in looking at the dynamics between her and her partner until the issue of being sexual came up. At that point she would use whatever defensive behaviors she needed to avoid facing the lack of ability to be sexual. Frequently she would turn on Joan, accusing her of bringing every issue back to sex. This and other accusations were ploys to divert attention away from feelings that were too terrifying to face. Benjamin (1996) describes the passive-aggressive personality pattern as "... compliance that culminates into avoidance, resentful compliance that culminates in blame ... masochism that indicts the oppressor ..." (p. 269).

Difficult partners' defensive behaviors can increase as therapy progresses and they feel more and more threatened. As the therapy comes closer to the issues the clients are defending, they may become more upset, may turn on the therapist, and/or may threaten to leave therapy (or actually leave). Another tactic difficult partners may use is to bring up other issues to divert attention, particularly issues about the other partner or the therapist. Benjamin (1996) recounts how passive-aggressive clients ask for help, seem willing to engage in the therapy, but then defy and sabotage the therapist's attempts to help.

Although defensive partners seem to have two different sides, they are not like the two-sided partners described below in several respects: The more defensive side is not hidden and does emerge in the therapy session, whereas the two-sided partner's angry attacking side is hidden, seems more calculated, and is more aggressive.

The Projector Onto Something Outside the Couple

Some difficult partners are convinced that the problem is something besides either of the two of them. Such partners may focus on another person, event, or situation as a way of not seeing the dynamic of the couple and thus not owning responsibility. They spare the partner, yet stonewall dealing with the issues. This is a form of projective identification (Lachkar, 1998) in which the partner is not the one receiving the projection. Examples of this behavior include:

1. Scapegoating one of the couple's children.
2. Focusing on someone they think the partner is attracted to, is attracted to him or her, takes too much of the partner's time, or influences the partner too much.
3. Worrying about outside forces such as difference of religion, male/female differences, illness, or finances.
4. Focusing on another person who affects their lives such as a mother-in-law, a neighbor, etc.

This type of difficult partner often won't look at how either member of the couple contributes to the issues, particularly not himself or herself. The partner engages the couple in these outside issues to keep them from facing couple issues. The other partner may make attempts to deal with couple issues, but is met with denial and resistance, often quite forcefully. The difficult partner may become quite agitated and angry, pouring more energy into convincing the partner and therapist that the outside issues are very real, troublesome, and urgent. To complicate getting to the couple's issues, there is often truth to the difficulty of the outside issues: The couple's child is acting out; the mother-in-law is too demanding; the partner's office mate is flirting. If the therapist does not give the outside issues their due, the couple, or the difficult partner, may become frustrated and close up further. Before getting to the couple dynamics, the couple often needs to deal more effectively with the external issue so that the difficult partner will agree to address the couple issues.

The Victim

One strategy that may thread through each of the above categories is being the victim. Difficult partners are the victim in an obstructive way. For example, Melissa, who lectures and castigates her husband about how he never appreciates her, complains about how she, "Sets the table for him at night," "Takes care of his children all day," "Takes his phone messages so carefully."

It may, in fact, be true that martyred partners take care of more. They may be quick to point this out and often are reluctant to give up the role. Being the victim wins sympathy (or is supposed to), shows virtue, and gives meaning to life events. Yet, in these partnerships there is often little reward or appreciation for the martyr. In fact, the victim role can be oppressive. The other partner, rather than feeling grateful for the things done "for him or her," feels guilty or resentful at constantly being reminded of the partner's virtues and his or her own shortcomings. This is aggressive victimhood. There are many ways of being a victim. Here I am discussing the particular way difficult partners play out being the victim in a very "in your face" way. There is actually little in their demeanor that suggests being a victim. Victimhood is a way of attacking the partner. They seem to take little joy in all that they do but are driven to take care of things. Difficult clients often complain that the way the partner does things is never good enough. In fact, the other partners would rather the difficult clients did not do so much and not rant so much about all they do.

Some partners, who are difficult by being a victim, exhibit passive-aggressive personality disorder. Carlson, Melton, and Snow (2004) describe some of the symptoms of this disorder as feeling misunderstood and underappreciated. The clients see themselves as encountering frequent misfortune. They describe a case example of Walter who "… saw himself as a victim" and "… lacked any insight regarding the role that his behavior might have played in the demise of the relationship [with his former wife]" (p. 258). In his work life his "… self-destructive pattern left Walter feeling very victimized, resentful and unappreciated by others" (p. 259).

The Two-Sided Partner

There is a type of difficult client who acts one way in the therapy session and in a very different way at home. In the therapy session, the client seems quite reasonable, open, and willing to engage in therapy. The partner, however, describes a very different person at home: someone who is angry, controlling, scary, or dominant. It may be difficult to tell initially which persona is real. After a while, it becomes evident that the person at home is quite real. For example, the descriptions by the scared partner are too vivid and consistent; the difficult client may slip in the session and show another side; or he or she doesn't adequately deny some of the behaviors at home. Yet, in the session the difficult partner, for the most part, seems quite cooperative. One signal in the therapy session occurs when the two-sided partner's behavior becomes too calm or even slightly condescending. At this point, he or she may be controlling feelings that at home would erupt. In the session, he or she is invested in appearing controlled and reasonable.

If the couple has children, it can be telling to ask how the children react to the difficult partner. If the behavior described at home is accurate, the partner will often be quite ready to describe how the children are upset and scared by the difficult partner's behavior. The rawness of the children may evoke the angry, controlling, scary side.

Another way to know the reality about this other side is to ask about the difficult partner's work relationships. Because work is a place where people interact day in and day out, chances are coworkers have experienced both sides of the client. Usually there is a pattern of troubled work relationships, and the difficult client consistently will describe these troubled relationships as the other people's fault. His or her descriptions of the others can be quite convincing. What is not so convincing is that the issues persist and show up with various people.

The two-sided partner can clearly be a challenge for the therapist in a number of ways. First, the therapeutic alliance is built with the more cooperative side of the client. Therefore, the client may feel a kind of betrayal if the therapist shows too much attention to the other side, which he or she is denying. Second, if the other side is too exposed in the therapy, the client may need to verbally attack his or her partner or the therapist (Benjamin, 1996). Third, as the other side is exposed, the client may need to build greater defenses around this other side. This may involve engaging in more secretive behavior, threatening the partner directly or indirectly, and/or turning others who don't know of the other side against the partner.

In order for the couple's therapy to progress, it is essential that the therapist be able to get to this other side of the client. This is a gradual process and must be built while allowing the client to save face. In the beginning, the therapist needs to address the difficult side by describing it in a way that sounds less destructive than it truly is. Yet, if you don't make it sound serious enough, you may lose the other partner.

Some two-sided partners may have characteristics of narcissistic personality disorder. Solomon (1998) writes about how people with narcissistic disorders come across as appealing, sympathetic, and successful yet exhibit destructive, blaming, and primitive behaviors: "Many people with narcissistic disorders appear to function as highly successful, accomplished, creative, and attractive individuals" (p. 249). On the other hand, Solomon (1998) writes, "Interpersonal exploitativeness, in which others are taken advantage of in order to achieve one's end, or for self aggrandizement, is common" (p. 244). Benjamin (1996) describes the rhythm of the borderline personality client in intimate relationships. In one part of the cycle of the relationship, the borderline client exhibits active love and trust. Yet, he or she is quick to experience being ignored, which leads to blaming and attacking behaviors.

For example, Dirk was the epitome of a cooperative client while his wife, Hannah, seemed closed and angry. He seemed more than ready to talk about issues. He was apologetic when Hannah brought up issues describing negative behavior on his part. He seemed ready to do homework when assigned. He got along well with me, the therapist. Hannah, on the other hand, was wary, critical of Dirk, and reluctant to try new behaviors. As the therapy progressed, Hannah expressed more and more frustration about many aspects of Dirk's behavior: his unwillingness in past therapy to participate in homework, his scary anger at home, his twisting of "facts" as he recounted incidents between them, and his secretiveness. It became clear that she was describing a very different person than the man presenting in the room. Some telltale stories appeared to validate her accounts: their son's extreme anxiety about his father's behavior during the couple's arguments, his contentious work relationships, and unaccounted for gaps in his descriptions of their disagreements. Gradually, Dirk's difficult side came out in the therapy as it became clear that he was manipulating accounts of interactions that happened right in the room. Yet, it was striking that he would explain these manipulations in the nicest of ways. In reality, at home Dirk was verbally abusive, argumentative, and emotionally quite unavailable. It was very difficult to get to these behaviors in the session because of his calm, friendly, articulate, and manipulating manner.

The Avoider

A partner can be difficult in therapy in still a very different way. He or she may have a wall deep inside that doesn't let much through. The person blocks the therapy by not participating in the process either overtly or covertly. The overt avoider doesn't have much to say, and may even say things are fine (except for the partner's issues with him or her). Or the avoider may say he or she doesn't see the point in talking about a certain subject or any issues, or doesn't see the point of therapy at all (yet is willing to come for "my partner's sake").

Avoiders can act in more subtle ways also. They may see a "simple" solution to the issues (such as getting more sleep or taking a pill). One of my favorites is "That's just the way I am." This is an example of a showstopper. Other examples include: "I don't know" or "I don't see what the big issue is." Some avoiders can be quite engaging. They are talkative, charming, but they don't connect with meaningful issues. They may just talk and talk and do nothing differently week after week.

Some avoiders are aware of what they are doing and don't want to expose their issues. They may even be carrying a secret. However, many of them are unaware that they are avoiding. They are so well defended that they don't know any other way. This way of being has worked well enough for them for years. They may see being open as weak, dangerous, stupid, unnecessary, and useless. Certainly, it is unfamiliar. It is not only that they don't want to open up, but also that they have no clue about how to open up. Some of the baseline behaviors of avoidant personality disorder are, "RECOIL, WALL OFF, SULK, **BLAME**" (Benjamin, 1996, p. 292). A trap for the therapist is to see these clients as simply resistant. Even if they get to the point where they want to try, they often don't know where to begin. The pattern of avoiding is usually lifelong. It is well learned in their family either through modeling, from cultural tradition, or as a response to family issues.

In many cultures, men are not supposed to have feelings, express emotions, or deal with relationship issues. In our mainstream American culture, more often the man is the avoider. Real (1997) writes of the prevalence of hidden depression in men who downplay weakness, vulnerability, and pain. This hidden depression leads to denial and avoidance.

In some cultures, neither men nor women are supposed to be open. In some couples, the woman may come from a more restrictive culture and the man from a more expressive culture. Then it can be the woman who is closed and sees no purpose in dealing with feelings and the man who wants emotional contact and expression. She is the avoider.

Underneath the "not caring" attitude of avoiders may be depression, lack of ability to attach, anxiety, or hidden anger. They may have grown up in an environment with intense parental control, emphasis on social image, or humiliation (Benjamin, 1996). It is often difficult to tell what is going on inside avoiders because they are so defended. Avoiders do not usually come to couple therapy easily or willingly.

Some avoiders are also passive-aggressive. The passive-aggressive client does not merely avoid, but also has an aggressive side that can emerge unexpectedly. Beck et al. (2004) describe the passive-aggressive client as having an "interpersonally contrary style" (p. 342). Avoiders thus may resemble defensive difficult clients who also may show passive-aggressive behavior. The difference is that the defensive difficult clients' nonaggressive side does not appear to be avoidant, but is engaging and cooperative.

For example, Jake was a classic avoider. He didn't understand what all the fuss was about. His wife Diana wanted more intimacy. As a result of her individual therapy, she had come to a point where she had refused to have sex unless they could have some intimate connection.

Jake wanted, in his own words, "dick and pussy" sex. He thought it had worked for them for years. He believed it was what sex was about. He claimed they had everything else they wanted together. He was angry that Diana was changing the rules. Jake was a meat and potatoes guy. He went to work. He was successful. He had come out of the city streets and become a successful business owner. What was done was done. No need to look back. Life was simple. He saw no need for more, for this thing called "connection." Jake resented his wife for making things so complicated. It appeared that Jake's main issue was resistance. Yet underneath this resistance were rigidity and a complete lack of understanding and experience with intimacy. He was afraid and locked up. And he couldn't understand what on earth his wife was talking about.

The Precursors Model of Working With Difficult Clients

Fred Hanna (2002) in his book, *Therapy With Difficult Clients* developed a model that puts forth seven precursors for change that are critical for assessing a client's ability to effectively use therapy. In addition, he gives specific methods for working with difficult clients on each precursor. The precursors are:

1. A sense of necessity
2. Willingness or readiness to experience anxiety or difficulty
3. Awareness
4. Confronting the problem

5. Effort or will toward change
6. Hope for change
7. Social support for change

To help describe clients who are difficult, one can turn Hanna's precursors into qualities that may be low or lacking in these clients. Thus, in a difficult client a therapist may encounter:

1. A low sense of necessity for change
2. Little readiness to experience anxiety or difficulty
3. A low level of awareness of self, others, and interpersonal dynamics
4. Little ability or willingness to confront issues
5. Low effort or will to take action toward change
6. A low level of hopefulness for change
7. Little social support from others toward change

Hanna's descriptions of how to work with difficult clients in individual therapy complement and dovetail with the strategies presented in this chapter for couples.

The Essence of the Difficult Partner's Behavior

To be simplistic, difficult partners have three main goals in their relationships. They are to

1. Control
2. Blame and disown
3. Disconnect and hide

The six types of difficult partners described above provide examples of these behaviors.

Beck, Freeman, Davis, and Associates (2004) illustrate these behaviors in narcissistic individuals: "Other people are viewed as objects or tools in the quest for distinction" (p. 250); "Narcissistic individuals also use power and entitlement as evidence of superiority" (p. 251); "Narcissistic individuals can be quite judgmental, opinionated, and forceful in communication" (p. 251); and "Narcissistic individuals believe that 'image is everything' because it is the armor of self-worth" (p. 252).

The primary ways for the therapist to work with these three dominating behaviors are discussed in Chapter 2.

Summary

This chapter has explored six types of difficult partners. Hanna's Precursor's Model of Working With Difficult Clients was discussed. The chapter concluded with looking at the essence of the difficult partner's behavior. Reading about the numerous and convoluted ways a couple member can be difficult and may exhaust the therapist. Or it may whet the therapist's hunger for help in dealing with a difficult partner: "What on earth can I do with this person?" The next chapters offer guidance, reassurance, condolences, and most of all, sustenance in the form of strategies.

2

Overview

Introduction

"Where do I begin?" "This work seems overwhelming."

Chapter 2 offers an overview of couple therapy with a difficult partner by exploring several primary issues: the therapist's experience, building a connection with the difficult partner, a systems view of the couple, an overview of the techniques presented in further chapters, and a model for the work that addresses the essence of the difficult partner's behavior.

The Therapist's Experience

Working with difficult partners should come with a warning label: This work may be hazardous to your health. You will probably experience heart palpitations, hot flashes, twitching, uncontrollable urges to scream, aggressive tendencies, feelings of total incompetence, helplessness and depression, and a desire to leave your profession. Hanna (2002) comments, "Working with difficult clients can make one feel foolish and inept" (p. 176). You will certainly need colleagues on standby to help you survive the journey. You will have unexplained feelings of longing for that session coming up with that wonderful couple who listens to you, likes each other, does homework, and makes progress. You may even have an urge to pay them just to restore your sense of competence as a therapist.

This work is not for the faint of heart. It will test your patience, your skills, your empathy, and your love for your profession. It is exhausting work and not the most rewarding. Linehan and Dexter-Mazza (2008) describe the burnout therapists experience with borderline personality clients who cross the personal boundaries of the therapist. Benjamin (1996) writes about how the borderline client first basks in the therapist's nurturance. However, when it becomes clear that the therapist cannot give enough, the borderline client goes into crisis and acting out, which leads the therapist to withdraw, feeling both dread and fear. Even when you make progress with difficult people in couple therapy, the experience is more one of relief than satisfaction. It is advisable to deal with only one or two of these couples at a time. As a therapist, you do need to feel hope and belief in the human race. This work will test that belief. Difficult partners are often not nice people. One of mine once said after 9/11, "I don't know what all this fuss is about a couple of towers falling down." Underlying the hostility and the aggression there is often a softer, kinder, and more caring person. The challenge of the therapy is to find that person.

There are many things going on in the therapist's mind during a couple session. Weeks and Treat (2001) discuss some of the questions marital therapists need to ask themselves in observing a couple's interactions: "What was the behavior for? How does the behavior fit into the relational pattern? Where does the behavior come from?" (p. 40). To answer these questions the therapist needs to be attending to such issues as:

- Body language
- Potential traps
- Feelings
- Alliances
- Pacing
- Triangulation
- Balance between the couple
- Underlying issues
- Resistance
- Timing

When working with a couple with a difficult member, the therapist needs to operate on all cylinders at once. Just tracking the issues can be a major task. The primary tasks for the therapist with such a couple include:

- Watching for hidden issues
- Watching for surprises
- Keeping track of the difficult person
- Monitoring one's own reactions
- Keeping control of the session
- Grabbing fleeting opportunities
- Watching for a side swipe and/or derailment
- Doing the unusual

- Making minute-to-minute decisions about what to do next
- Staying on track while also being willing to follow a tangent

Scharff and Bagnini (2003) write of the therapist's experience of working with a narcissistic partner, one of the types of difficult partners that a therapist may see:

> They want us to feel impressed by them. They want us to want them as patients and to dedicate ourselves to their every need, to gratify their requests for special treatment, and to provide them with phenomenally intuitive understanding. We may find their expectations daunting. We may feel flattered. ... Often we feel bored and irritated because they are unable to take in our interpretations. Loaded with honor, we may sink without a trace. We feel frustrated when we are unable to reach them ... Any intervention can be felt as an assault ... (p. 292)

This work is like playing a soccer game in which the rules keep changing. However, a discussion follows of some of the strategies that can help make sense of what sometimes may feel like chaos, running in circles, and falling into Alice in Wonderland's hole. Toward the end of Section I there is a also section on countertransference issues that may arise for the therapist.

Building a Connection and an Alliance

When the difficult partner is an unpleasant ranting and raving blamer, it is hard to imagine building a connection with him or her. You would probably rather run out of the room or give the client a piece of your mind. How do you find a connection with someone who is lecturing, manipulating, covering up, twisting, and even lying? This behavior is both offensive and (let's admit it) obnoxious. Yet, if as the therapist, you cannot build a connection, you will get nowhere. A connection is necessary to get beyond this entrenched facade—a facade that sometimes covers up desperation, loneliness, self-doubt, isolation, and pain. This connection is the key. The therapist must be able to reach through the wall to find a well-hidden person suffering from pain that may come from early years of neglect, judgment, abuse, aloneness, and/or feelings of inadequacy. How do you get to this hidden person? Carefully. There are many minefields on this road. The difficult client needs his or her defenses, which have been reinforced over many years. Reaching the hidden person can be a long, excruciating, slow process. For example, Kreisman and Kreisman (2004) write, "The therapist has a monumental task in establishing a therapeutic alliance with the borderline patient ..." (p. 135). However, when you do reach the person, it can be a transforming process. Following are some ways to begin the journey. Many of these strategies are explored in more detail in Chapter 3.

1. Listen carefully to the difficult partner's concerns and issues and let him or her know that you hear them. Often the difficult partner is used to being turned off by his or her partner and others. The intolerable behavior increases exponentially over time as the difficult partner feels unheard.

2. Follow the details of the story that the difficult partner weaves, and let him or her know that you hear and understand the story. The partner needs to know that you can keep up. This is a way to win his or her respect. Overwhelming the other partner with intricacies and details is one way the difficult partner gains control, and the difficult partner needs to know that this tactic is not going to control you.

    This takes a lot of mental work on your part. You need to operate on several different levels simultaneously. For example, as the therapist, you need to listen for how the story hangs together, the strategy the difficult partner is using, his or her motive, his or her underlying issues, his or her partner's reactions, what the partner needs from you, and how you can keep an alliance with both.

3. Validate the difficult partner's concerns when you can. Fruzzetti and Fruzzetti (2003) and Linehan and Dexter-Mazza (2008) describe the importance of validation in working with borderline clients. Validation involves communication to the partner that his or her responses "make sense and are understandable within his current life context or situation" (p. 393).

    When validating the difficult partner's concerns, it is important not to *in*validate the other partner's concerns. Often the way to do this is to validate each person. For example, the therapist might say to the couple, "I can see that you (the difficult client) feel unfairly burdened and that you (the partner) feel unrecognized for your efforts."

4. Show empathy for the difficult partner's concerns and feelings. Winston, Rosenthal, and Muran's (2001) research shows that supportive therapy is effective with personality disordered clients. They describe outcomes of recently published data that show such results as, "...change not only at termination of treatment but also sustained change at a 6-month follow-up..." (p. 356). Benjamin (1996) describes how empathy with narcissistic clients provides affirmation and soothing that helps them learn self-regulation as long as the empathy does not enable old narcissistic patterns.

5. Purposely work on an issue that the difficult partner presents show-ing that you take his or her concerns seriously. The issue may not be the most important or relevant issue for the couple at this point. As the therapist, focusing on the difficult partner's issue helps to build a connection to the partner, contributes to the partner feeling heard by you, and builds trust in you. Because difficult partners are obstructive and often exasperating, they may not be used to having their concerns addressed.

6. Explain how each person's concerns are part of a system in which each plays a role. This is a way of stepping aside and looking at the relation-ship together without blame. Show how there is a circular system in which each person's behavior is a reaction to the other and a trigger for the other's behavior. Show how they are stuck in this circle together. This can give the difficult partner some responsibility without blame and without making him or her feel picked on. This approach is described in more detail below. Piper and Joyce (2001) write about social skills training as a basic part of behavioral therapy with person-ality disorders.

7. You may need to address the other partner with one of the difficult partner's issues (for example, irresponsibility or addiction) in order to keep the difficult client in the therapy. The difficult partner may need to see that you will support him or her on a legitimate issue about his or her partner. This can be a powerful step in gaining trust and leeway with the difficult partner. However, I would only recommend this step if you have built some alliance with the other partner and have made it clear that you see the issues as part of the couple system. There is always the risk of losing the other partner and being co-opted by the difficult one.

8. When possible, bring humor to the sessions. Beck et al. (2004) write of working with clients with personality disorders, "The art of therapy involves the judicious use of humor …" (p. 76). Hanna (2002) describes how humor can be effective: "If a difficult client can be helped to see the humor in his or her situation or behaviors, the aura of seriousness and tragedy can diminish and make it easier to confront" (p. 170). This may not be easy because difficult clients are often quite serious. The humor needs to be about the situation or about something external and not about the difficult client or his or her partner.

9. Talk with the couple about something external such as their vacation or baseball. This may help the therapy lighten up and create a bond with the couple.

Keeping the Balance: The Couple Part of Couple Therapy When One Partner Is Difficult

Many of the techniques that follow are geared to dealing with the difficult partner. Yet, this is couple therapy ... or is it? At times the difficult member of the couple may be so dominating and obstructive that the therapy seems like individual therapy. Yet, the other partner is in the room, which changes the dynamic entirely. (Sometimes it makes the work more challenging, sometimes it makes it easier, or often it makes it possible at all because the difficult client often would not come for therapy alone.) There are several issues to consider when the couple is in the room.

As much as possible, especially in the beginning, keep a systems-oriented focus (Weeks & Treat, 2001). It is tempting to focus on the difficult partner most of the time. It may even seem unfair, or worse, collusive, to keep the couple looking at the couples system. To point out how the more cooperative client is part of the system may feel like adding more blame to the one who is already being unfairly blamed by his or her partner. Yet, it is important to focus on the couples system because there are important ways that the partner participates in the couple's issues and focusing on how the partner, as well as the difficult client, contributes to the issues may help the difficult client buy into the therapy.

One of the main challenges in this work is keeping a balance. Weeks and Treat (2001) state that keeping balance in marital therapy is central to systems work. As the therapist, you must constantly watch this balance to see if you are (1) losing one of the couple members; (2) overwhelming the other partner with more responsibility than he or she can handle or (3) letting the difficult client off the hook.

A Systems Focus

What does keeping a systems focus mean in this work? First, it means showing patterns of interaction in the couples system. Weeks and Treat (2001) write:

> Systemic thinking includes cause and effect, but extends the concepts to include identification of circular and reciprocal patterns ... discovering who is at fault or who began the problem is secondary to exploring how each partner, family member, influences of family of origin, societal values and so on contributes to the original patterns. (p. 49)

Systemic thinking includes looking at how circular patterns of behavior emerge in which the partners play out certain predictable roles and scripts. Cottraux and Blackburn (2001) write about how each client brings his or her own schemas (unconscious structures) that interact with the partner's schemas to create relationship patterns. Tracking these patterns, pointing them out, interrupting them, and providing alternative behaviors is a cornerstone of systems couple work. It is particularly helpful with a couple with a difficult member because it takes the blame out of the system and asks each member to be responsible for contributing to the pattern and for trying new behaviors.

Second, a systems focus also means breaking negative cycles of behavior, such as anger and abuse that may exist in the relationship. Third, it may empower the more cooperative client to see his or her contribution and to see possible ways of being proactive in the relationship dynamics.

Sometimes a difficult partner rebels against a systems approach and feels unfairly "blamed" by you, the therapist, because you are implying he or she has some responsibility for the couple's issues. The opposite may also happen: The other partner joins with the difficult client and takes on the bulk of the responsibility (and maybe turns against you). In either case, you need to be ready to acknowledge the difficult partner's concerns and feelings. You may need to change the focus of the therapy either to keep this partner engaged or to help the other partner differentiate from the difficult client.

One of the challenging issues for the therapist in working with a systems approach is considering if the issues really are caused by the difficult client? Keeping a systems approach may unfairly put responsibility on the more cooperative partner, or worse contribute to his or her abuse and low self esteem. As the therapist, you must constantly watch this balance and know when to turn the focus primarily on to the difficult client because the relationship is so out of balance.

When you focus on the difficult partner, you also need to stay aware of the other partner and how he or she is reacting to what is happening. The balancing may come in how the other partner is included. It is important that this partner be brought into the work in order to understand his or her reactions. You need to watch out for this partner undermining the work by defending the difficult partner or by joining with you and coming out against the difficult partner. In this case, you may need to speak directly to the partner about this behavior and show how it is undermining, or you may need to ask him or her not to join you, but rather to let you be the leader.

Overview of Techniques

Many of the techniques discussed come directly from my work as a couple therapist. Some come from cognitive-behavioral therapy and strategic family therapy, which are familiar to seasoned therapists. These approaches lend themselves especially well to this clientele because they deal with concrete behavior and with specific behavioral changes. Cognitive therapy deals with understanding meaning and restructuring cognitions, something difficult clients greatly need. Both types of therapy also work with problem-solving skills and strategies. Some examples of cognitive behavioral therapy described later include "Cognitive Restructuring," "Showing the Consequences of Behavior," and "Trying on a Behavior as an Experiment." Examples from strategic therapy include "Paradoxical Intervention" and "Outlasting the Difficult Partner at His or Her Own Game." The application of these techniques to working with *difficult* clients in *couple* therapy is included in this discussion.

I have also included techniques from various therapies that involve clients' developing a deeper level of awareness. These techniques are less likely to be effective early in the couple therapy. The therapist must first build a relationship with the couple, especially the difficult partner. In addition, some movement forward in the couples relationship first needs to have taken place through the more concrete techniques. Examples of awareness techniques described later include "Identifying Some Small Part of the Self That Is Uncomfortable" and "Appealing to a Positive Picture of Self as an Open Person."

Another group of techniques used in this work is what I call therapist–client relationship techniques. Because this work is challenging, the therapist often must be very engaged with the clients. This requires a high level of awareness from the therapist and an ability to use himself or herself in interaction with the clients to promote change. Examples of these techniques include "Going Toe to Toe," "Controlling the Session," and "Outlasting the Difficult Partner at His or Her Own Game."

Working with a couple with a difficult partner requires the therapist to be flexible and able to adopt a variety of different roles. Harmon and Waldo (2004) describe the role of the therapist in working with a client with narcissistic personality disorder: "… explaining, demonstrating, coaching expression and listening, and negotiating role changes" (p. 345).

Fruzzetti and Fruzzetti (2003) describe the roles of the therapist when working with a borderline personality: "… teacher, coach and traffic cop … identifying, encouraging or cheerleading progress; and interrupting reactive or invalidating responses" (p. 252).

Working With the Essence of the Difficult Partner's Behavior

As described in Chapter 1, at the essence of the difficult partner's behaviors are three main goals: (1) controlling; (2) blaming and disowning, and (3) disconnecting and hiding.

The goal of the therapist in addressing these problematic behaviors is to help the difficult client develop the following:

- Mutuality in responsibility
- The ability to own his or her behavior
- Openness and connectedness

These experiences are extremely frightening and foreign to difficult clients. Their fear has developed over years of experience of self-protection, abandonment, or abuse. The stories difficult clients could tell of their own growing up are sobering, hair-raising, and frightening. They come by these behaviors out of survival and practice.

Summary

This chapter provided an overview for working with difficult partners in couple therapy. With support for how this work can be so demanding, guidelines about how to begin this work, and a model for working with the essence of the difficult partner's behavior, we now have the skeleton. Next, we need the meat on the bones, the content to fill in the structure.

3
Therapy Strategies:
Offensive Difficult Partners

Introduction

This chapter is the beef. Specific techniques are presented to work with the couple with an offensive difficult partner. The techniques are organized into categories that deal with (1) issues of control; (2) the difficult partner owning his or her behavior; and (3) the difficult partner coming out of hiding to discover himself or herself. This chapter is designed to help the therapist dive in. The techniques focus on working with the offensive difficult partner although, as discussed in Chapter 4, they may also be applicable to work with other types of difficult partners.

To help difficult partners move from their very entrenched behaviors is a challenge. The following therapy techniques are grouped in categories that fit with the difficult partner's primary issues.

Dealing with Control

1. Dealing with control
   a. Taking control of the therapy session
   b. Giving control to clients
   c. Directly challenging the difficult partner's control
2. Helping clients own their behavior and issues
3. Helping clients come out of hiding and discover themselves

Taking Control

Controlling the Session

One of the dilemmas in dealing with difficult partners is how to keep control of the session. They will challenge you constantly by interrupting, negating what is happening, changing the subject, not letting you guide the session, ignoring you, persisting in disruptive behavior, overriding you, or accusing you. Weeks, Odell, and Methven (2005) and Goldenberg and Goldenberg (2004) discuss the importance of being in control of the session in doing couple therapy. Benjamin (1996) emphasizes the importance of the therapist keeping clear boundaries in working with borderline clients.

Some specific strategies to control the session include the following:

1. Early on, stop what is going on and take charge. For example, "OK. Time for you to stop so I can give you some feedback and look at where to go from here." Weeks and Treat (2001) give as an example, "I am going to speak to one of you and then the other, insisting the other partner does not respond" (p. 82). Slavik, Carlson, and Sperry (1998) write of the effectiveness of clear limit setting with a passive-aggressive partner.

2. Tell the couple what you are doing periodically. For example, "I am going to go back to the issue we started with so we can make some headway. We have too many issues on the table." Another example, "I am going to stop you now because you are blaming each other and this is not going anywhere. I want you to … "

3. Talk about your role and the issue of control. For example, "In order for us to get anywhere in these sessions, I need to be the one in control. You need to let me guide the session. Otherwise I can't do my job and help you."

4. Ask the couple to agree to letting you be the one guiding the session (in reality you are addressing the difficult client). If both will agree, you can then remind them of this when necessary. If not, you cannot do therapy.

5. As appropriate, set specific ground rules and boundaries, such as no interrupting, no walking out of the room (Hanna, 2002).

6. Stop difficult partners with specific and consistent action after you have laid the above groundwork. For example, I will sometimes hold my hand up and say, "Stop." Sometimes I will say nothing else and repeat "Stop" until they stop. Other times I will repeat simple feedback such as, "You are pounding him and it is not working." Weeks and Treat (2001) advocate using strong confrontation that structures the discussion when

the intensity in a couple's session has become *
examples, "Stop!" or "Don't speak" (p. 82).

7. Show difficult clients how their behavior is no'
can see that you want your partner to hear
them, but what you are doing is not accomp.
turning your partner off."

8. Then suggest they find an alternative behavior. For example,
to find another way to get through to your partner. What else ca..
do besides pounding him?"

9. Since it is likely that difficult partners will not have another strategy
(and are not interested in finding one), suggest an alternative. For example, "You could ..."

10. Sometimes you may need to sidestep confrontation. For example, seeing that difficult partners are building up to a battle, you can change the focus, reinterpret what is happening, put the focus on yourself, or ask the difficult partners what they need right now. You may need to be direct. For example, "This is going to lead to an argument, so I'd like to come back to the main issue" or "We know this is one of those times that it can get ugly, so what can we do differently now?" This second approach engages the couple so they can see what is happening and participate in finding new behavior.

Emotional Regulation

Part of taking control is regulating the emotionality of the sessions. Difficult clients can raise the emotional level of the sessions to a point where the emotions are out of control. It is the couple therapist's job to help bring the emotions down and to teach emotional regulation skills (Linehan & Dexter-Mazza, 2008). Emotional regulation is discussed in Chapter 3 as a technique for discovering oneself.

Picking the Right Issue

What issue will be most effective in reaching the difficult partner? It may not be the issue the couple presents, they most want to address, or the most obvious issue. It may be a low-key issue. It may be an issue important to the difficult partner. It may be an issue for which there is a concrete solution. How do you, as the therapist, decide? There are a number of factors to consider including the following:

• The intensity of the issue
• The immediacy of the issue
• The probability of getting anywhere with the issue

ιe couple's history with the issue
ɹow much trust is built between you and the couple (particularly the difficult client) and what has gone on in prior sessions?

- Where you intend to go in the next sessions
- What the couple is willing to discuss
- What is going to most help the progress of the therapy?
- What you are ready to handle
- Who has been the focus of the sessions lately?

You must be ready to weed through the many issues that the couple throws out on the table in a session. Be ready to keep coming back to an issue, to change midstream, to be alert for a breakthrough. In working with a couple with a difficult member, picking the right issue is a high priority. It is all too easy to be mired in an impossible issue, in an intransient interaction, or in a hopeless argument. Picking the right issue is like running an obstacle course.

Sometimes you may find the right issue by picking the wrong issue. This can work in two ways. First, the wrong issue may be the one that the difficult partner reacts to most strongly or defensively. Seeing the strong reaction and making some guesses as to what is causing it, you may decide to slow the work. This delicate issue may be a later avenue through which to reach the difficult partner. Second, the wrong issue may provide a launching pad to approach the right issue. It may give you time to think about where to go. It may motivate the difficult client and partner to deal with the right issue because it is more productive.

How do you know when you have picked the right issue? In the beginning of the therapy, picking the right issue often involves working with the concerns of the difficult partner. Often you do not know until you are into the issue and, seemingly by luck, you are finally getting somewhere. With a difficult person, there is a certain amount of trial and error. There also can be whole sessions that go by in which you don't know whether you have picked the right issue or not. As you work with the couple and get to know them, you look for the issues that are more likely to bring any kind of openness, any admission of responsibility, or any shift in the couple's interaction pattern.

Dealing With a Low-Key Issue That Could Be Resolved

In the beginning of the couples therapy with a difficult partner it can be helpful to work on a "safe" issue. This is an issue in which the couple is not highly invested, is not highly charged, and has a low level of disagreement.

The issue must be one in which the difficult client does not have a high level of ego involvement. It further must be one for which a "reasonable" solution is possible. The solution may be one in which each can modify his or her behavior or try a new non-threatening behavior that makes a difference. Baucom, Epstein, and LaTaillade (2002) discuss the importance of creating a safe atmosphere before working on difficult issues. It is helpful to tell the couple that you are looking to find a non-threatening issue to begin with so that they can understand the goal and are therefore less likely to be frustrated at the lower significance of the issue.

Hanna (2002) discusses "assigning graduated tasks" (p. 256) as a way to build success. When this approach works, it also helps the couple to engage in the therapy. Working on a low-key issue also allows you to work with the couple to learn the process of constructively interacting and working through an issue. The couple needs to learn very different ways of interacting. This approach can provide a way to begin to teach the tools of better communication.

For example, with Barbara and Ian, who were constantly fighting and blaming, we worked on a schedule for Ian to be able to go to the gym three times a week. Barbara was frequently criticizing and deriding him. In this interaction, she was sarcastic and obstructing. I kept holding her off in order to arrive at a schedule that worked for her as well as for him. Ian provided the positive energy to find a solution. In the end, Barbara begrudgingly admitted that they had found a solution. I then used this as an opportunity to talk about how to have a dialogue that searches for a solution rather than butt heads.

Letting Difficult Partners Walk Into Their Own Trap
Difficult partners will contradict themselves, say things that make no sense, trivialize important issues, back themselves into a corner, attack when no attack is needed, lie when it is pointless, or get angry when there is nothing to be angry about. These are only some examples of their inappropriate behaviors, and there are plenty more. There are times in a session when the difficult partner's behavior speaks for itself. How can you, the therapist, highlight this? Sometimes by doing nothing as the behavior becomes evident, sometimes by being silent for a minute. Sometimes you might say, "I'm not sure where you are going with this," "I don't quite see how this fits here," or "Can you explain what you are saying?" On occasion, the other partners will sigh, roll their eyes, or tune out at that moment. You can use these behaviors to make a point to difficult partners.

For example, "Your partner isn't listening anymore. Can you see how your behavior is affecting him?"

Sean had told his wife Angela that he had gone to a certain store after work. She figured out that, indeed, he had gone somewhere else and not to the store as he claimed. As we discussed this during the session, Angela presented her information that showed Sean had not gone to the store. He eventually agreed. It also became clear that there was no particular reason that Sean had lied. He was not covering anything. He did not gain anything by the lie. The senselessness of his lie was striking and exposing. It seemed he had lied because he could, because it gave him a sense of control, and because he liked being secretive. We were able to discuss these issues because Sean had walked into his own trap.

Cognitive Distortions
Difficult partners in a couple therapy setting will often use distortions of thinking. This is one of the main ways difficult partners handle relationships. They will use overgeneralizations, arbitrary inferences, selective abstractions, and/or catastrophic outcomes. Baucom et al. (2002) describe cognitive variables, such as selective attention and assumptions that underlie cognitive distortions. It is critical for you as the therapist to address these distortions because they directly impede the couple therapy. A number of the techniques in this book address these distortions. It may be necessary to address them directly, set boundaries, and give alternative communication techniques. It cannot be acceptable for difficult partners to say, for example, "You never think about my interests" or "You always interrupt me." Beck et al. (2004) discuss that one of the cognitive techniques that is helpful in working with personality disorders is "...labeling of inaccurate inferences or distortions, to make the patient aware of bias or unreasonableness of particular automatic patterns of thought..." (p. 11).

Difficult clients may use these distortions so often that the couple therapy will be bogged down if you regularly call the clients on their use of distortions. Timing is important and there are times when you may cringe as you let some distortions go by because you are headed in another important direction.

Jeremy regularly used cognitive distortions to avoid taking responsibility for his behavior. For example, when his wife Zoe was upset with him, he would claim that she had "written him off" so he could not deal with her. When Zoe had difficulty with Jeremy's behavior, he would claim with great disdain that she acted like a mother to him. There were times when

Zoe was unhappy with the way Jeremy treated their daughter. He would justify his behavior of hammering and lashing out at their daughter by telling Zoe that their daughter was deliberately setting out to undermine his effectiveness as a father and therefore he needed to put her in her place. It was important with Jeremy to validate his concerns about his wife and daughter's behaviors and at the same time point out his overgeneralizations and his exaggerated attributions. This had to be done clearly and in a way that did not shame him.

Paradoxical Intention

Some of the interventions that can help difficult partners face the implications of what they are saying include "I don't think this is going to get anywhere," "Maybe you need to think through whether you really want to be in this relationship," or "Given how negative you are about your partner, I would think you wouldn't want to be in a relationship with him." However, they can only be meaningful when the therapist speaks sincerely. The strategy here is to preempt difficult partners by saying something worse than what they are saying, to get them to back off from the obstructions and blaming, and/or to have difficult partners face how bad things really are.

Sometimes when I say "I'm surprised you'd want to be in a relationship with him (or her)" the difficult client will say, "Oh, he (or she) has some good qualities also." I pick up on this and say, "Tell me about them." This may nudge the partner into uncharacteristic (and short-lived) positive statements. Even though this will not last, it can briefly move the partner out of the negative patterns and it gives you, the therapist, something to come back to later at a strategic time. Goldenberg and Goldenberg (2004) describe that one of the goals of paradoxical interventions is to help the client(s) abandon dysfunctional behavior.

Another form of paradoxical intention with difficult partners involves saying something negative about one's own behavior as the therapist. For example, Whitney would get annoyed with me when I asked her to repeat an obscure detail of her story. On a few occasions I would say, "I may be dense right now, so could you tell me that part again." Rather than being sarcastic, I was being purposely self-critical to ward off her annoyance. She would then retell the detail without as much anger at me. This strategy can be used only when you are saying something about yourself that is not entirely true, but is believable to difficult clients.

Staying Stuck

Difficult partners want results. They want action. Although their behavior perpetuates being stuck, they cannot stand having nothing happen. Sometimes pointing out that nothing is happening, that they are going around in circles, and that they are repeating the same behaviors, can build the difficult partners' frustration. You can then play into their need for action by challenging the couples: "What can you do right now?" or "Here is where you could try this behavior that we have discussed." It may also be important not to move too quickly away from being stuck. This may be particularly true if you are working too hard, harder than the clients. This is a major trap with difficult clients. They often want you to do the work (especially since they think the problem is not theirs anyway). You can feel very frustrated and inadequate racking your brain for what to do next. It is important to remember that the therapy may not work. It certainly will not work when you are doing more work than the couples are. You may need to point out how they are stuck and focus the therapy on this.

Giving Control to the Client

Moving Beyond Being Stuck

As the therapist, you can take control by pointing out that the couple is stuck and by having them stay in the stuck place. When they are stuck, you can also give control to the partners when you turn over the responsibility for progress to them.

You might say, "It's up to you as to whether you want to ..." or "You have the opportunity here to change what you are doing, if you decide to take it." Interventions like this may be important for you as the therapist as well as for the couple. They give you a chance to remember who needs to do the work and to decide your next move.

When the trust is established and the therapy relationship has gone on for a while, it is sometimes helpful to say, "We're stuck. It's not clear where to go next" or "I don't think there is much more new to do. What do you think needs to happen?" This strategy can be risky, however, because you may be giving up too much control.

Another way to work with being stuck is to make it a challenge. Difficult partners like to feel like heroes. You might say, "We are stuck. Something needs to happen here. I wonder if either of you can step up to the plate to make something different happen. It takes someone with courage to step out and do something different. Who will take the risk? Who will dare to take the ball in their hands and come back here next week having made a step forward?" Difficult partners do not like to look bad. They also like to look as if they are moving forward without having to own any responsibility for the problems. This can give them an out: change without having to admit to any responsibility.

Leading Difficult Partners to an Idea or Change That Comes From Them
Sometimes, as a therapist, you can lead difficult partners to an idea and let them discover it and name it. Questions such as "How would you handle this?" or "What do you think is going on here?" may lead the way. However, groundwork must be done to create a productive pathway before difficult partners can identify something helpful rather than merely self-serving.

For example, the therapist can show numerous times how the couples' fights are unproductive. Neither gets what they hoped. Both end up upset and frustrated. All efforts to get anywhere fail. The therapist may then ask, "What do you think the two of you need to do in these situations?" leading the way for difficult partners to come up with a helpful suggestion. If they do contribute something helpful, the therapist can compliment the idea and work with the couple on how to implement it. This strategy is similar to techniques used when a couple is stuck. The emphasis here is on the clients leading the way.

Appealing to a Positive Picture of Self as an Open and Cooperative Person
Most of us, even difficult people, either believe or want to believe ourselves to be open and willing to learn. As a therapist, you can sometimes appeal to this part of difficult partners to cooperate in the therapy. You can point out how they appear to not be open and give alternative behaviors that could come across as more willing to cooperate. For example, "When you immediately refute what your partner says, you appear to be closed. I suggest you say something different such as, 'Let me think about that' or 'I don't quite see it that way. Can you explain what you are saying?'" In the beginning, the difficult partner may only mouth the words, but changing the behavior may lead to better interactions.

Creating an Acceptable Story
Difficult clients love to tell stories, exaggerated stories. The stories recount the many things they do wonderfully, thoughtfully, valiantly. They also point out the many things their partners do that are wrong, ridiculous, and thoughtless. When the other partners can speak up, the difficult

partners become defensive and then the couples are at loggerheads. "He said, she said" only becomes worse. Getting more information out on the table only increases the disagreement and increases the difficult partner's disdain. Soon there are at least 10 issues out on the table at once.

As a therapist, it is easy to get lost in the "facts." Sometimes I will say, "There isn't much hope that the two of you are going to come to any understanding or agreement about what went on, so I am going to try a version that represents what I am hearing and is somewhere in between what each of you is saying." I then describe a scenario based on what I know of this couple and on patterns of relationships in general. The goal is to depict a scenario that incorporates enough of what each of them has said to bring in perspectives they have not considered and ask each to tone down his or her viewpoint. Usually the partner who is more reasonable and desperate readily agrees with the scenario. To get difficult partners to buy in, your explanation has to allow them to admit to something small and to save face. To admit to some responsibility can be an important step in the therapy. This technique is a form of cognitive restructuring (Goldenberg & Goldenberg, 2004). Winston et al. (2001) describe reattribution (a form of cognitive restructuring) as the therapist redistributing clients' sense of responsibility in a more reasonable way.

For example, Gabrielle was furious at Carlos because he had supposedly flirted with a woman at a neighborhood party. Gabrielle had built up the incident to a frenzy, quoting friends and neighbors as exclaiming to her (Gabrielle), "How could he have done this to you?" She accused Carlos of violating their vows and piercing her trust. He claimed he was not doing anything and that the same friends and neighbors had told him they had seen nothing inappropriate. Gabrielle then refused to attend any event that the woman neighbor was attending. Carlos did admit that he found the woman attractive.

To create an acceptable story I described the following: "Here is what I imagine happened. I imagine that you, Carlos, were giving off signals that you were attracted to the neighbor and were unaware of doing so. Women are very acutely aware of such signals, often more than their male partners are. Women grow up paying close attention to such things and men often don't. Then I imagine that you, Gabrielle, presented this to Carlos and he denied it. That drove you crazy and you got much more upset. Carlos, you couldn't understand Gabrielle's fuss and downplayed what went on even more hoping she would realize her exaggeration. This further infuriated you, Gabrielle. Then being even more upset, you built a case about the incident to try to get through to Carlos. In reality there was something that you, Gabrielle, were reacting to, but it got exaggerated because of your lack of ownership of any of your behavior, Carlos."

In fact, Gabrielle's response was way over the top given the size of the event. Yet, the explanation gave both Carlos and Gabrielle an out and allowed each to take some ownership of something. Gabrielle could admit she had overreacted (this was huge for her) and Carlos could see how his lack of awareness and his reaction to her response exacerbated the situation.

Directly Challenging the Difficult Partner's Control

Staying Ahead of Difficult Partners and Letting Them Know

It is important in working with difficult partners to look ahead and try to figure out their next moves. Difficult partners have certain unique sequences of behaviors. Once you figure out some of these sequences, they will try to change them. It seems in the beginning that difficult partners have an unlimited repertoire. Yet, most of this repertoire actually becomes more and more rigid and predictable as you work. Soon you can anticipate what is coming next or what array of behaviors they may choose next. You learn to anticipate through tracking the behavior of the client. Weeks and Treat (2001) give as an example of tracking "… to listen to the specific words and language used by the client" (p. 75).

Once you know the difficult partner's next steps and have tried different responses and found some that work, you can see what to do before you get there. This is a relief (but you can never be sure), and being ready helps enormously. Telling the difficult client that you anticipated the next comment ("I had a sense that is what you were going to say") or describing what is likely to happen ("The next step for you would be to start lecturing your wife") can create tension and anger but also respect, and eventual relief (it may take a while to get to relief). Difficult partners depend on thinking they can outsmart others. Discovering this does not work with you, the therapist, is critical. At first, when difficult clients realize this, they may increase the maneuvering to stay ahead of you or to see if you can keep up. As the therapist, you must be ready for this escalation and know how it will affect the other partner. There are times when it is best not to let on that you are staying ahead of difficult partners and can anticipate their next moves.

Showing the Consequences of Their Behavior
There are times when I am very direct with difficult clients about how their behavior is affecting the partner, the therapy, or even me. When addressing how the behavior affects the partner, it is most effective to be able to show what is happening right then in the room. I show difficult partners how the other partner has tuned them out, is crying and shaking, or is furious. Often I say, "Can you see that you are not getting the response you want right now?"

For example, Ralph, after verbally castigating his partner Devon in the session, claimed that his berating worked in that it got Devon to do what he wanted. I turned to Devon and asked him if this was true. He sneered at Ralph, "Yeah, but I hate you for it." Ralph had not bargained on hearing that from Devon.

Linehan and Dexter-Mazza (2008) describe the importance of the therapist discovering the environmental and behavioral consequences of beliefs and actions of a person with borderline personality disorder. The goal is to find the consequences that will weaken the problem behavior of the client. Benjamin (1996) advocates working with borderline clients to give up maladaptive patterns of behavior by helping them understand the negative results of the behaviors.

Sometimes I explain the consequences in terms of human nature. For example, I might say, "When a person is put down by another, that person tends to get defensive and closed. Most of us do not respond well to blaming." As another example, "When a person feels controlled by another, he or she tends to find indirect ways of regaining control and may cover things up, withdraw, and placate."

Outlasting Difficult Partners at Their Own Game
There may be times when, as the therapist, you join with difficult clients and track with them. One of my difficult partners, Melissa, loved to tell tangential stories. It was very difficult to follow these stories because she changed the subject often, talked about obscure issues, and didn't tell the point of the stories until after many details and digressions. On occasion, I would follow the story in minutia repeating back to her some important detail to show I was following. Eventually she would talk herself into nowhere, then wave her hands and say, "Oh, let's just get on with what we were talking about." She was lost in her own story. The listener was supposed to have been long ago distracted, lost, and given up. When I tracked with her, she could not keep it going. When she got lost herself

before I did, it helped her to eventually curb her stories. Her own behavior embarrassed her.

A variation of this strategy is "playing devil's advocate" as described by Linehan and Dexter-Mazza (2008, p. 391). The client may say, "My wife doesn't appreciate what I do at work, so I might as well quit." The therapist agrees with the client's dysfunctional belief in order to counter it. The therapist may say, "Yes, since she is so ungrateful, you might as well quit." The purpose here is to bring out the self-defeating nature of the partner's position.

Another extension of this technique that Linehan and Dexter-Mazza (2008) suggest is "Irreverent Communication" (p. 399). Effective irreverent communication is unexpected and comes from a warm compassionate place. It has an "offbeat" flavor to it designed to push the client into awareness (p. 399). They write, "For example, if the client says, 'I am going to kill myself,' the therapist might say, 'I thought you agreed not to drop out of therapy'" (p. 400). Clearly, this approach can be used only when there is trust and a good connection with the client.

Going Toe-to-Toe

Difficult partners are used to steamrolling over people, particularly their partners. There are times when you, the therapist, need to give them a run for their money. This may involve following their logic detail by detail and "out logic-ing" them, or out detailing them, or remembering a part of the story that contradicts what they said. It may mean looking at the situation in a way that refutes what they are saying. Or it may mean showing how the big picture refutes or challenges their viewpoint. Difficult partners will not like this approach. They may get angry, dismiss you, or turn on you. Thus, this approach can backfire. Yet, it may gain you respect and control in the session. I have seen slight smiles on the difficult clients' faces when they realize they can't get me. One client even said to me, "I have never had someone who can keep up with me the way you do." Most difficult clients can outsmart or out bully most people, particularly their partners. In some manner, it is crucial that they learn that that does not work in the therapy.

Ultimately, at some point in the therapy, it is inevitable that you will have to go toe-to-toe with difficult partners. It is almost a rite of passage for them in dealing with people to gain respect for the person. The difficult partners' behavior is provocative. It is meant to rile people up, to bring on confrontation, to win, and to control. Thinking and hoping that you can get away without such an encounter is likely to sink the therapy. You need to be ready to take them on and you need to pick your time rather than have difficult partners pick it for you. Hanna (2002) stresses that confrontation with a difficult client not be done in anger, but with compassion and the intention to help.

Working With the Partner
Sometimes you can make an impact on the difficult client by working with the partner. There are different ways of going about this and each has its pitfalls. Partners can be a source of information about their difficult partners. This information may be very useful for you in helping the couple in a number of ways. It may

- Show another side of the difficult client
- Show an extreme in his behavior that is hard to deny
- Reveal past successful and unsuccessful efforts at change
- Help address specific issues or reveal other's reactions to him

Sometimes this information is hard to get because the partner is afraid to share it, fears retaliation, is protective of his or her partner, or thinks it is unimportant because the difficult client has minimized it. As the therapist, it is important that you proceed cautiously to get this information so that the partner does not shut down or the difficult partner feel too exposed. It is important that you get the information in as an objective manner as possible.

Sometimes you can reach the difficult partner with information from the other partner that someone else reacts the same way. The difficult partner needs to care about how this other person reacts or to feel embarrassed about the behavior. For example, Grady was annoyed when his wife described how his judgments and harshness scared her. However, when his wife told him that the behavior also frightened their children, Grady was concerned. This strategy can backfire if the difficult client thinks the partner is just loading the dice against him or her.

When the partner reveals another side of the difficult client, perhaps a softer more caring side, it can be helpful to bring this side out and to build on it. By discussing this side, you can encourage the difficult partner to show this side in the therapy. For example, Craig talked about Kristen's strong love for horses. Kristen could be warm and affectionate with the horse she owned, but not with Craig. Kristen was quite defensive and unwilling to own any part of the lack of sex in their relationship. We worked to bring out the softer side of Kristen through her horse and then to bring that softer side into the relationship with Craig. I asked Kristen at one point to talk to Craig like she talks to her horse. With laughter and joking as she did an imitation of herself, she could open up a little.

When there are trust and confidence on the part of difficult partners that you are fair and balanced, you can sometimes use a precarious strategy that involves cornering them with information the partners give. When you are feeling the trust of difficult partners and you are quite certain the other partners are giving you accurate information, you might turn to the difficult partners and say, "Did you say that?" or "Did you do that?" or even, "Help me understand what was going on for you when you did that." This last statement risks assuming that the difficult partners will not dispute the other partners' account and is willing to talk about their own experience. It actually can give difficult partners an out by allowing them to explain the behavior without directly owning it.

There are times when you can show difficult partners the negative impact they have on their partners by helping the partners talk about the feelings they have in a given situation. If the partners' feelings include fear, pain, or vulnerability, the difficult partners may be surprised and uncomfortable in a way that help them think twice about the behavior. However, this strategy can also backfire if the other partners' feelings trigger anger and defensiveness in the difficult partners.

Another way of working with the partners is to help them be willing to own some part of the issue. This allows the difficult partners (with much guidance from you) to also own a piece of the issue. Sometimes I am very direct with difficult partners and say, "Your partner has owned that she has a role in the issue. What are you willing to own?" They will usually evade the question. Then I press further and repeat myself. If they will not own any part, I will state that. "So, you don't think you have any role in this." The difficult partner may even say, "Yes." One of my clients in couple therapy recently said very boldly, "I'm right and he's wrong." Most people, even difficult partners, do not want to look that unfair, that pigheaded, so this may buy you some willingness on the difficult partner's part to admit to something later. It is not uncommon for difficult partners to back off a little after making a comment like the one above. Their declaration, which makes them feel strong, may also make them feel a bit uncomfortable.

A further possibility in working with difficult partners is to get them to take the first step in making a behavioral change in the relationship. Particularly if the difficult partner has a clearly legitimate issue with his or her partner, it can make a difference if that partner makes a change. For example, I worked with a couple in which the wife was relentless in her criticism of her husband. She took no ownership of her own behavior. When he took a step of cutting back on his drinking, she, for a moment, said she was grateful he had cut back. It was then important for me as the therapist to praise her for recognizing the step he had taken and to praise him for taking a significant step. She, of course, added her skepticism that the behavior would last. It was also vital for me to support her skepticism, talk to her husband about the importance of continuing his cutback, and reinforce that this was a significant step for both of them. It is evident in this example how fragile the process is and how easily it can be knocked off balance. I sometimes feel like I am walking on a tightrope carrying fragile figures of glass.

Sometimes the partners can help calm the difficult partners and become an "accessory to the treatment" (Peven & Shulman, 1998, p. 23). When difficult partners are interfering with the therapy directly, the partners may be able to reason with them, appeal to their ego, agree with their view, or support difficult partners in a way that helps them become more cooperative and engaged. The danger here is that difficult partners will feel ganged up on or put in the position of being the "problem."

Cognitive Dissonance

Cognitive dissonance involves showing the difficult partners ways in which there is dissonance between two different parts of themselves: for example, two ways they are acting, two beliefs, or a belief and a behavior that are contradictory (Festinger, 1957). Hanna (2002) writes:

> It begins with the presentation of incongruency, inconsistent or contradictory information concerning the self, beliefs, behaviors or lifestyle. This then produces a sense of anxiety in a person that is followed by a desire to resolve the incongruency and anxiety. (p. 202)

In couple therapy, the therapist may point out how difficult people believe they are doing something for the partners' good, but it is in fact bringing negative consequences to the partners or to themselves. For example, difficult partners may be very critical of the partners "for their own good," yet this results in the partner's not wanting to be close and sexual. In order for the dissonance to have an effect, the partners must care about the consequences of the contradiction.

A specific form of creating cognitive dissonance is to point out to partners, who blame everyone else, that this means others control their life.

The result of blaming others for one's own ills is that one's life is then controlled by others. Difficult partners value their independence and control and may not like the idea that blaming means they have, in effect, given up control to others.

Paradoxical Intention
This technique can be used in a challenging way when the paradox you are pointing out hits at the core of the partner's behavior. For example, the therapist might say, "I suggest you go to a hotel for the night when your partner is so thoughtless." This statement could challenge difficult partners to back off in the attacks on their partners. By suggesting something extreme, the therapist dares difficult partners to see the extremes in their behavior.

Helping Clients Own Their Behavior and Issues

Notice Your Reaction

Difficult partners are very careful about how they react to interactions and situations. The following technique is designed to move them away from their carefully controlled reactions and evoke a reaction in the room. First, you, as the therapist, tell the difficult clients that you are going to say something and you want them simply react to it. You then say something deliberately provocative that you think will get a response from the difficult partners. More specifically, you say something that could provoke discomfort, dissonance, or anxiety. Then you ask the difficult partners to notice their reaction and talk about it.

For example, you might point out a contradiction in what difficult partners have said: "You are saying you want your wife to trust you enough to be sexual with you, yet you do things that are upsetting to her as you begin lovemaking. It appears maybe you do not really want to make love." Then you say, "Now, notice what you experience when I say this to you. How do you feel?" You can then process the clients' discomfort, dissonance, or anxiety with you and with their dilemma. This can possibly lead the difficult partners to see some of their negative behavior.

This reaction exercise has a specific structure to help difficult partners notice feelings. "Notice Your Reaction" can also be used in a more general way. As the therapist, you pick moments in the couple therapy when you see difficult partners reacting emotionally and ask them to stop and notice their sensations, feelings, and thoughts. Then you ask the difficult partners to talk in a more objective way about what is being experienced. Carlson et al. (2004) describe the use of "noticing" (p. 255) in couple therapy with a partner who has passive-aggressive personality disorder. Fruzzetti and Fantozzi (2008) also discuss the use of partners' developing the skills of noticing and observing their own and their partner's experiences as part of mindfulness skill development in couple therapy with a partner with borderline personality disorder.

From noticing comes awareness. Hanna (2002) presents awareness as one of the precursors for successfully working with difficult clients. In fact, he summarizes numerous studies that show that "...awareness has been identified as a common factor closely tied to the change process across a wide spectrum of therapies" (p. 63).

Discussing a Story in Which the Partner's Difficult Behavior Was Inappropriate

Occasionally partners will tell of an incident in which the difficult partners' alienating, blaming, or angry behavior is blatant. Usually these incidents involve other people who react to the difficult partner in a strong way. There were consequences to their actions that they cannot easily avoid. Usually the behavior was way over the top. Someone else complained, got upset, expressed dismay, or anger. These other people may have set a limit on the difficult partners such as refusing to associate with them, not inviting them back, not doing business with them, etc. This can be an opportunity in the therapy to show the difficult partners' effect on others and to get them to take some responsibility for this behavior. This type of story may be less charged and less open for debate than an issue in the relationship. To focus on such an incident the therapist needs to be sure the difficult partners are ready to look at some aspect of their behavior and can tolerate the embarrassment. The difficult partners need to trust that they won't be humiliated in the session.

Another situation that may help difficult partners see their behavior as inappropriate occurs when the behavior would be acceptable in one situation, but not in the situation being discussed. As the therapist, you can reinforce the positive aspects of the partners' actions in another context while showing how they may not realize that, in the current situation, the behavior doesn't fit or work. For example, a man's participation in harsh humor may be fine with his friends, but not with his wife.

Another example occurs when the difficult partners have acted in a way that they judge to be inappropriate. The difficult partners will not volunteer this, but you, as the therapist, may see that the behavior goes against their values. An example is the difficult husband who prides himself on being a giving son-in-law, yet became very short-tempered with his mother-in-law for trying to "interfere" in the couple's life. One such client was able (barely) to admit that he (maybe) overreacted after explaining how demanding his mother-in-law was. This is also an example of cognitive dissonance.

Identifying Some Small Part of the Self That Is Uncomfortable
Difficult partners often show bravado that they are not the least bit concerned about their behavior and its effect on others or on their life. Sometimes it is possible to access some small part of the person that *is* a bit concerned, that *does* worry. This part may be accessed when some obvious negative consequences have resulted from the behavior. This is particularly true when the negative consequences have hurt the person for example, by losing a job or being rejected by a friend.

Another way to access this part is to ask the dificult clients directly if indeed there isn't some small part that occasionally is uncomfortable with their life or relationships. If they say, "Yes," they will be only too happy to tell you that it is someone else's fault (the boss, the friend). You then may need to ask again very carefully whether they have any small concern about their own life. For example, "I know your boss is a very difficult woman who seems to not particularly like you and not appreciate you. I do wonder if, in addition to this, you have some small concern about how you got into this situation and if there is any way you may have done something to trigger your boss being upset with you?" It is possible that they may be uncomfortable with their behavior and willing to admit to having done something inadvertent or even provocative. This may be a small stepping-stone for the therapist to help difficult clients look at their own behavior. Hanna (2002) writes about helping the difficult partners identify a part of themselves that does want to work toward change.

Gabrielle, as described earlier ("Creating an Acceptable Story"), hammered and criticized her husband Carlos constantly. She often criticized him for how he handled the children. He rarely said anything about her behavior with the kids although he was concerned about how critical she was with them. In one session he did describe her "losing it" with the kids earlier that day. It turned out that she was, in fact, uncomfortable with how angry she had become with the kids because she pictured herself as a loving devoted mother. She was able to admit to this discomfort and, for a short time, see her reaction as being overboard.

Owning the Resistance

One of the goals with difficult partners is to have them own their behavior. One such behavior they may be willing to own is their resistance. They will, however, not see this behavior as resistance, but rather as appropriate and justified. The goal here is to help the difficult partner openly say, "I won't cooperate," "I think this is a waste of time," or "I don't see how I contributed to this." Hanna (2002) describes the technique of "immediacy" (p. 258) in which the difficult partners admit that they have no use for therapy. As the therapist, you can then make a point of feeding back what they are saying in such a way that they can take ownership of it and feel acknowledged by you. For example, "So, you see this as his issue and it has nothing to do with you" or "You believe that trying to change someone's personality is a waste of time." This acknowledgment can help build trust with them. Often difficult partners will be surprised that the therapist would say something like this and not try to counter their opinion. Sometimes after owning the resistance, difficult partners will be more open because they have been acknowledged and don't want to look so obstinate.

Trying on the Behavior as an Experiment

Difficult partners often don't see any need to change. The other person needs to change. One way around this is to suggest that they, "Just try on a behavior," "Think of it as an experiment," and "See what happens." This does not require any ownership of the problem. In fact, it may let them off the hook for the moment because the difficult partners can change without having to see that they have contributed to the issue.

Alex was often very critical of Ben. In addition, Alex was sometimes unaware that his "feedback" and "suggestions" were negative and demeaning. Furthermore, Ben argued back, giving Alex justification (in his own mind) for coming on strongly to Ben. Alex saw himself as blameless and only well intentioned. He resisted owning his behavior as problematic unless he had acted in an extreme way. He was, however, willing to take suggestions from me about alternative behaviors that would help the couple to interact in a more constructive way. He would even enact these behaviors in a way that showed he was not to blame. Eventually, after some of these new behaviors did help improve the couple's interactions, Alex was minimally able to say that his previous behavior had been problematic. Cottraux and Blackburn (2001) discuss the use of role-play as an effective way for clients with personality disorders to rehearse new behaviors.

Paradoxical Intention and Cognitive Distortions
As previously discussed, paradoxical intention and cognitive distortions can help the therapist gain control in the therapy. These techniques can also lead difficult partners to own their behavior. They are designed to help them see contradictions in their thinking and behavior. They may surprise or jolt the difficult partners, opening the door for them to take more ownership for their thoughts and behaviors.

Techniques to Help Partners Come out of Hiding and Discover Themselves

Discussing the Difficult Partner's Positive Qualities
Difficult partners may be quite smart, funny, accomplished, competent, or knowledgeable in a certain area. They may have some good parenting skills, be very mechanical and helpful, or may be successful executives. In fact, these difficult clients may possess any number of positive qualities. It is important in the therapy to bring out these qualities and find ways to use them in the therapy. For example, if they have good problem-solving skills, you may ask difficult partners to use them to help the couple get out of a jam. If they have good financial skills, you may ask difficult partners to help figure out how to get a deal on something that would help the relationship. Many therapies advocate focusing on the positive qualities of the client as a healing tool (Wile, 1999; Linehan & Dexter-Mazza, 2008; Hanna, 2002). In working with difficult partners, this approach can be particularly important to help build connection and to counter difficult partners' negativity.

Self-Observation
Self-observation and difficult partners seem to be an oxymoron. In fact, one of the central issues in working with difficult clients is their unwillingness or inability to look at or see their own behavior. A classic exercise in therapy is to send clients home and ask them to notice their behavior

in general or in regard to something specific. This exercise differs from the exercise "Notice Your Reaction," which focuses the partners on their experiences and feelings rather than on their behavior.

It may seem to be a waste of time to ask difficult clients to notice their behavior. Yet, there may be times this approach would be helpful (Hanna, 2002). For example, the difficult partner may notice the absence of positive behavior. If, for example, the difficult partner insists that he does do supportive things for his wife, you might ask him to notice the supportive behaviors he does that week and share them in the next session. It may be that he has little to report or that he, in fact, does do some supportive things that he then undermines, or that his idea of supportive is doing basic things like getting the mail.

Difficult partners may insist that they do not enact the negative behavior that the other partner describes. As the therapist, you may want to ask the difficult partners to notice for the week if they do something specific that troubles the other partner. For example, do the difficult partners interrupt or lecture? Chances are that if the difficult partners do admit to such behavior, they will justify it or minimize it. As the therapist, you may need to then employ some of the other strategies to illustrate how the behavior is, indeed, negative.

Several previously mentioned techniques in other categories could also help difficult partners come out of hiding and discover themselves. Building a connection with the partners helps them feel safe and reveal more about themselves. The techniques "Notice Your Reaction," "Discussing a Story in Which the Difficult Partner's Behavior Is Inappropriate," and "Identify Some Small Part of the Self That Is Uncomfortable" help difficult partners emerge and learn more about who they are.

Speaking for the Client

There are times in working with difficult partners when they will not or cannot speak about what is inside. They can't lose face, don't know how to express themselves in a constructive way, or do not have the tools to talk about themselves. If, as the therapist, you determine that the difficult partners will accept you intervening and acting in their stead, it can be very helpful for you to speak for them. Dan Wile (1999) describes the power of speaking for a client as a way to help the client open up at a deeper level. It is vital after doing so to check in with the difficult partners to validate whether what you have said as them is correct. If possible, it is then important to have the clients say their own version of what you have said. This technique may also be particularly helpful for the difficult clients' partner. They may be too numb, too intimidated, or too unaware to be able to say some important things for themelves. You speaking for difficult partners may open the door for the other partners to talk more openly. However, there is also a danger in your speaking for difficult partners because they may well then see you as lining up against them.

At one point in couple therapy with Kay and Joan (see Chapter 1) I spoke for Kay about her resistance to being sexual. Kay was unwilling to address the lack of sex in their relationship, often blaming Joan for, "making everything about sex." Speaking as Kay, I talked about how I associated sexuality with being high on drugs and was afraid of re-experiencing that out-of-control feeling. I continued that my sobriety saved my life and I feared doing anything to threaten it. Being sexual felt very frightening. Kay was able to acknowledge this connection between sexuality and her drug addiction. This helped Joan be more understanding of Kay and it helped Kay be less angry with Joan.

Emotional Regulation

Difficult partners often escalate quickly to intense emotions such as anger. They do not know how to recognize the emotions they have or the signals that they are about to explode. Fruzzetti and Fruzzetti (2003) describe the importance of learning emotional regulation with partners with borderline personality disorder. This involves awareness of your own and your partner's emotions and accurate labeling of emotions. Further, Fruzzetti and Fruzzetti discuss the role of couple therapy in helping borderline clients learn to differentiate between primary or normative emotions in a situation and secondary emotions such as shame, sadness, and anger. An important part of the therapist's role is to teach the difficult partners to deescalate and find a more appropriate way to express their feelings, needs, and opinions. Weeks and Treat (2001) present techniques for managing couple interactions that become too intense. They suggest, for example, (1) "asking process questions that demand the couple's reflection and insight" (p. 82) and (2) "intervening … to take the focus off anger and judgment and redirect the discussion into more primary feelings of pain, hurt and rejection" (p. 82).

Going to a Deeper Level

Often the issues the couple is struggling with are not their deepest issues. They may be fighting over what days of the week he goes to the gym or whether she cleans out the sink. To the couple, these may seem like life and death issues. Even when the issues seem more significant, such as whether he drinks too much or how he handles the children, there well may be yet deeper issues that underlie the couple's intransigence and fuel the difficult partner's behavior. For example, Jill was relentless in her criticism of Paul. There was no owning of any responsibility on her part, rather just a steady barrage of stories and condescending lectures about what Paul did wrong. Using many of the previously mentioned techniques, we were getting nowhere. I decided to look deeper to see what else might be going on inside Jill. What emerged was her unfinished grief about her father's and her aunt's deaths from cancer. In the emptiness left by these losses, she had turned on her husband, who could not possibly make up for her losses. Bringing this issue out did not suddenly change her behavior, but did build an alliance with me and helped her act more humanely in the sessions.

Going to a deeper level may (1) involve specific tragic events; (2) open up family history (which many difficult partners will resist); or (3) confront the difficult partners' deeper disappointments, fears, and self-doubts. Often access to this deeper level comes through the partners who will reveal important clues. The partners have spent much time trying to figure out their difficult partner and likely have a number of theories to explain who they are. It can be tricky for the partners to express these ideas in a constructive way. They may have accused, analyzed, or challenged the difficult partners in a way that has closed them to any of the partners' theories. Sometimes it is helpful to meet with the partners alone to hear some of these ideas and discuss how to raise them in the couple's therapy.

Scharff and Bagnini (2003) write of using an object relations approach to working with a narcissistic partner in couple therapy. Their approach can be helpful in working with the various types of difficult partners discussed in this chapter. Using object relations is an in-depth therapy focused on recognizing the childhood experiences that create projections in the partner relationship. Scharff and Bagnini (2003) write:

> Our theory and clinical experience guide us to tread softly and gradually with these patients. We attend to the developmental deficits, tranferences between the partners, and their projections onto the therapist. Most importantly, we work with the couple's conflict over longing for intimacy and fearing intimacy, wanting to give love but needing to protect the self from imagined attack and depletion. (p. 305)

The therapist's role in this work is central. Scharff and Bagnini (2003) further write:

> ... therapists must study their own reactions, their countertransference to the couple's transference. ... The therapist's analysis of how he feels helps him to understand what is being projected from one partner to the other and from the couple to him. (p. 298)

This level of work requires that the therapist consider his or her own feelings and must be carefully supervised. The reader is referred to Scharff and Bagnini (2003) for an in-depth and rich discussion of their approach.

Summary

This chapter is one of two that presents specific techniques for working with difficult partners in couple therapy. The focus here has been on a three-part model of work that gives the therapist tools for working with the primary issues in this therapy: control, owning behavior, and coming out of hiding. These techniques are primarily for work with an offensive difficult partner. Chapter 4 presents appropriate techniques to use with different types of difficult partners.

4

Therapy Strategies:
Various Types of Difficult Partners

Introduction

Chapter 4 introduces additional techniques to work with specific types of difficult partners as described in Chapter 1. The similarities and differences to working with offensive difficult partners in couple therapy are described, as well as alternative therapy options. Chapter 4 concludes with a case study.

Working with Defensive Difficult Partners

When a partner is truly a defensive rather than an offensive difficult partner, he or she may need a different approach. Some of the therapy strategies for working with offensive difficult partners do also work with defensive difficult partners. These include "Working with the Partner," "Going to a Deeper Level," and "Showing the Consequences of His Behavior." More aggressive techniques such as going "Toe-to-Toe" and "Letting Them Walk Into Their Own Trap" often do not work with defensive difficult partners because they quickly mobilize the partner into self-protection. Approaches that build trust, do not surprise the difficult partner, and allow face-saving are more effective.

Benjamin (1996) advocates that the therapist be friendly, collaborative, and straightforward with passive-aggressive clients. The primary approach is to come in slowly and show that the partner's defensive behavior is not necessary. However, the defensive behavior can become so offensive that other more assertive therapy techniques may be necessary. The most effective approach, if possible, is to get the defensive partner into individual therapy. The individual therapist can help the partner open up, learn how to navigate the couples therapy, and discover the issues behind the defensiveness.

Working With Partners Who Project on Something Outside the Couple

As described earlier, some difficult partners are convinced that the problem is something outside of the relationship. However, it may be clear to you, the therapist, that the real issue is within the couple. However, difficult partners may not be interested in looking at the couple's issues. If you try to focus on the couple's issues, you will likely lose them. You need to start with talking about the outside issue. Often the outside issue interacts with the couple in a way that creates a real problem. The first steps in addressing the outside issue include getting a history, helping the couple find some new understandings of the issue, and developing some action that they can take to help address the issue. This helps them to engage and develop some investment in therapy. However, the first steps need to be small steps that are doable and that don't take the issue away. Difficult partners are not ready to have the problem resolved because it serves as a hiding place. (In some respects, you don't need to worry about this because they will make sure the problem can't be solved.)

Suppose the outside issue is a child who is doing poorly in school. The child's school issues reflect the inability of the couple to get along and the inability of the difficult partner to relate closely with the child. The first step is to discuss the child's issues. Then the couple therapy would focus on finding some strategies to help the child or set some appropriate limits on the child. It may take some improvement on the part of the child (and the parenting behavior) before the difficult partner is willing to see how his or her individual behavior as well as the couple's behaviors affect the child. As the therapist, you can slowly and indirectly venture into discussing this. For example, you might talk about another couple whose child is also doing poorly in school and show how those parents learned to adapt their behavior in a more helpful way. You might also gently focus on how a disagreement between the partners affects the child in the family.

Often, with partners who project onto something outside the relationship, you will need to teach them basic skills of self-awareness and communication. These partners do not know how to look at issues or at themselves. Finding skills that produce positive consequences without great discomfort is important in the beginning to motivate the partners to want to look at this behavior. "Speaking for the Client" can help the partners feel understood and interested in participating in the therapy.

Working With the Victim

As a therapist, you may ask yourself, "Why do I feel so tired and vaguely annoyed rather than supportive toward this difficult partner who is the victim?" The answer is because the difficult partners are using being a victim aggressively as a way of blaming their partner. It takes patience to work with this behavior. In the beginning, you need to listen and support without reinforcing the difficult partner's victim stance and without losing the other partner who is likely, in fact, a victim of this indirect verbal attack. Sometimes you can distract the couple from this behavior as a way of diminishing it. As trust builds in the couple's therapy, you can begin to show the negative consequences to the relationship of the victim behavior.

It is important to get to the feelings and issues that underlie the difficult partner's need to be a victim. One important intervention is to show the difficult partners that they have choices. Rather than being a victim, they can set limits and boundaries. In fact, being a victim can be a way of controlling others' behavior. Explaining this is a form of cognitive dissonance in that the "victims" believe they are out of control, but their "victim" behavior can actually be controlling.

Sometimes difficult partners will be mea culpa victims ("It's all my fault"), which is another form of being an aggressive victim. They will go on about how they caused the problems and they are the ones who have to do all the changing. Clearly, the difficult partners do not really mean this and the behavior is a way of deflecting real responsibility. For example, when Zach felt pressure from Heather to face his difficult behavior, he would start to turn the discussion around and claim how it was all him, that he was the problem, that he never learned how to relate as a child. Heather then reassured him that it was not all him. Zach's victim strategy worked! Eventually I called him on this behavior and showed him how it disempowered Heather and him. Eventually, I told him he could not go there any more in the sessions and that I would stop him when he did. He then began to engage more genuinely in the discussions.

Working With Two-Sided Partners

One of the goals of two-sided partners in couple therapy is to seduce you. You need to be seduced and yet resist seduction at the same time. The difficult partners need to build trust in you. To build this trust, you cannot expose them right away. On the other hand, you need to build credibility with the other partners. If you appear too seduced, the other partners will not trust your ability to help. How do you accomplish these conflicting goals—slowly and carefully. In the beginning, it is important to support and validate each person's experiences and feelings, but not get caught taking sides. This may be obvious, but it is more difficult than it seems because the partners are likely to question you and pull on you strongly. Two-sided partners want to keep up their image and the other partners are often desperate for someone to see and validate the two-sided partners' difficult behavior.

As you wade into these stormy waters, it is important to take a systems approach. Show relationship patterns to which both people contribute so that no one person feels blamed and pinpointed. To do this, begin with communication patterns and circular dynamics, processes that don't go too deeply yet. Cognitive behavioral techniques such as reframing and contracting can be helpful. "Creating an Acceptable Story" is a useful technique for keeping balance and building trust.

Another contradictory bind for you as the therapist is how to divert couples from stories that expose two-sided partners while encouraging these stories to surface. In the beginning, if you hope to reach two-sided partners, you need to allow them to save face. At the same time, you need to learn more about the two sides and allow the other partners to bring out their deep concerns and frustration. This is a time when careful pacing is crucial. You must gauge the timing of the stories as they emerge as well as control the session to keep the pacing you think will work.

As trust builds, it becomes more pressing that the two sides of difficult partners do come out and are addressed. A step in this direction is to help two-sided partners look at the consequences of their behavior without actually owning the behavior. Seeing the consequences may help difficult partners recognize how their behavior needs to change to get results that are more positive. The technique entitled "Letting Difficult Partners Walk Into Their Own Trap" may be effective here. More direct techniques include "Discussing a Story in Which the Partner's Difficult Behavior Was

Inappropriate" and "Cognitive Dissonance." All these techniques from Chapter 3 work to help two-sided partners facing their hidden side.

Working With the Avoider

The strategies for working with avoiders are usually quite different from those for working with offensive difficult partners. Whereas offensive difficult partners are aggressive, avoiders are passive and quiet. The main issue with avoiders is drawing them out and engaging them. Benjamin (1996) emphasizes the importance of therapists giving warmth and empathy in generous doses to clients with avoidant personalities: "The need for therapist warmth and protectiveness cannot be overstated for work with AVDs [avoidant disorders]" (p. 302). The partners have probably been trying, sometimes desperately, sometimes with threats, to draw the avoiders out. As a result, the avoiders may well see you, the therapist, as an extension of the partners. You must differentiate yourself from the partners in several ways. First, you need to show understanding of the avoiders' position and behavior. Second, avoiders need to feel you are not judging them. Developing trust in you is crucial (Benjamin, 1996). It is indeed tricky to show avoiders acceptance at the same time that you are working to help them change.

As the therapist, you need to help avoiders see a reason for opening up. There are a number of ways to do this. You can look for an opportunity for them to open up just a little with a positive result. Usually this will involve discussing an issue that is important to them. For example, you might get avoiders to talk about something difficult related to their job. This may be a safer subject than others. You must pick an issue that is likely to draw a positive response from the partner and use it as a small example of the merits of opening up.

Maureen avoided dealing with couple issues as much as possible. She came to couple therapy to pacify Bethany. Engaging her in the therapy was a challenge. I searched for a subject that was of concern to her. She wanted to return to school to study physical therapy. Discussing how she could do this and how she needed Bethany's help drew her into the therapy and opened the door to looking at couple issues.

You will likely need to inform and educate avoiders. For example, it may help to give examples of others who have benefited from opening up. Talking about the barriers to opening up and suggesting appropriate reading material may help. Another technique that can be effective with avoiders is "Speaking for the Client" (see Chapter 3). Often I will role-play for avoiders what they might really be feeling or wanting to say. I then turn to the avoiders and ask if this is accurate. If they say, "Yes," I will then ask them to put what I have said into their own words. I am surprised at how often avoiders are then able to voice real feelings and concerns.

Sometimes the avoiders can use the safety and structure of the therapy session to open up in a way they cannot outside therapy. The great advantage of the therapy session is that it lasts only 50 minutes and then the avoiders can leave. Another advantage is the safety you provide as the therapist. You can give the right support at the right time for the right amount of time, if you are careful. In addition, you can set some limits on the partner's reactions. I am still amazed at how avoiders can open up during a session and then close right up when they leave the room.

Avoiders often claim that nothing bothers them. The challenge is to find a way to help avoiders experience what they are shutting off. Real (1997), in his therapy with depressed men, states the importance of men facing the disavowed parts of themselves. This includes the vulnerable boy and the aggressive harsh boy. At times, a more aggressive side of an avoider will emerge. If so, you may need to use techniques for working with offensive difficult partners (see Chapter 3).

Gestalt therapy helps people focus on what they are experiencing in the here and now. When avoiders show body expressions of emotions that they will not acknowledge, you can guide them to describe these body sensations (Hanna, 2002). They may not see this as acknowledging a reaction. If they can describe their body sensations, however, this may open the door to recognizing (1) they are having a reaction and (2) they are having feelings. A classic example is the client who is tapping his or her foot impatiently while not acknowledging any emotion. Getting the person to describe what is happening with his or her foot can open a door. You may need to repeat this with different body reactions before the clients will make any connection to themselves.

Other Therapy Options

Getting Difficult Partners Into Individual Therapy

As discussed earlier, referring defensive difficult partners to individual therapy can be very effective. They are usually far more open to individual therapy than are offensive difficult partners. Because offensive difficult partners see the problem as outside themselves, they usually don't see any need for individual therapy—except for their partners. Sometimes offensive difficult partners will go to individual therapy to complain about their partners and get support for their viewpoints. Yet, without the other partner in the room, the individual therapist may have better luck than the couple's therapist in getting offensive difficult partners to take some responsibility. The consequences for taking some responsibility are less direct in individual therapy than in couple therapy. Individual therapy can help the difficult partners learn how to explore issues that they will not or cannot bring out in couple therapy. The danger is that the individual therapist may develop a very different picture of the difficult partner and unwittingly support this partner in a way that is detrimental to the couple therapy. The two partners need to give the two therapists permission to talk because communication between the therapists is crucial. Fruzzetti and Fantozzi (2008) write, "… it is important to make sure that the individual therapist is not working at cross purposes to the couple therapy …" (p. 573).

Doing Co-Couples Therapy

On occasion, I have worked with a couple with the therapist of one of the partners, usually the therapist of the difficult partner. Each therapist is there primarily to support one of the partners. At the same time, each therapist is functioning as a couple therapist. Each of the partner's individual therapists can support his or her client as an ally since the other partner also has an ally. In addition, one therapist can play the "bad guy" role with the partner who is not his or her client. This may help to get at issues that the other client's individual therapist may have trouble raising. The therapist playing the "bad guy" can also speak for his or her client who may have trouble speaking for himself or herself.

When Nothing Works

Sometimes nothing works. You ask yourself, "Is it me? Is it this impossible client?" Yet, as therapists we are not supposed to blame. When dealing with difficult clients, it is hard not to want to blame (after all, they do it so readily). There are times when the therapy is going nowhere and there is nothing more to do. It goes against our nature to give up. This tests our sense of competence, our confidence, and our boundaries.

Some therapists will persist and persist. Usually the therapy deteriorates. The dynamics of the couple get worse. Then they blame you, the therapist. Alternatively, you may get angry with them (or him or her) and express your feelings inappropriately. We need to know when to stop and how to stop. It is essential to be able to stop without blame. The therapist should be the one who acknowledges that the therapy is not working. This acknowledgment may recharge the therapy. If it does not, then the therapist should be the one who suggests that it is time to stop. Some time to process the ending and to look ahead is vital. At that point, the therapist should help the couple consider their options including the following:

- Take a break
- Accept things as they are
- See another therapist
- Consider a separation (if appropriate)
- Do individual therapy
- Do a couples workshop

It is not helpful for the therapist to point out how impossible the difficult person is or to apologize for his or her work. In fact, any steps that the couple has made must be acknowledged. A good ending can in fact be therapeutic.

The Therapist

We have seen how working with a couple with a difficult member is very challenging work. Whatever issues the therapist brings to the table will likely be evoked. This couple work is loaded with countertransference mines, and it is easy to step on one or several at once. Following are some of the therapist's issues that may be evoked.

Authority

Difficult clients will challenge your authority regularly. Therapists need to be aware of any personal issues they may have about authority: a controlling mother or husband, a reluctance to take charge, a need to be in charge, or life circumstances that challenge their sense of authority. There will certainly be times when you need to address the challenge directly and assert your authority as the person running the session. You must be ready to use your authority objectively and appropriately.

Intelligence and Creativity
It is very easy in working with difficult clients to think you have lost your innate intelligence. You may well get lost, have no idea what to do, and even feel quite stupid. Remember that this is part of the client's strategy to gain control and avoid change. You need to be comfortable saying things like, "Could you go back over that again. I didn't follow what you were saying." You may see yourself as quite creative in your work. With this client, you may well experience "therapist's block," in which nothing comes, no new ideas. Or you may come up with 10 ideas that go nowhere. Breathe and detach. Remember that the success of the therapy is not totally up to you.

Helplessness and Ineffectiveness
Difficult clients will often push whatever buttons you have about feeling helpless or ineffective. It is important to look at your own history to know where those buttons might be: a father who didn't listen; a teacher who treated you as stupid; a job in which you felt ineffective. Benjamin (1996) states, "The BPD's [borderline personality disorder] perceptiveness and knowledge of unfair rules of interpersonal play make her capable of shredding the therapist's confidence and effectiveness" (p. 132). You need strategies for handling these feelings. The first step is to recognize when these feelings are being evoked and what in you is responding to your client's behavior. Second, you should know your patterns of responding to these feelings and whether or not they are productive. Third, you need choices of how to respond so you are not locked into an old behavior. These steps involve being able to keep some detachment and objectivity. You may also need to look at what you can learn from this difficult client. What can working with this person teach you?

Frustration and Anger
Kreisman and Kreisman (2004) describe the frustration and anger that therapists can feel at a client with borderline personality disorder. A therapist can be seduced by the clients' flattery, only to be outraged at their judgments and threats of litigation. Kreisman and Kreisman write:

> Some therapists may be charmed by the patient's idolizing and deferential behavior. They may succumb to flattery and accept the implications that both the therapist and the patient are special...More commonly, the therapist eventually suffers the borderline patient's disappointment at failing to satisfy needs. Frustration and rage may replace the previous empathy. (p 139)

Difficult partners by definition obstruct the therapy process. They make your job hard, unpleasant, or downright awful. The anger that comes up in you may come from a primal place or from the frustration of not being able to function effectively.

Dread and Avoidance

It's Tuesday and the Girards are coming for a session. Is there a reason you cannot go to work? Your child is sick, it's a vacation day, or you are sick. There is that knot in your stomach. How will you get through the session? Time to think about other situations you have been in where you have felt dread and avoidance: the time you had to read in front of the class, the time you got a D, the time your parents caught you, the time you were berated. Look for what is compounding your feelings. You will likely find a number of situations that you can identify and separate from this session with the Girards.

Benjamin (1996) writes that in the cycle of the borderline personality client attacking the therapist for not caring enough, storming out of the therapy and then wanting to return, the therapist comes to "...dread the appointments with the BPD [borderline personality disorder]" client (p. 131).

Anxiety

Your heart is racing. You are watching the clock. You want to scream. You begin to squirm. Yes, it's anxiety! Difficult clients can raise your anxiety levels for all the above reasons. This is the time to use those self-soothing techniques you learned in graduate school, the ones you teach your clients. Breathe. Detach. Change the subject. Bring in some humor. Give yourself some empathy. These are strategies for you. Sometimes you need to do things that help you so that you can help them.

Loss of Hope

Hanna (2002) writes, "When working with difficult clients, it is common to feel discouraged, disgusted, or hopeless" (p. 172). When you experience loss of hope for the couple, you may need to end the therapy. First, however, look at your own experiences of loss of hope. Also, look at ways you may be taking too much responsibility and may need to scale down your expectations. Hope is an essential part of therapy. You may need to get some help from a colleague or supervisor to restore your hope.

Lack of Support

As stated previously, you need support when working with a couple with a difficult member. Hopefully you had your first experience of this when you were in regular supervision with a good supervisor. You now need some peer support or you will need to seek some supervision. Cottraux and Blackburn (2001) stress the importance of arranging for peer supervision when working with clients with personality disorders. Kreisman and Kreisman (2004) write of the importance of getting supervision and consultation when working with borderline clients because of the intensity of the transference and countertransference feelings. Do not go this alone. You need to maintain your love of your work. Being able to vent, to get suggestions, and to look at yourself with other professionals is vital.

Case Study: Doug and Jill

One of the more difficult couples I worked with was Doug and Jill, or rather I should say one of the more difficult members of a couple I worked with was Doug. Jill was quite reachable and open to learning. She was also beaten down and depressed by Doug's constant put-downs, anger, and blaming.

Doug and Jill came into therapy in a very dispirited and stressed state. They had difficulty getting along and had no sex life. This had gone on for years. As they approached their late 40s, they wanted help finding a sex life and finding a way to like each other again. The previous therapist, one of a number, had told them he couldn't help them. It was clearly going to be a challenge to get anywhere with Doug. He often talked in a circuitous, tangential way and changed the subject by bringing in quotes and stories from sports that had little relevance to the subject at hand. Or he would talk about the rotary club meeting or his last golf game to illustrate some point that existed in his own mind, but was unclear to anyone else. He could be overtly hostile to both his wife and to me.

Frequently, Doug made assumptions about what I was saying and drew conclusions as if they were mine, misconstruing what I had said. For example, at one point in a session, I stopped one of his detailed stories about an issue that had happened several years ago, a story illustrating an egregious error by his wife. I explained that I wanted to stay in the present in order to deal with the current issue between them. From then on throughout the therapy, Doug would throw back at me that I had said that we could never talk about that particular issue despite numerous subsequent occasions when that issue had been discussed.

Doug also frequently deflected responsibility for his behavior by taking a point and exaggerating it to absurdity. For example, with heavy sarcasm he would talk about how he was a healthy cave man, but Jill was anorexic.

One of the most infuriating things for Doug was not to have everything he said heard exactly as he said it. In his long talks, he wanted each point to be completed and the listener to hear everything. He would check to see if I had followed everything he had said. When I asked for clarification of points or told him that I couldn't follow him, he would sarcastically say, "I just said that three times," or "Weren't you listening?"

Doug took no responsibility for any of the issues in the relationship. They had no sex because Jill "had no juice left in her." He claimed he needed to repeat himself because she didn't listen. They didn't get along because she was too cold and unavailable. She spent too much time with her girlfriends. These were just some of the attributions he would make about her behavior. Doug had little sympathy for anyone in his life. His relationship with his two elementary school-aged children was distant at best and often argumentative and hostile. They had learned to avoid him.

Jill tried to stand up for herself. She would argue with Doug and then give up. She suffered from low self-esteem and loneliness. Her health issues were numerous and included asthma and arthritis. She often felt helpless in dealing with Doug. She was desperate. In the therapy, she was hungry for feedback and someone who could deal with Doug. Jill wanted help, was open to suggestions, and was more than ready to accept responsibility for her issues. At times, she would take too much responsibility for situations to avoid Doug's anger. Jill contributed to the couple's issues by allowing Doug to browbeat her and by trying to please him.

Doug's behavior in therapy came to a head in one session during an argument—or rather during one of his rantings at Jill. She was attempting to stand up for herself when he argued back and ended by saying, "Shut your face." The gauntlet was down. Those three words were a direct challenge to me, the therapist. Would I allow him to control the session? Would I allow him to be abusive? My mind raced. Do I say something now while he is hot, or do I wait until he can hear me better. Is Jill watching to see what I do? How do I get through to him and not alienate him? (Or do I stand up and dramatically order him to leave, as in a scene from a movie?)

After Jill made a comment, which I barely heard as I was deciding how to handle the situation, I was calm and direct with Doug. Looking straight at him I said, "I do not allow people to speak to each other in that way in my sessions. It is disrespectful and harmful to a relationship. There are other ways you can express your feelings." He argued back without much punch. I stood my ground, repeated what had I said, and moved on. I had drawn the line in the sand. Doug did not cross it. We had come to a milestone and the therapy could continue. Doug decided in that moment to allow me to be in charge, which was no small concession for him.

Many of the strategies described earlier in this section were part of the therapy with Doug and Jill. One of the first and most critical tasks before the therapy could go anywhere was to build an alliance with Doug, which was a challenge. The first step was to let him know that I listened to him and could follow his detailed ramblings. He was delighted (and tried to hide his delight) when I talked with him about the details of his stories, laughed at some of his remarks, and showed interest in his point of view. I knew I needed to do this to have any hope of eventually curtailing his ramblings. This also gave me a way of knowing him and connecting to his way of being in the world. I also made it a point to start the therapy with issues important to him as well as to Jill. He was a man who alienated people such that they didn't engage with his concerns. He needed some validation.

At times, I worked with Jill to try to help Doug see her reactions as a way to understand the impact of his behavior. This strategy did not work in the short run. In fact, Doug would sometimes use her reactions against her. What did help was me pointing out to Doug the consequences of some of his behavior, particularly that he was not getting what he wanted. We discussed how his style was hard to follow and Jill would stop listening. We discussed how their styles were different and that she could not understand what he was saying at times. I pointed out how his criticism of her made her withdraw and did not open her up to change in the ways that he wanted.

There were occasions when Jill brought up an issue that showed that Doug's way of being in the world was a problem. At the time, I had to judge if he could tolerate being embarrassed. On one occasion he had humiliated the father of one of their children's friends so much that the man's wife called him to complain and to say that their child could no longer play with Doug and Jill's child. Jill was embarrassed because this family was part of their social network. I decided to pursue the issue judging that (1) it would be difficult for Doug to deny his insulting behavior; (2) it was a step removed from the couple's direct interactions and therefore less charged; (3) we were at a point in the therapy where Doug could—maybe—take some small responsibility for his actions; and (4) if Doug could own some part of the problem, it could set a precedent for him to own something (anything, please). After explaining, justifying, denigrating the father, plus castigating Jill for being too influenced by others, Doug did admit "perhaps he had gone too far." This was huge for him. I praised him for admitting this in an understated but clear way. Later I drew on it as an example of how he could own some responsibility and how that could be positive.

There were many times where Doug and I went toe-to-toe. I challenged him about how he was interacting with me. When he said things about what I intended that were not true, I told him calmly and directly that I did not mean what he interpreted. I would go on to tell him what I did mean and why. When he carried on as if performing for an audience, I told him that we were getting away from the point, that he was losing me, and that his style was difficult to follow. At times, he would threaten not to come back to therapy. I expressed regret if he chose to do that because I thought we were making progress. I also told him that I could imagine that the sessions were very uncomfortable for him. He did come back. Often the next session after the threat would proceed as if nothing had happened in the last session. This was his way of saying "I am staying with this. Don't rub it in my face."

Control was a constant issue in the therapy. Often I chose to sidestep the head of steam building up in Doug by shifting the conversation slightly without Doug realizing I had done so. When he started on tangents, I brought him back to the main issue. I pointed out his misconceptions to him. I stayed with my point, walking through minefields with him. Often I had to tell him that he needed to let me guide the session in order for me to be able to do my job and to help them. Gradually he backed off when I took control. Eventually he would try to get the control back, but his attempts were weaker.

One of Doug's main concerns was the lack of a sexual relationship. Jill was currently about 30 pounds underweight. Doug was quite upset about her weight loss. He saw it as a direct affront to him because he claimed that Jill knew how much her being sexy and attractive meant to him. She was upset that Doug would not accept her for who she was. Doug kept trying to get her to join a gym and pay attention to her health. Doug's pressure only led to Jill detaching more. Underlying these issues were past sexual issues in the relationship. In the beginning of their relationship, sex had been mutually satisfying for both of them. Then part way through their marriage Jill began to feel sexually rejected by Doug because he was critical of her lack of expressiveness and because he started to have erectile issues. Gradually she withdrew sexually. They had not had sex in four to five years. Doug blamed Jill for this situation.

In fact, Jill wanted to have a sexual relationship with Doug. Despite his blaming and negativity, she expressed interest in learning how they could recapture their early sexual feelings together. Doug kept focusing on her weight. It was clear that he was deflecting the discussion any way he could from talking about their real sexual issues, particularly his own. Jill's persistence and her openness about sexuality helped create a different atmosphere. Doug tried to insert his sarcasm and judgments to derail the process. At times, I ignored his inputs and stayed on a more positive course toward sexual learning and connection. Gradually, Doug entered into these discussions with more openness and candor. We were able to discuss issues of sexual functioning, weight, and past hurts. They were able to do exercises at home including touching, hugging, and eventually sexual stimulation. Doug never admitted that his behavior had a negative impact on Jill, but he was able to make enough adaptations in his behavior for Jill to try again to be sexual.

After several years of therapy, Doug and Jill had resumed a sexual relationship. They enjoyed touching and cuddling. Regaining their sexual relationship had a major impact on toning down Doug's difficult behavior. The intensity and the directness of the therapy in dealing with his behavior right in the room also had a great impact. Working with Doug was not for the faint of heart. It drew on all my therapeutic skills and stamina. I learned a great deal about myself and I stretched my abilities as a therapist. In the end, I came to like Doug and to admire him for sticking with the therapy. Many others like Doug don't stay with the process.

Summary

Dealing with a difficult partner in couple therapy is one of the most challenging dilemmas that confronts couple therapists. The work is demanding, exasperating, intricate, nail biting, and even at times exhilarating. To work with these issues you need to be in top form: fully attentive, perceptive, versatile, compassionate, fair and balanced, sharp, and strong. You may need protective gear and plenty of colleague support. Many strategies are described to help you to be effective and to help you handle your own reactions and countertransference. I hope that you, as the therapist, are now feeling more prepared to do this work. Filled with possible approaches to this work, you may feel less dread and more empowered. Each of us needs to work with a couple with a difficult partner to earn our stripes, to remain humble, to appreciate our cooperative clients, and to experience the grand failures and amazing successes of this difficult work. Doug was one of my best teachers, someone I will always remember and treasure.

Bibliography for Section I

Baucom, D.H., Epstein, N., & LaTaillade, J.L. (2002). Cognitive-behavioral couple therapy. In A.S. Gurman & N.S. Jacobson (Eds.), *The clinical handbook of couple therapy* (3rd ed., pp. 26–58). New York: Guilford Press.

Beck, A.T., Freeman, A., & Davis, D.D. and Associates (2004). *Cognitive therapy of personality disorders.* New York: Guilford Press.

Benjamin, L.S. (1996). *Interpersonal diagnosis and treatment of personality disorders* (2nd ed.). New York: Guilford Press.

Carlson, J., Melton, K.A., & Snow, K. (2004). Family treatment of passive-aggressive (negativistic) personality disorder. In M.M. MacFarlane (Ed.), *Family treatment of personality disorders* (pp. 241–272). New York: Haworth Press.

Cottraux, J. & Blackburn, I. (2001). Cognitive therapy. In W.J. Livesley (Ed.), *Handbook of personality disorders* (pp. 344–358). New York: Guilford Press.

Festinger, L. (1957). *A theory of cognitive dissonance.* Stanford, CA: Stanford University Press.

Fruzzetti, A.E. & Fantozzi, B. (2008). Couple therapy and the treatment of borderline personality and related disorders. In A.S. Gurman (Ed.), *The clinical handbook of couple therapy* (4th ed., pp. 567–590). New York: Guilford Press.

Fruzzetti, A.E. & Fruzzetti, A.R. (2003). Borderline personality disorder. In D.K. Snyder & M.A. Whisman (Eds.), *Treating difficult couples* (pp. 235–260). New York: Guilford Press.

Goldenberg, I. & Goldenberg, H. (2004). *Family therapy: An overview.* Pacific Grove, CA: Brooks/Cole Publishing.

Golomb. E. (1992). *Trapped in the mirror.* New York: Quill William Morrow.

Hanna, F.J. (2002). *Therapy with difficult clients: Using the precursors method to awaken change.* Washington, DC: American Psychological Association.

Harman, M.J. & Waldo, M. (2004). Relationship enhancement family therapy with narcissistic personality disorder. In M.M. MacFarlane (Ed.), *Family treatment of personality disorders: Advances in clinical practice* (pp. 335–359). New York: Haworth Press.

Keim, J. & Lappin, J. (2002). Structural-strategic marital therapy. In A.S. Gurman & N.S. Jacobson (Eds.), *The clinical handbook of couples therapy* (3rd ed., pp. 86–117). New York: Guilford Press.

Kreisman, J.K. & Kreisman, J.J. (2004). Marital and family treatment of borderline personality disorder. In M.M. MacFarlane (Ed.), *Family treatment of personality disorders: Advances in clinical practice* (pp. 117–148). New York: Haworth Press.

Lachkar, J. (1998). Narcissistic/borderline couples: A psychodynamic approach to conjoint treatment. In J. Carlson & L. Sperry (Eds.), *The disordered couple* (pp. 259–284). Bristol, PA: Brunner/Mazel.

Linehan, M.M. & Dexter-Mazza, E.T. (2008). Borderline personality disorder. In. D.H. Barlow (Ed.), *Clinical handbook of psychological disorders* (4th ed., pp. 365–420). New York: Guilford Press.

Miklowitz, D.J. (2001). Bipolar disorder. In D.H. Barlow (Ed.), *Clinical handbook of psychological disorders: A step-by-step treatment manual* (3rd ed., pp. 523–561). New York: Guilford Press.

Millon, T. & Grossman, S. (2007). *Overcoming resistant personality disorders: A personalized psychotherapy approach.* Hoboken, NJ: John Wiley & Sons.

Peck, M.S. (1983). *People of the lie.* New York: Simon and Schuster.

Peven, D.E. & Shulman, B.H. (1998). Bipolar disorder and the marriage relationship. In J. Carlson & L. Sperry (Eds.), *The disordered couple* (pp. 13–28). Bristol, PA: Brunner/Mazel.

Piper, W.E. & Joyce, A.S. (2001) Psychosocial treatment outcome. In W.J. Livesley (Ed.), *Handbook of personality disorders* (pp. 323–343). New York: Guilford Press.

Real, T. (1997). *I don't want to talk about it.* New York: Scribners.

Scharff, J.S. & Bagnini, C. (2003). Narcissistic disorder. In D.K. Snyder & M.A. Whisman (Eds.), *Treating difficult couples* (pp. 285–309). New York: Guilford Press.

Slavik, S., Carlson, J., & Sperry, L. (1998). The passive-aggressive couple. In J. Carlson & L. Sperry (Eds.), *The disordered couple* (pp. 299–314). Bristol, PA: Brunner/Mazel.

Synder, D.K., Schneider, W.J., & Castellani, A.M. (2003). Tailoring couple therapy to individual differences: A conceptual approach. In D.K. Snyder, & M.A. Whisman (Eds.), *Treating difficult couples* (pp. 27–51). New York: Guilford Press.

Solomon, M.F. (1998) Treating narcissistic and borderline Couples. In J. Carlson & L. Sperry (Eds.), *The disordered couple* (pp. 239–257). Bristol, PA: Brunner/Mazel.

Solomon, M.F. & Siegal, J. (1997) (Eds.), *Countertransference in couples therapy.* New York: W.W. Norton.

Waldo, M. & Harman, M.J. (1998). Borderline personality disorder and relationship enhancement marital therapy. In J. Carlson & L Sperry (Eds.), *The disordered couple* (pp. 285–297). Bristol, PA: Brunner/Mazel.

Weeks, G.R., Odell, M., & Methven, S. (2005). *If only I had known: Avoiding common mistakes in couples therapy.* New York: W.W. Norton.

Weeks, G.R. & Treat, S.R. (2001). *Couples in treatment: Techniques and approaches for effective practice* (2nd ed.). Philadelphia: Brunner-Routledge.

Wile, D.D. (1999). Collaborative couples therapy: Integrative couple therapy. In J.M. Donovan (Ed.), *Short-term couple therapy* (pp. 201–225). New York: Guilford Press.

Winston, A, Rosenthal, R.N., & Muran, J.C. (2001). Supportive psychotherapy. In W.J. Livesley (Ed.), *Handbook of personality disorders* (pp. 344–358). New York: Guilford Press.

Zinker, J.C. (1994). *In search of good form: Gestalt therapy with couples and families.* San Francisco: Jossey-Bass.

Section II

Secrets in Couple Therapy

5

Issues About Secrets

Introduction

Jason and Eliza have not had sex in six years. Early in their 20-year marriage, sex was rich and satisfying. What happened? Jason had developed difficulty with low sexual desire related to depression. He started to avoid sexual encounters. Sex diminished and gradually stopped. For years, Eliza poured herself into raising their son and her work. Recently, having scaled back her work to part time, she became very frustrated at the lack of affection and sexuality in the marriage. She initiated couple therapy to try to revive these aspects of the marriage. Jason came as a willing participant, having previously had therapy for depression. In the couple therapy they worked on both underlying issues and on homework to bring back their intimacy. Assignments to have a date night and to touch and hug more often were successful.

Jason and Eliza had a 13-year old son, Ethan. Jason and Ethan were quite close. Eliza often felt left out by Jason's attachment to Ethan. At the same time, she worried that the closeness was not good for Ethan who was showing signs of depression like his father. Eliza wanted Ethan to spend more time with friends out of the house and less time with Jason. Jason became very annoyed at Eliza's interference in his relationship with Ethan. Jason and Eliza argued about their differences over Ethan.

There was a turning point in the therapy when Jason blew up at Eliza and humiliated her in front of some of their friends. Eliza was mortified and outraged. From then on, Eliza pulled back from Jason markedly. Her interest in intimacy diminished. She had said from the outset that she had to have more intimacy or she couldn't stay in the relationship. In the therapy sessions, she seemed to be primarily interested in keeping peace with Jason. Had she decided to leave the marriage? She had a history of alcohol abuse, although she had been in recovery for seven years. Did she fear a divorce would jeopardize her rights for custody? On the other hand, was she simply reacting to the blowup by Jason? As the therapist, I came to believe that Eliza had given up on the marriage.

I was in a bind. The couple therapy was going nowhere. Efforts to resolve the blowup were not working largely because Jason did not see his behavior as problematic. I feared that trying to surface Eliza's possible "secret" of having given up on the marriage would push her out of the therapy and make the family tensions worse. I thought there were probably other secrets in the relationship and wondered if Eliza had had an affair. I wondered if Jason had had sexual trauma.

What do I as the therapist do? Should the couple therapy continue? Should I surface the potential secret(s)? Should I refer both partners to individual therapy? This case shows the complex and confounding nature of secrets. It also illustrates the binds that therapists confront in dealing with secrets: What does the therapist "know"? What should the therapist bring out? How does the therapist handle the disruption secrets can cause?

This chapter addresses basic issues about secrets, beginning with defining "What is a secret?" Background material is presented including Sissela Bok's book *Secrets* (1982) and John Bradshaw's book *Family Secrets: What You Don't Know Can Hurt You* (1995) plus a discussion of issues of privacy, secrecy, and intimacy. The theoretical approach discussed in the Introduction of this book is applied to dealing with secrets.

What Is a Secret?

Marion is no longer attracted to Damon. She is frustrated and lonely, but she hasn't said a word about this to Damon. Is this a "secret"? Should she tell him? Aiden is in charge of the money. His wife Lindsey doesn't know about money and doesn't want to know. She is happy to have Aiden take care of things. Aiden has made some risky investments and lost some significant family money. He has not told Lindsey about this. Is this a "secret"?

What is a secret? In fact, there are many types of secrets. According to Webster's Dictionary (Agnes, 2001) a secret is, "Something known only to a certain person or persons and purposely kept from the knowledge of others" (p. 1296). For purposes of this discussion, I define a secret as information that is knowingly or unknowingly withheld or denied and that would be hurtful, harmful, or upsetting to one's partner. My definition goes beyond Webster's in several ways. I include information that is unknowingly withheld, and I include specific consequences to the partner. In addition, my definition of a "secret" includes information that a partner may not want to know, even though it would be devastating. Using my definition, an affair, for example, would be a secret.

By my definition, Aiden's action would not be a secret if the result were not hurtful, harmful, or upsetting to Lindsey. Perhaps Lindsey has her own assets. Perhaps she understands that Aiden will, from time to time, lose and gain money.

As therapists, we come across secrets that the people holding them do not realize are secrets. They may not even recognize that they have the information. For example, perhaps Marion does not realize she is no longer attracted to Damon. Yet, the effects can still be hurtful and harmful to Damon. Marion may avoid contact and sex with Damon without even knowing why.

Sissela Bok's Work on Secrets

In her book *Secrets*, Sissela Bok (1982) writes a comprehensive work on secrets that covers such topics as personal secrets, secret societies, government secrets, and issues of morality. Her scope is wide and thought provoking. In this book I explore a much narrower area of secrets: those within an intimate couple relationship. However, it is worth looking at some of Bok's concepts as they apply to couple relationships. Early in her book she writes of the magnitude of secrets in human experience:

"In exploring secrecy and openness, I have come up against what human beings care most to protect and to probe: the exalted, the dangerous, the shameful, sources of power and creation, the fragile and the intimate." (p. xvii)

Bok (1982) discusses that secrets have both allure and danger and include concepts of "sadness, intimacy, privacy, silence, prohibition, furtiveness and deception" (p. 6). She incisively describes the positive and the negative aspects of secrets:

> Secrecy is as indispensable to human beings as fire, and as greatly feared. Both enhance and protect life, yet both can stifle, lay waste, spread out of all control. Both may be used to guard intimacy or to invade it, to nurture or to consume it. (p. 18)

Having the capacity for secrecy, Bok (1982) believes, is necessary to protect how a person is seen by others, thus protecting one's sense of identity.

Secrecy gives one freedom of choice. Children do not develop the ability to keep secrets until they develop a sense of separateness. Keeping some of one's thoughts and actions secret is an essential part of being separate. Secrecy is also necessary for formulating and developing thoughts and plans. It allows us to be creative without interruption or challenge. Yet, Bok writes, secrecy can also harm, control, manipulate, and isolate. By shutting out feedback and criticism, secrecy can both debilitate judgment and give rise to erroneous beliefs and ways of thinking. Secrecy allows people to maintain facades that conceal negative traits. According to Bok, secrecy can "… lower resistance to the irrational and pathological" (p. 25), and it ultimately "… shuts off the safety valve between the inner and the shared worlds" (p. 26).

For Bok (1982), concealment is the defining aspect of secrecy. Concealment requires separation and exclusion. It involves methods of disguise and camouflage. Yet, she also discusses self-deception, acknowledging the psychological concept of how the split self guards against anxiety-producing knowledge through avoidance and ignorance. It is interesting that Bok points out that ultimately avoidance, which is a self-protective defense, does not defend the self because it opens people to threats that they are keeping out of their awareness.

Bok makes another important point: "What we keep secret requires our most intense and often most active attention" (p. 10). This is particularly relevant for couples in which this attention may create distance in the relationship.

Privacy Versus Secrecy

What is the difference between secrecy and privacy? It is much easier to define how they are similar. Both involve withheld information, concealment, consequences to others, and separateness. Bok (1982) defines privacy as "… the condition of being protected from unwanted access by others, either physical access, personal information or attention" (p. 11). Secrecy, she believes, is much more hidden and serves as an additional protection beyond privacy. Merriam-Webster.com (2008) defines privacy as "The quality or state of being apart from company or observation." Wikipedia.org (2008) defines privacy as "The ability of an individual or group to seclude themselves or information about themselves and thereby reveal themselves selectively." Secret is defined by Merriam-Webster.com (2008) as "kept from knowledge or view," and "designed to elude observation or detection," and Wikipedia.org (2008) defines secret as, "Information kept hidden from others." Thus, privacy seems have to do more with the self, and secrecy has more to do with one's relationships with others. The focus of privacy is on what we need to control that defines our sense of self and our boundaries. The focus of secrecy is keeping others out for positive or negative reasons. Privacy is less concerned with consequences and more with personal definition and freedom.

In his book *Family Secrets: What You Don't Know Can Hurt You,* John Bradshaw (1995) discusses the importance of privacy in human relationships. He writes that our need for privacy is biologically based in that we have a natural sense of modesty and shame that protects us from being violated (pp. 9–10). Shame is the signal that we are being exposed involuntarily, and modesty allows us to be hidden and protected appropriately. According to Bradshaw (1995, pp. 9–10), privacy protects us in the following four areas of human life:

1. The basics of the human life cycle such as eating, elimination, death and sexuality
2. Individuality and selfhood
3. Expansion of the soul
4. The realm of the sacred and the holy

Bradshaw (1995) emphatically makes the point that the less privacy one has, the more one must resort to secretiveness. He quotes Gay Sanders, a doctor from the University of Calgary: "Secrecy is the *necessity* of keeping something to oneself whereas privacy is the *choice* of keeping to oneself" (p. 12). Thus, secrecy involves some internal feeling of pressure that is not true of privacy.

The opposite of healthy privacy are dark secrets, which Bradshaw believes result from the perversion of privacy. Dark secrets are based in toxic shame. Toxic shame develops when natural shame is violated. Bradshaw (1995) writes about how we then take on a false pretend shamelessness:

> Toxic shame forces us to literally lose face and then try to save face. In order to save face, we go into hiding and isolation. We seek ways to always be in control. We guard lest we ever be caught off guard. We live covering up our pain. (p. 30)

Lies and deception are often understood to mean behaviors that are purposefully undertaken to cover up a truth and to be taken by others as true. However, throughout the literature, lies, lying, deception, and deceiving are used in many different ways with regard to the degree and level of awareness and intentionality. Because of this, the words lies and deception are used interchangeably with the word secrets in this chapter. They are only used when referring to other authors' writings in which the authors use the words lies or deception.

Privacy and Secrecy in an Intimate Relationship

Following from Bradshaw's (1995) point that the less privacy there is, the more one must resort to secrecy, we can see how challenging an intimate relationship can be. Eric Erikson (1964) describes the stage of human development during which an individual learns to become intimate with a partner as "intimacy vs. isolation." The dilemma of intimacy is how to be close without losing a sense of self. In a couple relationship, there is an ever delicate and moving balance between closeness and separation. Too much of either can create problematic issues. Each partner's need for closeness and separation often varies from time to time and from each other. Thus, the ground is fertile for tensions over issues of privacy and secrecy. These issues often underlie many couple issues. Intimate relationships touch on all the areas Bradshaw (1995) defines as important areas of privacy: the human life cycle, selfhood, the soul, and the sacred.

Where are the lines between privacy and secrecy? Welter-Enderlin (1993) stresses the importance of keeping secrets in an intimate relationship as a way of gaining individuation and avoiding the "tyranny of intimacy" (p. 50) (e.g., getting lost in a regressive fusion). At the same time, she describes how secrets in an intimate relationship can be divisive and destructive.

There is little available research on secrets in an intimate relationship and even less on working with secrets with couples in couple therapy. Imber-Black (1993) writes of the lack of research on secrets in the field of family and marital therapy. This continues today. Much of what has been written is based on clinical experience and psychological theory. There are numerous rich explorations of secrets written by psychologists and other authors available. References to these works which are not research based are made throughout this chapter.

Theoretical Approach to Dealing With Secrets

In this chapter, as throughout this book, my approach to working with secrets in a couple relationship is phenomenological. (For a fuller description see

Introduction.) I explore the phenomenon of what is happening in the couple relationship and in the therapy. This includes the dynamics of each person's perceptions, feelings, and experiences. Because secrets are complex, it is particularly important to explore the levels of experience involved. What does each person know? What are the underlying dynamics that influence each person's decisions regarding the secret? Doing this work is like confronting a huge jigsaw puzzle with confusing images, scenes, and subsections. Throughout this section, I focus on the partners' and the therapist's experiences, feelings, and meanings. Spinelli (1989) writes:

> Common to the various "attitudes" within phenomenological psychology is the acknowledged emphasis placed on the clients' consciousness and experience of being-in-the-world ... In this way, clients' various choices or assumptions about being-in-the-world can be exposed, examined, questioned and evaluated in relation to the problems encountered throughout their lives ... (p. 128)

Working with secrets in couple therapy requires that the therapist observe and understand the partner's experiences of and choices about "being-in-the world." Secrets involve a choice to keep part of oneself out of the world of one's intimate relationship.

The strategies suggested are influenced primarily by systems therapy, cognitive behavioral therapy, and Gestalt therapy. These therapies work well with a phenomenological viewpoint because they help partners understand their immediate experience, develop strategies, and find new meanings. Because secrets can profoundly affect a relationship system, it is necessary in working with secrets to have a systems perspective. The choices you make, as the therapist, about how to handle a secret must consider the dynamics of the relationship. Cognitive behavioral therapy and Gestalt therapy provide strategies for working with secrets through their emphasis on understanding and working with perception and meaning.

Summary

Secrets are necessary, dangerous, and protective. They are a fundamental phenomenon of human relationships. This chapter introduced some of the intensely thorny issues we encounter in grappling with the presence of secrets in our lives. The differences and overlap of secrecy and privacy were explored. The theoretical foundation for the book was discussed. The chapter showed how secrets in an intimate relationship are endlessly confounding, enduring, and challenging.

6

The Dynamics of Secrets

Introduction

So what do we know about secrets? What kinds of secrets are there? What are the level of awareness and the intentions of the secret keeper? Why do couples keep them? How do they keep them? What are the consequences of secrets and how are they maintained? Chapter 6 delves into the nitty gritty intricacies of secrets, giving important information about the "what" and "hows" of secrets.

Types of Secrets

Levels of Awareness and Intentions of the Secret Keeper

Do the secret holders know they are holding a secret? Do they consider the information not a secret because it is "private"? Are the secret holders manipulating their partners with the secret?

There are any number of types of secrets and ways of categorizing the types. First, I'll look at secrets in terms of level of awareness and intention of the secret holder. Some types of secrets include the following:

1. Secrets of which the holder is unaware.
2. Secrets the holder does not consider to be secrets because:
   a. The secret holder believes them to be private.
   b. The secret holder believes them to be information not to be shared for cultural, social, family, etc. reasons.
3. Secrets the holder knows are secret yet believes they shouldn't be shared.
4. Secrets the holder knows are secrets and knows the secrets are destructive.
5. Secrets the holder uses to control and manipulate the partner.

Secrets of Which the Holder Is Unaware
There are secrets of feelings, beliefs, or actions that a person can be holding and not know. Clearly, these secrets have consequences. If the consequences are negative enough, it becomes harder not to realize something is wrong. For example, Frank is wildly spending money without admitting it and without telling his wife. Jake fears being fired from his job, but is unaware that this is why he is overcompensating and working all hours into the night driving his wife, Sally, crazy. When Sally confronts him about his behavior, Jake denies that he fears losing his job.

What keeps a secret from being known to the secret holder? According to Lerner (1993) factors such as denial, lack of awareness, fear, or self-deception can prevent the secret holder from knowing he or she is holding a secret. Lerner writes, "Because of the enormous human capacity for self-deception, we may fail to recognize when we are lying ..." (p. 13). The person may even be aware of the consequences and wonder why this is happening. Or the person may attribute the consequences to another source. Frank may see that he has less money and think prices have skyrocketed, his wife is spending too much money, or his kids' school expenses have jumped.

Denial may be operating because it would be too startling, upsetting, or frightening to know. Denial is also a good defense against having to be responsible for what is being denied. Denial may be useful to get one's way. In fact, denial is a very convenient and often effective way to get rid of something unpleasant, unacceptable, or overwhelming. Krestan and Bepko (1993) describe the power and prevalence of denial in families dealing with addiction. The effects of denial include "... the blocking of evidence that prevents a person from possessing information, revealing it or *making use of it*" (p. 141). Because denial blocks out awareness, the denier can go about his or her business without the struggle awareness would bring. Denial of a secret can be active or passive. It becomes active when information from the inside or outside threatens to expose the secret to the secret holder.

Lack of awareness of a secret may also stem from lack of learning. Frank may not know how to understand and manage money. He also may not know how to communicate important information in an intimate relationship. Jake may know he fears losing his job, but he may not have connected this fear to his behavior. To be aware that you are holding a secret may require that you be in touch with both your feelings and the connection between your feelings and your behavior.

Secrets the Holder Does Not Consider to Be Secrets

Another type of secret people can hold is a secret of which they are aware, but which they don't qualify as a secret. They may think that they are not supposed to share the information. They may consider it a "private thought," "no one's business," a "burden" to someone else, "inconsiderate," or "inappropriate." There may be cultural or family values that define this information as not to be shared. Imber-Black (2000) writes of "Internet infidelity" as a new type of secret that a partner may not consider a secret because it doesn't appear to hurt anyone (p. 57). Internet infidelity involves a partner sending sexual messages back and forth with an unknown person over the internet.

For instance, Aaron may not tell his wife that the doctor has diagnosed him with cancer because it would be a "burden" for her to know. He doesn't believe he is holding a secret. Rather he believes he is being considerate of his wife. Alicia may not share with Ilana that she received a poor work review because she considers that information private.

Pretending is a type of secret keeping that is considered mild and not as serious as lying in part because the person pretending often does not consider what he or she is doing as secret keeping. Lerner (1993) describes pretending as "… feigning or faking that neither rattles the conscience nor demands careful examination" (p. 121). Lerner also writes, "Pretending reflects deep prohibitions, real and imagined, against a more direct and forthright assertion of self" (p. 14).

Secrets the Holder Knows Are Secret Yet Believes They Shouldn't Be Shared

There are secrets that partners know are secrets but believe they shouldn't share. They may be concerned about the consequences to their partner and may not want to:

- Hurt the partner
- Create stress for the partner
- Alienate the partner
- Drive the partner out of the relationship
- Put the partner in a bind with respect to someone else who doesn't know
- Put the partner in a dangerous situation

In this situation, the secret holders know they are holding a secret and may therefore have feelings of unease, guilt, or ambivalence.

Secrets the Holder Knows Are Secrets and Knows the Secrets Are Destructive
An affair is an example of a secret that the secret holders know is a secret, and they usually know that the secret is destructive for the relationship and the partner (Spring, 1997). These kinds of secrets usually create a great deal of stress for the secret holders. They need to find some justification, some reason to hold the secret. Or they may be so driven by the need behind the secret that this need overrides being in touch with the secret's destructiveness. For example, Jim and Marina had had no sex in the relationship for years. Jim was a very sexual person. Desperately and secretively, eventually he went to escorts because his drive for sex overrode his conscience and his concerns about the negative effects of his behavior.

Secrets the Holder Uses to Control and Manipulate the Partner
Some partners keep secrets in order to have control and power in the relationship (Welter-Enderlin, 1993). Imber-Black (1989) writes, "Power, powerlessness and struggles for power contribute to many secrets. I've seen couples where one partner's secret constitutes a scornful exercise of power" (p. 189). The secret may allow partners to do as they wish without consequences and without accountability. The secret may keep the partners in a position of powerlessness that keep the secret holders feeling safe. The secret holders may keep a secret out of anger and revenge for a betrayal, for unmet needs, for disappointment, or for lack of fulfillment. The secret holders may be involved in dubious or suspicious behavior that they believe requires keeping the secret and keeping control. Webster (1991) writes about secrets as a tool to exercise power over others.

Content of Secrets

There are many types of secrets in terms of the content of them (Brown-Smith, 1998). Some examples include the following:

1. Secrets of information
2. Secrets of emotions
3. Secrets of beliefs, attitudes, values
4. Dangerous secrets
5. Secrets of betrayal
6. Illegal secrets
7. Secrets meant to protect
8. Secrets that involve consequences to others outside the couple

9. Old secrets from some time ago
10. Recent secrets
11. Current ongoing secrets
12. Family secrets
13. Other's secrets (such as a parent withholding a child's secret from the other parent)
14. A secret where the issue is not the content, but the secretiveness. Secretiveness has an air of excluding and cover up (such as a partner avoiding discussing work in a way that says to the partner, "Stay out"). [See below for a discussion of secretiveness.]

Secrets of information involve events, behaviors, and knowledge. Marcy knows that her type of cancer is deadly, but stoically withholds this from her partner. John's vice president has dropped strong hints that the company is about to have a layoff, which could include him, but he does not tell Belinda. Roberts (1993) gives a thorough exploration of many types of secrets of information that can emerge in therapy. She includes such topics as adoption, addiction, eating disorders, AIDS, and violence.

Secrets of emotions are common in relationships. Joe is furious at Bruce and buries his anger inside. Grace is jealous of Peter's intense relationship with his boss, but does not say a word because she fears Peter will blow up. Inez feels terribly lonely every night when Luis comes home and spends the evening holed up in the basement working on the computer, but she fears for his job and says nothing. Secrets of emotion are tricky in a relationship. Some need to be shared or they create distance and distrust. Others will create distance and distrust if they are shared.

Maurice has no use for the church and what it stands for. He is tight-lipped about this with his wife, but his scorn leaks out. Secrets of beliefs, values, and attitudes often create distance because they are fundamental to who we are. Not sharing them means not opening up and not really knowing each other. It is not easy to hide our beliefs, values, and attitudes in an intimate relationship. Keeping them secret requires shutting off one's partner.

Secrets to protect one's partner are often kept in order to keep the partner from being hurt, frightened, or overwhelmed. They are held also to keep the partner from facing things that may be unpleasant, disturbing, or beyond the partner's ability to handle (Webster, 1991). One difficulty is that the secret keeper is playing God and controlling the situation. Another difficulty is that the secret keeper has to be careful to keep the secret even though it is apparently to "help" the partner. There are times when a partner lets it be known directly or indirectly that he or she doesn't want to know the partner's secret. Also, the secret keeper may be correct in assessing that the partner can't handle the secret and may suffer more from knowing than not knowing.

Sometimes secrets involve or affect people outside of the relationship. Skip does not dare tell his wife that his business is floundering financially because she would feel obligated to tell her brother whose business is tied in with Skip's. Her brother might then stop giving business to Skip, hurting both Skip and his wife. Secrets, in fact, rarely affect only the couple. Others are often affected at least emotionally if not in more concrete ways.

One member of a couple may hold a secret about something prior to their relationship or from a time earlier in the relationship. Is the secret relevant now? If not, is it necessary or helpful to share it? Telling may bring the couple closer or push them further apart.

Family secrets are legend. They are part and parcel of family life. Most families have any number of them. There is the uncle who "had to marry" the aunt, the great aunt who is an alcoholic, the grandfather whose business went bankrupt, etc. John Bradshaw's (1995) book *Family Secrets: What You Don't Know Can Hurt You* goes into the many types of family secrets. Family secrets tend to go on through a number of generations and tend to be around aspects of the human and family life cycle. Couples may or may not reveal their family secrets to each other. Toxic family secrets wield a kind of power over families that may perpetuate through branches and generations if they are not addressed.

Vangelisti (1994) researched types of secrets in families and found three main categories: (1) taboo secrets (activities that are condemned or stigmatized); (2) rule violations; and (3) conventional secrets (activities that are not to be discussed with non-intimate others). These types of secrets were kept for various reasons including privacy, defense, and bonding.

Sometimes one member of a couple is holding someone else's secret. This may be particularly important if the "someone else" is one of their children. Rita's daughter revealed to her mother that she was gay and begged her mother not to tell her father. What does Rita do? The secret can create distance or suspicion or it can protect.

Bader and Pearson (2000) describe many types of lies in an intimate relationship including lying by omission, "Yes Lies" (p. 64), "Gray Lies" (p. 65), self-deceiving lies and "five-alarm" (p. 69) lies. "Yes Lies" are "minor fibs" (p. 61). "Gray Lies" misrepresent or hide "... certain aspects of who or what you are ..." (p. 65) by not giving the whole story. Self-deception lies involve lying to one's self, and "five-alarm" lies are fraudulent lies

"... when a person deliberately misleads a lover about who he is ..." (p. 60). Bader and Pearson (2000) explore how certain types of lies emerge at different stages of a couple's relationship. Lerner (1993) also describes different types of deception such as constructive lies, silence, concealing, and exaggerating.

For some couples, particularly those who value openness, the primary issue when one member keeps a secret may not be so much the secret, but the secretiveness or secrecy itself. Schlein (1987) writes, "Secrecy is the whisper in which the secret is told or hidden. This is how 'learned ignorance' comes into being" (p. 392). Secrecy is a separate layer above secrets. It involves an air or cloud around secrets that keeps others out and unknowing. Secrecy, if discovered, can create distance, distrust, and exclusion—all the things secrets cause and more. It may lead a partner who discovers the secrecy to panic about what else the partner is not sharing and why. It raises issues about the character of the secretive partner.

Why Couples Keep Secrets

Why do couples keep secrets? Sometimes a partner will keep a secret believing that the secret protects the relationship. Sharing the secret might, in that person's view, threaten the relationship. Bader and Pearson (2000) write, "We fear that the truth will unleash conflict that will endanger the relationship—so we lie" (p. 2). Kim may hide from her husband Jake that her sister Anne dislikes Jake and secretly wishes Kim had married Bob, Anne's good friend. What would be served by telling Jake? With time, Anne may come around to like Jake, but Jake would resent Anne if he knew her feelings. In addition, his knowing would stress the couple's relationship and bring up potential arguments and jealousies between Kim and Jake.

A secret may be time limited in that it may go away or be resolved. Thus, not sharing it avoids consequences that will also potentially go away (as in the above situation). In another example, Mira is desperate in her marriage because she is feeling suffocated and has lost her independence after six years of being at home taking care of the children. She keeps her misery to herself hoping that getting a job and returning to her career will get rid of these feelings.

Sometimes partners keep a secret because they believe that their partner would not understand or would misinterpret the secret. Bader and Pearson (2000) stress the importance of understanding the inability to trust or to be heard as underlying many martial lies. Colin does not tell Mark that he has lunch at work every day with Fred because Mark tends to get irrationally jealous. Mark certainly would not understand that Colin must talk over business with Fred regularly to keep up with the competition. Colin believes Mark would misinterpret these lunches, get very upset, and then jeopardize Colin's position at his job.

A closely related reason partners may keep a secret is that they believe that although the secret has no impact on the relationship, their partner would think otherwise. Thus, differences of point of view and understanding can lead to partners keeping secrets.

Sometimes partners keep secrets because they are not resolved themselves about the secret. They fear revealing both the secret and their ambivalence about the secret. They are straddling conflicting realities and feelings and are unable to resolve the conflict. Yet, they know they need to resolve this conflict and that the secrecy is destructive to themselves and to their partner.

A partner may keep a secret because he doesn't really know his own thoughts. Lerner (1993) writes:

> Then there are lies, secrets, and silences that begin with the self. We are not clear about what we think, feel and believe. Our priorities and life goals are not really our own…As a result we are not fully present in our most important relationships. (p. 13)

There are times when partners keep a secret because they feel it is of no use to share the secret. They may have shared such things in the past with their partner with negative results. Feeling put down and mowed over, they now keep things to themselves. For example, Lakisha doesn't bother to tell Duane about her issues at work because she feels ridiculed by Duane. As a result, she doesn't share important issues and concerns that might affect the relationship.

Based on their extensive clinical experience, Bader and Pearson (2000) describe a number of other reasons people lie in a marriage:

> We want to look good—so we lie … We feel foolish about something we said or did—so we lie. We have trouble putting the whole truth into words—so we manipulate it. We're reluctant to admit the darker sides of ourselves, our greed, envy and selfishness—so we try to hide them. We lie because lies come with being human, and we are probably never so exposed as we are with our mates. (p.2)

The Consequences of Secrets

Many of the consequences of secrets are evident throughout this chapter. In summary, secrets primarily protect and control. The consequences of this protection and control depend upon the nature of the secret, the circumstances, and the secret keeper. Consequences can range from safety to destructiveness.

Some of the positive consequences of secrets are similar to the consequences of natural privacy. They include having a sense of boundaries and of order. Secrets may contribute to my having a sense of self. My thoughts are my own. What I think and feel help make up who I am. Deciding when, where, and with whom to share my thoughts and feelings gives me a sense of myself as well as a sense of control. My cultural and family values and beliefs about secrets, proprieties, and boundaries strongly help to define me and give my life meaning. For example, my culture may have rules that forbid mentioning sexuality. With this belief go a whole host of behaviors, mores, rituals, and expectations that help me make sense of my world. Without these I would not know how to act or how to carry out my relationships.

Secrets in a couple relationship also allow partners to surprise each other and to be creative. Joshua is excitedly working on a financial plan that will allow Janice to have more time off when the baby comes, but he doesn't want to tell her until he has secured the funds he needs.

Bader and Pearson (2000) write about productive lies, which they define as lies done in a spirit of generosity, love, and respect for your partner and the relationship. A loving lie promotes your partner and your relationship. Productive lies may not be exactly true but are emotionally true. You may not really want to go through the hassle of giving your partner a fiftieth birthday party, but you tell him or her that you are excited to do it.

In working with couples, it is important for the therapist to distinguish when a lie seems to be "productive" and loving, but is, in fact, manipulative. For example, a husband may tell his wife that he likes how she dresses when, in fact, he does not. He is complimenting her to throw her off guard so she won't discover he is having an affair. A partner who is loving may make the same compliment not so much because of how he feels about his wife's choice of clothes, but because he knows how much time and effort she puts into looking nice.

Then there are all the negative consequences of secrets, which include the following:

- Isolation
- Lies
- Shame
- Illness
- Guilt
- Deceit
- Ignorance
- Fear of discovery
- Internal pressure
- Betrayal

Some secrets are dangerous or toxic because, if known, they would break trust, jeopardize the relationship, or endanger health. Certainly, secrets of illegal activities are likely to be dangerous. Secrets of betrayal are particularly dangerous because they involve the betrayer living a life that is unknown to the partner. The betrayers may be putting the partner and the relationship, as well as themselves, at risk.

These are the consequences primarily of toxic secrets. Yet they can also result from issues of privacy. For example, one's cultural value may include that health issues are kept private. As a result, treatable conditions may go undisclosed and untreated.

Bader and Pearson (2000) describe the many negative consequences of lies in a marriage including arguments, aloneness, distrust, pain, and loss. They write:

> ... lies can *infect* a relationship ... [They act] like a virus invisible to the eye, but with huge destructive potential (p. 23) ... Lies can also *infest* a relationship. Lies of all sizes and import can swarm around a couple constantly, provoking and distracting them. (p. 23)

Lerner (1993) describes how secrecy blocks possibility. If issues and feelings are not revealed, then couples cannot experience resolution, healing, and deeper intimacy. Imber-Black (1993) discusses how secrets can distort and confound communication, impairing the ability to solve problems and confront issues. Karpel (1980) writes about the anxiety and shame that holding a secret can create. Brown-Smith (1998) notes that the secret keeper may experience anxiety in dealing with subjects related to the secret and in fearing that the secret will be disclosed or discovered.

Probably the most devastating negative consequence of secrets in a couple relationship is the breakdown of trust (Brown-Smith, 1998). Toxic secrets lead to distance. Distance leads to lowered trust. Certainly toxic secrets revealed or discovered lead to a breakdown of trust. The unknowing partners, upon learning or suspecting the secret, begin to question the basic premises of the relationship. How do they know what is real? The unknowing partners begin to question their perceptions of reality and their partners' intentions, caring, and judgment. The unknowing partners' world may be thus turned upside down depending upon the severity of the secret. Hidden financial problems, affairs, or secretive visits to doctors can be alarming and shattering. The consequences will depend a great deal on the nature of the secret, the length and methods of keeping the secret, how the secret is uncovered, and the real world consequences of the secret.

How Secrets Are Maintained

Secrets require active attention. Conversations, actions, and thoughts must be diverted to maintain a secret. Signals must be covered, ignored, or redirected. Stories must be changed, reconstructed, and made up. Intuitions and looks must be thwarted. Excuses must be made. It takes a lot of work. Brown-Smith (1998) describes strategies that secret holders develop to maintain secrets including fabrication, withholding information, and clouding information to disguise it. Roberts (1993) writes about the importance of therapists focusing on the process of secret keeping.

There are many ways secrets are maintained, including the following:

1. Social and cultural mores and traditions
2. Psychological defense mechanisms such as repression, denial, projection, displacement
3. Lies and deceit
4. Collusion
5. Manipulation, coercion, threats
6. Fear, anger, pain
7. Conscious decision

Certainly if the social and cultural traditions support the secret, it is easier to maintain. The social mores and behaviors may provide the cover-up and redirect the focus. Expectations in a couple relationship may govern perception in a way that makes it fairly easy to keep the secret. Psychological defenses are very handy and often essential for keeping secrets. Denial works particularly well to help secrets stay hidden. The other defenses may also work well, but are more prone to creating stress and being detected. Lies and deceit require a great deal of work.

Saarni and Lewis (1993) write about the elaborate cognitive capacities that lying requires. One must remember previous lies and make sure that current lies are in line with them. Inconsistencies may be a giveaway to a partner. Deceitful behavior requires planning, cover-up alibis, and often dependence on another's cooperation. Lies and deceit bring with them stress and anxiety, which may show through in the secret keeper's behavior. Collusion with others makes the secret keeper more vulnerable. Others may not be so careful with one's secret. They may have other motives for colluding that make them unreliable. Manipulation, coercion, and threats are tactics often used when the stakes of the secret are high, the secret is in danger of being known, the partner is being challenging, or the secret keeper is desperate. These tactics are more obvious and thus may give away that there is a secret. Emotions may well drive the maintaining of secrets. Fear, anger, and pain can be strong motivators for perpetuating a secret. The emotions may override other concerns such as fairness, caring, and honesty.

For example, Dwayne may justify keeping his affair secret because he is angry at his wife for controlling many aspects of their life. Conscious decision often is used to maintain a secret when the secret keeper feels justified in having the secret. Derrick may consciously maintain the secret that he has cancer because he thinks his wife could not handle knowing.

Summary

At this point, as therapists, our heads are spinning. What do we do with all this information? This chapter has explored many issues regarding secrets including types of secrets, content of secrets, consequences of secrets, and maintaining secrets. Levels of awareness, the intentions of the secret keeper, and why couples keep secrets were discussed in depth. Understanding the complexity of these issues about secrets engenders a respect for the intricacy and intensity that secrets create in couples and in their therapy.

7

The Challenge of Working With Secrets in Couple Therapy

Introduction

"What am I facing in working with secrets in couple therapy?" This chapter explores the therapist's experience working with secrets and outlines many of the possible situations and contingencies the therapist may face in this work. Why therapists hold secrets is also discussed. The chapter concludes with strategies for dealing with these situations.

The Therapist's Experience

Each of us has stayed awake some night debating what to do with a client's secret. Each of us has felt the stress of the responsibility as we formulate a plan as to how to deal with the couple about a secret. Each of us has felt the dread as we approach a couple therapy session knowing we have to address a secret. These are the times when we ask ourselves, "Why did I decide to become a couple therapist?" and "Isn't it easier to stick with seeing just individuals?"

On the one hand, dealing with secrets in couple therapy is common fare for a couple therapist. A good part of our work is bringing out issues that are hidden from awareness and from one's partner. During couple therapy, hopefully much will emerge that the couple didn't know so that they can heal, grow, and improve their relationship. On the other hand, dealing with secrets creates particular dilemmas and challenges for the therapist. One of the main dilemmas is "playing God." When we, as therapists, know something secret within the couple, we are in a potentially powerful position. What we do with the secret can profoundly affect the couple's relationship and the lives of the two individuals. For example, the secret, if known, could break up the relationship. Once revealed, the secret could hurt children and family members of the couple. The secret revealed could ruin a career, wreck friendships, or cause financial distress. Thus, it is vital that as therapists we know how to deal with secrets. We need to have a well-developed approach and belief about secrets. We need to have the skills to handle that approach.

Secrets can also pose a challenge to our career as therapists. Clients may become angry with us, leave us, or sue us as a result of how we handle secrets. How we handle secrets poses ethical and legal dilemmas. Most of us are familiar with the Tarasoff decision that involves "duty to warn." This decision states that if we determine from information from a client that a person is in imminent danger of being harmed, we must warn the endangered person and the appropriate people who can protect the individual. We are also mandated reporters, meaning that we must report child abuse to the proper authorities. We may be called to the witness stand in a divorce trial. We may be required to submit our therapy notes to a court. How do confidentiality and limits of confidentiality affect how we deal with secrets? We may, at times, have to decide how to handle a secret based more on what we are required to do and on protecting ourselves than on what we think is right for our clients.

Thus, we must be knowledgeable about our ethical and legal obligations. We need to be prepared for how to handle secrets that involve these dimensions. We also need to be clear about the limits of confidentiality with the couples we see. What is our obligation with regard to affairs, financial deception, destructive lies, or one partner's plan to leave the relationship when the other doesn't know? What are our professional beliefs about how to best help a couple get through a dilemma that involves a secret? Some couple therapists won't hold secrets. They make it clear up front that anything revealed to them in an individual meeting is open to be shared with the other member of the couple. This may apply to affairs, lies, betrayals, etc. But it is not so easy or clear-cut when it comes to feelings, thoughts, and perceptions. Does this therapist share that one member of the couple finds the other's body unattractive? Does the therapist share that one member of the couple is having thoughts of leaving the relationship when these thoughts may be an expression of frustration? Because secrets encompass a wide variety of issues, we often have to decide what is right in the particular situation. This goes back to "playing God." We need some guidelines to help us through the maze and some ways to handle the dilemmas that arise about secrets in general and particular types of secrets specifically.

Weeks, Odell, and Methven (2005) explore the complexity of dealing with confidentiality and secrets in couple therapy. They describe three ethical approaches for couple therapists with regard to confidentiality: "… keeping all individually revealed information confidential unless there is a waiver; sharing all information; and having accountability with discretion" (p. 57). The latter option involves the therapist maintaining "… information in confidence unless he or she believes it will be detrimental to the progress of the couple therapy" (p. 61). They explore the advantages and disadvantages of each position and describe the accountability with discretion option as being preferable because it allows the therapist the most flexibility and ability to control the therapy. They warn that whichever position therapists choose, they must be clear about their position with the clients and understand that no position is without ethical and legal risks and complexities. I believe that accountability with discretion is the most realistic and helpful position for the couple therapist given the complexities of secrets, their gravity, and their consequences, and given that some secrets are better shared and some are better not shared. Karpel (1994) gives an example of accountability with discretion in working with an undisclosed extramarital involvement (EMI). He writes:

> In some cases, you may feel that the EMI should not be disclosed immediately, for example, if there is a preexisting crisis or if the uninvolved partner is seriously depressed. In these situations, as long as the involved partner agrees that disclosure might be necessary at a later point in treatment, you can offer to proceed. (p. 341)

On the other side of the coin, helping a couple navigate carefully and successfully through secrets to a healthy outcome is immensely gratifying, relieving, and exciting. It is part of what makes our work fascinating and exhilarating. The challenge keeps us sharp and alive. We may want a week off when we feel we have helped a couple to safe shores, but we can take home the feeling that this is what it's all about. This is, in fact, why we do this work: to help people through extremely difficult situations toward relationships that work and are meaningful rather than destructive and hateful.

Who Knows What: Therapy Strategies for Each Experience

"I know, but the couple does not."

"She knows that I know, but he doesn't know anything."

"He is lying to both of us."

Who knows what? There are multiple complex possibilities as outlined below. Much of the literature on who knows what discusses only a few of these options, particularly "the secret holder tells the therapist privately" (see 2e below). Yet, the realm of possibilities is much more complex than that as the list below indicates. Each variation explores a different scenario regarding couple secrets in therapy.

1. Both clients don't know.
   a. The therapist doesn't know.
   b. The therapist senses the secret.
2. One partner knows and the other doesn't.
   a. The therapist doesn't know.
   b. The therapist hasn't been told, but figures out the secret.
   c. The therapist hasn't been told, senses the secret, and doesn't want to know.
   d. The secret holder implies the secret so the therapist will know.
   e. The secret holder tells the therapist privately.
   f. The therapist finds out from another source (another therapist, a child, etc.).
3. The partner lies about the secret to the other partner.
   a. The therapist doesn't know the secret or the lie.
   b. The therapist picks up the secret and the lie.
   c. The therapist knows the secret and the lie and the lying client doesn't know this.
   d. The therapist knows the secret and the lie and the lying client does know this.

Both Clients Don't Know and the Therapist Doesn't Know

Ali is still angry with his wife Kala for not supporting him when he started his fledgling business. Since that time, he has been gradually withdrawing and the relationship has become icy. Neither the couple nor the therapist knows how this began. It has been years since Ed and Elise have had a fulfilling sex life and the cause of this is lost to their memories. In fact, the tension and distance between them began during a time they were experiencing infertility. Specifically, Ed gave up emotionally connecting to Elise when he felt he had become a baby-making machine.

In situations like these, the feelings were not shared and have become calcified into distance. The work of the therapy is to uncover the secret in order to release the couple from its effects. The person holding the secret may at one time have been aware of holding these secret feelings and attitudes, but time has covered them over. When the therapist begins to uncover the secret, he or she needs to be cautious about whether and how the secret emerges. There may be circumstances when it is more harmful for the secret to emerge. Sometimes one of the partners discovers the secret.

The examples above involve secrets of feelings. There can also be secrets of information, secrets of values, and family secrets that fall into this scenario. There may be an illness that is undetected yet is affecting the partners. There may be a family secret that is affecting the partners and is unknown. The therapist should be aware of the possibility of something secret and unknown that could be influencing the therapy. Therapists need to be on the watch for these secrets.

Self-deception may underlie why partners do not know that they are holding a secret. Self-deception may be the result of selectively ignored information, resistance to information, or unconscious processes. Ego defense mechanisms such as repression, dissociation, denial, projection, rationalization, and displacement lead to self-deception (Ford, 1996). Ford writes, "…a common feature of defense mechanisms is that they assist in the process of self-deception…these are the means by which we fool ourselves" (p. 38). This is the stuff of therapy about which much has been written (Saarni & Lewis, 1993; Goleman, D., 1985). Krestan and Bepko (1993) describe the self-deception and denial that often occur with alcohol and drug abusers: "'I'm not doing what I am doing' or 'What I'm doing doesn't have the consequences it appears to have'" (p. 142).

Both Clients Don't Know and the Therapist Senses the Secret

How does the therapist sense a secret? There are many clues a therapist can pick up: inconsistencies, defensiveness, guilty affect, withdrawal, unexplained behaviors, and protectiveness are examples. Ford (1996) cites research on the most prevalent nonverbal signals of lying. Examples include: reduced rate of speech, increased pitch of voice, disguised smiling, lack of head movement, and pause fillers such as "uh" and "er" (p. 213). Ekman (2001) describes facial cues to lying, which include blushing, blanching, blinking, false smiling, and tearing. Research also shows that a liar's credibility is an important factor in whether the lie will be detected (Bond & DePaulo, 2008).

When therapists sense a secret, they need to decide whether they want to pursue the secret and find out whether what they sense is true. A number of factors involved in this decision include the following:

- Will it help to know?
- Will it compromise the therapist to know?

- Will pursuing it make it known to the person or partner?
- What will be the consequences of pursuing it?
- How important is this issue at this point?

Suppose, as the therapist, you sense that Vinnie is a closet alcoholic and that neither he nor his partner Sam are aware of this. To determine whether this is true, you observe Vinnie's behavior and physical presentation. You could also ask questions that would help you to make an assessment. You will need to think about whether to ask direct questions (how much Vinnie drinks, under what conditions, how high he gets etc.) or indirect questions (how is he doing in his job, how is he when he gets up in the morning, how is their sexual relationship). You need to base the decision to pursue these questions in part on whether you think one or both of the partners will realize why you are asking these questions and what the consequences will be if either is aware. Because your questions could clue one of them into the issue, you need to be aware of the timing of raising the questions. Do you have the trust built to open up this issue yet? How fragile is Vinnie, and how fragile is Sam? There are any number of considerations to weigh. You also need to decide if Vinnie's potential alcoholism is a central issue for the therapy.

One Partner Knows, the Other Doesn't, and the Therapist Doesn't Know
Think of the potential problems this situation causes for couple therapy. The therapist is operating partially in the dark. In addition, the partner who holds the secret is living in a different reality than the therapist and the other partner. Thus, the therapy may have limited effectiveness for this partner and the couple. The partner who knows may also control the therapy in some ways. For example, the secret holder may carefully steer clear of certain topics. He or she may come across as cooperative and congenial, but if the secret were known, he or she would be defensive and protective. Usually, but unfortunately not always, the therapist can begin to sense that something is not right. The behavior of the partner with the secret becomes cagy, inconsistent, or exaggerated. The partners seem to be living in two different worlds.

Sometimes the unknowing partner may not want to know a secret. Ekman (2001) writes "… we collude in the lie, unwittingly, because we have a stake in not knowing the truth" (p. 343). He gives as an example a wife who doesn't want to know her husband is having an affair because of how disruptive it would be to the family.

One Partner Knows, the Other Doesn't, and the Therapist Figures Out the Secret
The therapist doesn't just sense the secret at this point, he or she now *knows* the secret. The therapist doesn't have to decide whether to pursue learning about the possible secret, he or she has already figured it out. As the therapist, you realize that Laura is hiding financial problems from Jan. Or you realize that Sal's father abused his mother, but Sal's wife has no clue about this. When you pick up on the secret, the knowing partner may or may not realize that you now know. Usually the knowing partner does not know. This becomes a very difficult position for you as the therapist. What do you do? Do you hold the secret? Do you reveal to the secret holder that you know? If so, do you urge the secret holder to tell his partner? In some situations, as discussed, the therapist must reveal the secret. In many more situations, the therapist must judge what to do based on all the variables. When the secret-holding partner realizes that the therapist now knows, there are more issues. Does the therapist who knows the secret also know that the secret-holding partner knows she or he knows? How does the therapist determine if the secret-holding partner knows he or she knows?

One Partner Knows, the Other Doesn't, Plus the Therapist Hasn't
Been Told, but Senses the Secret and Doesn't Want to Know
Therapists may not want to know because of the awkward and compromising situation in which knowing puts them. Therapists may decide to continue the therapy as if they don't know. There may be several reasons for this: therapists may judge that if they "know," they cannot keep moving ahead with the therapy and may feel that the couple therapy is on a good course. The therapists may feel the couple is not ready to face the secret, but if they "know," the secret will have to be addressed. The therapists not "knowing" mean that they don't let the clients know they know or that they avoid knowing.

The Secret Holder Implies the Secret so the Therapist Will Know
This situation creates a double bind for therapists. Clearly if they let the implying partners know they understand, the therapists are keeping a secret in collusion with the secret-keeping partners. On the other hand, if the therapists ignore the signals the secret-holding partners are sending, the therapist may miss an opportunity to know and address the secret. The secret-keeping partners may also feel shut off by the therapists. The therapists must determine whether to (1) have an individual session with

the implying partners (2) surface the implications in the couple session; or (3) ignore the signals and keep going.

The Secret Holder Tells the Therapist Privately
The secret holder may reveal the secret in a private session, over the phone, in a letter, or in a voice mail. In their research of subjects documenting many secret-sharing sessions, Rodriguez and Ryave (1992) put together a step-by-step outline of how secret sharing often occurs in an organized way. How will the revelation of a secret to the therapist affect the therapy? As discussed previously, the therapist needs to discuss the limits of confidentiality. This should happen at the beginning of the couple therapy and then, depending on the nature of the secret, it may need to be addressed again later. If it is agreed that the therapist will not reveal the secret, there may need to be a discussion with the secret-holding partner about how couple therapy will proceed from here. As the therapist, you now have extra responsibility. You will be walking a thin line between helping the couple relationship move forward and holding the secret. Sometimes knowing makes this easier because you understand what is happening and sometimes it makes it harder because you are keeping one partner in the dark. Roberts (1993) discusses the complexity of the therapist's position and how therapeutic planning can become contorted. If the unknowing partner discovers that you have known the secret, that person may feel angry, hurt, or betrayed.

Weeks et al. (2005) describe the sense of betrayal and anger that a partner might feel. They write of a therapist working with a couple in which the man is having an affair that the therapist, but not the wife, knows about. "Had the wife found out about the therapist knowing this secret she would have felt betrayed by him, at the very least" (p. 53). Karpel (1980) describes the binds, such as collusion and guilt, which the therapist may experience.

The Therapist Finds Out From Another Source
When this happens, the couple members may not know that the therapist knows. The therapist may find out from a number of possible sources such as a referring therapist, another family member, a public source, or another client. Weeks et al. (2005) give the following example: "...a therapist may learn that a client that he or she is seeing in couple therapy is having an affair with another of his or her other clients" (p. 53). The bind for the therapist is similar to the bind when the therapist senses a secret that he or she hasn't been told. In addition, in this situation there is the added dynamic of how the therapist found out. Adam's referring therapist

tells the couple therapist that Adam has acquired evidence that his wife is having an affair, yet his wife does not know that Adam has this evidence. As the couple therapist, it is up to you to decide if the secret needs to come out and, if so, how it should emerge. You will most likely need permission from the source of the secret to bring the secret out, but you may not get this permission. Then you need to decide if you can proceed with the couples therapy knowing what you know and keeping it a secret, or whether you need to reveal the information without permission.

The Partner Lies About the Secret to His or Her Partner
Secrets are a lie in and of themselves. A further lie can be added if the secret-keeping partner makes up more lies to cover the secret, or denies the secret if confronted by the partner. Further lying compounds the difficulty and complexity of the situation. If the therapist becomes aware of the secret and the further lying, he or she needs to assess the seriousness of the situation. Is the lying client a compulsive liar? Is the lying client creating far more serious damage with the lying? What is the responsibility of the therapist to the unknowing partner? The more extensive the lying, the more difficult it becomes for the therapist not to be colluding if he or she doesn't take some action.

Why Therapists Hold Secrets

Why would we want the burden of holding secrets? Why would we take the risk of holding secrets? Knowing secrets gives the therapist a better picture and therefore an understanding of what is going on in the couple relationship. If partners know that whatever they share can be shared with their partner, they will potentially not reveal important information and feelings (Weeks et al., 2005).

Knowing secrets gives therapists the possibility of working with the secret keepers to face their secret holding and its consequences. In the process, the therapists can help the secret keepers make informed and better choices about the secret and what to do with it. If the secret holders decide to reveal the secret, the therapists can help the partners prepare to share it in an appropriate way. The therapist can also help prepare the unknowing partners for what they will learn.

Some partners hold secrets because they believe that the relationship can't handle the secret. Perhaps the couple has low trust or poor communication. Couple therapists can help the partners develop the skills to handle secrets. This may be part of helping the couple learn about closeness, separateness, and boundaries.

Sometimes therapists hold secrets because they are bound by confidentiality to do so. They do not have permission to share the secret or they have not stipulated that secrets told to the therapist will be shared in the couple therapy. Even if the therapist has stipulated that secrets are to be shared, there are some secrets that fall outside these parameters; for example, secrets of feelings that are too hurtful to the partner to know. In this case, the therapist would be inflicting pain to insist that the secret be shared.

Summary

Working with secrets presents an incredible challenge for a therapist! There are so many possible nuances to address including who knows what, who wants to know what, who found out from whom, how to deal with confidentiality, and the feelings that come up for the therapist. This chapter delved into these nuances, offered support and direction for the therapist, and concluded with a discussion about why therapists hold secrets.

8
Guidelines and Strategies for Therapists

Introduction

> What do I do? My head is reeling. How do I sort out who needs to know what and what is my responsibility? Am I in trouble?

To do this demanding work therapists need guidelines. This chapter presents a list of such guidelines plus strategies for dealing with three main possible courses of action for the therapist: holding the secret, helping the secret emerge, and facing the secrecy and the lying. Issues about revealing secrets are probed and the chapter concludes with a case study.

Guidelines

1. Address confidentiality.

This issue is discussed in Chapter 7 in the section entitled "The Therapist's Experience." It is vital that therapists include the limits of confidentiality in their contracts with couples. Certainly the legal limits must be included along with further limits particular to the therapist. Confidentiality contracts usually cover clear overt secrets. The more nuanced secrets, such as secrets of feelings, cannot be easily defined in terms of what is confidential and what is not.

2. Decide whether to see couple members individually.

Many couple therapists see each member routinely as part of the couple assessment. Then throughout the couple therapy, the therapist may meet with one or the other or both individuals. The more the therapist meets with the couple individually, the greater the chance of learning secrets.

Thus, this factor should be considered when deciding whether to meet with each member alone. There may be times when it is wise not to meet with the members individually because you, as the therapist, don't want to hold secrets. Karpel (1994) advocates meeting with each partner individually as part of the evaluation because he believes that the advantages of the individual sessions far outweigh the disadvantages of secrets emerging. At the same time he acknowledges that "The introduction of secrets ... may create ... serious complications" (p. 123).

3. Pay attention to the dynamics of secrets.

Since many secrets are subtle and complex, there is no one clear guideline a couple therapist can hang onto for all situations and couples. With some couples, as the therapist, you must constantly think through where you stand and how you will handle the therapy. One guideline is clear: be on your toes, be ready for discomfort, and watch for subtleties. When working with a couple with secrets, you need to pay extra attention to the dynamics of the therapy and to your role in guiding the process.

4. Do not jeopardize your own integrity in holding secrets.

This may seem obvious, yet you can easily find yourself in compromising situations in which you are over invested, trying too hard, or having difficulty holding both people's interests. You need to have a good sensor for when you can get in trouble. And you need to know what to do when your sensor is telling you to watch out. Warning signs can include: feeling too burdened, being too aligned with one of the couple members, or having too much power that you don't want. Welter-Enderlin (1993) describes her own wrestling with her role in temporarily keeping a secret in marital therapy.

5. Set limits on secrets.

You may need to tell one of the partners that there are certain things you don't want to be told. For example, if you know that one partner is thinking about leaving the relationship but the other partner doesn't know this, you will likely need to limit how much the first partner tells you about his or her desire to leave. You may also set limits by directing what is discussed. For example, if you suspect Mary is avoiding sex with Bethany because she finds her body unattractive, you may want to stay away from discussing attractiveness.

6. Focus on the couple as a unit.

It is important to remember to focus on what will help the relationship when dealing with secrets. It can be easy to get drawn into helping one member in particular. When you know a secret, it may be the unknowing partner that you find yourself wanting to help more. Secrets can pull apart your focus on the couple as well as pull the couple apart. Secrets can be divisive and can thus affect you in your work.

7. Focus on the larger relationship issues.

Secrets can be powerful. They can start to define the couple therapy if you are not careful. The secret is important, but it is likely to be one facet of the relationship. You need to keep the whole relationship in the therapy.

8. Check your own feelings and countertransference.

Secrets are compelling and may well stir up strong feelings in you, the therapist (Imber-Black, 1993). You should expect that you could have a personal reaction. There may have been a secret in your history that in some way affected you. Secrets can also be difficult because so much of our job is helping people to be more open, to share, and to grow. Secrets may directly challenge what we are about in our work. This can be quite disconcerting and even disorienting, provoking anger, frustration, and helplessness. We need to know when our ability to help has been limited by secrets. We may not be able to get beyond the immobilizing effects of the secret. Imber-Black (1993) writes about how the presence of a secret can block the progress of the therapy.

9. Know your threshold and know what to do.

What if a secret hurts the unknowing partner beyond the point that the therapist believes is acceptable? (Ford, 1996). This threshold of acceptability varies among therapists. As previously explained, you need to have informed your clients about your policy about confidentiality. The following applies primarily to those therapists who take a position of "accountability with discretion" (Weeks, Odell, & Methven, 2005) (see Chapter 7, "The Therapist's Experience"). Your limit may be when one partner is endangering the other's health by seeing prostitutes. Or it may come when one partner is secretly wrecking the family's finances. What can you as the therapist do when you reach that limit? The primary action you can take is to meet with the secret-holding partner and tell him or her that you can no longer participate in holding the secret because you believe that the harm to the unknowing partner is too great. Further, you can say to the secret-holding partner that either he or she needs to reveal the secret or the couple therapy will end. You will no longer do the couple therapy and hold the secret. You will need to explain why the consequences to the unknowing partner are too great for the therapy to be productive with the secret being withheld. The secret-holding partner will likely feel threatened, cornered, fearful, or angry. You will need to handle these responses and talk about the options for telling the secret or ending the therapy constructively.

10. Don't take too much responsibility.

It is all too easy to feel responsible and, in fact, to become responsible for a secret. This may happen particularly when the unknowing partner learns of the secret and learns that you knew the secret. This partner then may feel angry and betrayed by you as well as by the other partner (Weeks et al., 2005). Further, this partner may project responsibility for keeping the secret on to you because it is easier than holding the other partner responsible. You may become responsible for the secret in your mind because you took on too much responsibility for managing the couple's dynamic around the secret. Or you took on too much responsibility for helping the couple move to a point where they could face the secret. In the situation where the secret becomes known and the unknowing partner is upset with you, you will need to explain carefully your role in the therapy and why you didn't reveal or force the other partner to reveal the secret. You may, for example, need to explain that your role is to help each person discover his or her feelings and issues and work to a point where he or she can be more open with his or her partner. You may need to explain that your role is to help the relationship get to a point where the secret could be revealed productively.

11. Consider whether the therapy needs to end.

Couple therapy enhances the possibility that secrets will emerge. Yet, perhaps the relationship cannot handle the emergence of secrets. Continuing to do therapy will, then possibly jeopardize the relationship. Thus, there may be times when it is wisest to end the therapy in order to preserve the relationship. You may need to help the secret holder or the couple see the situation and the risks of continuing the therapy. One client alerted me to this situation when he said he didn't want to continue the couple therapy because he feared his wife would discover she wanted to leave the relationship. In fact, this was a real danger.

12. Put a ban on lying.

A partner overtly lying about a secret is unacceptable in couple therapy. Therapists need to set a limit on the lying or they are colluding in the cover-up. It is essential that therapists let the secret-holding partners know that they cannot be in that position. The couple therapy cannot continue if the secret holding includes the therapy in the deceit. The therapy then ceases to have credibility. For couple therapy, omitting and not admitting may be as unacceptable as lying. One might argue that omitting and not admitting are lying as much as telling a direct lie. This gets into a philosophical debate beyond the scope of this discussion. Yet, they can allow some room for the therapist to work with the feelings and issues toward some resolution. Overt lying is too much of a violation of trust between the partners and undermines the therapy. This is similar to the client lying to the therapist, which Gediman and Lieberman (1996) believe "renders the work meaningless" (p. 70).

Strategies

There are three main strategies that couple therapists can use in dealing with secrets:

1. The therapist holds the secret.
2. The therapist works toward the secret emerging.
3. The therapist addresses the secrecy and lying.

Ford (1996) states, "The art and skill of the family therapist are in knowing which secrets need to be disclosed and how to let them unfold in a constructive manner" (p. 247).

Holding the Secret

How do therapists hold secrets? They may avoid dealing with the secret by doing any of the following:

- Changing the subject.
- Working on other issues.

- Prioritizing the secret as of lesser importance than other issues.
- Telling the partners directly that there are certain issues they are not going to address at this point.

The therapist may also help the couple work beyond the secret. If, for example, one member secretly wants to leave the relationship, the therapist may work on strengthening the relationship with the possibility that the partners will grow closer and the person who wants to leave will have a change of heart. If one person is secretly flirting with someone outside the relationship, the therapist may help the couple to find more fulfillment together so that the need to flirt goes away. This strategy can be risky if the partner with the secret acts out in a way that makes it difficult for the therapist to maintain the secret. The therapist then needs to use a different strategy.

While couple therapists are holding the secret, they can work to detoxify the secret in such a way that it is no longer charged. It may then no longer be a secret, making revealing it unnecessary or able to be revealed. This work would most likely be done individually. Cognitive behavioral couple therapy (CBCT) may work well to detoxify the secret. Baucom, Epstein, and LaTaillade, (2002) write, "CBCT has established itself as an empirically supported intervention for treatment of distressed couples" (p. 28). The partners may see the secret as a negative reflection on them or as a poison for the relationship. Therapists can help the secret holder redefine this view through the cognitive behavioral concepts of faulty thinking and cognitive distortions such as overgeneralizations, inaccurate inferences, and catastrophizing. Then the therapists help the secret holders readjust their view of the consequences of the secret. This technique is called reframing, which Goldenberg and Goldenberg (2004) define as, "Relabeling behavior by putting it into a new more positive perspective ..., thus altering the context in which it is perceived and inviting new responses to the same behavior" (p. 511). For example, if the secret can come to be seen in the larger context of the relationship, particularly with regard to positive aspects of the relationship, it may diminish in importance. Other aspects of the relationship may take on more valence and meaning. A similar technique from narrative therapy is "unique outcomes." Through telling the story of the secret, the partners can come to see a new and different outcome than previously believed.

Therapists can also detoxify a secret by normalizing it. The therapists show the secret-holding partners that the issues that they imagined were unique to themselves are common to many people. The dire consequences they imagined are not so likely. For example, the wife may imagine that if she tells her husband that she has an illness her husband will lose interest and leave. When the wife understands that these are normal feelings, she may see that sharing the secret will not so likely lead to abandonment. Thus, detoxifying can also occur by the therapist helping the wife to see that the husband will not necessarily have the reaction the wife expects.

Helping the Secret Emerge

Some of the above techniques of holding the secret also help the secret to gradually emerge. They may make the secret become less charged and able to be shared. If the therapist's goal is for the secret to eventually emerge, there are a number of pathways to achieve this. Korelitz (1982) and Imber-Black (1993) describe various ways to help a secret to emerge. Bader and Pearson (2000) discuss many strategies for couples to face up to lies and to come clean in their relationship. They suggest, for example, confronting self-deception, sharing in a clear productive way, acknowledging responsibility, and being prepared for the partner's anger.

Stressing the Importance of Sharing the Secret
As the therapist, you can be clear with the secret holder that to be able to share the secret is an important and necessary goal of the therapy. You can then show how holding the secret is destructive to the partners and the relationship. You can also show how sharing the secret could lead to positive consequences such as relieving guilt, releasing tension, and building trust.

Preparing for Sharing
You can help prepare the partner for sharing the secret. This may involve initially facing the secret, discussing how it developed, determining what it accomplishes, and acknowledging the power it has. Sometimes partners are not even aware they are holding a secret. The techniques discussed above such as detoxifying the secret and reframing the consequences of it can help prepare the partner for sharing the secret. Facing the probable consequences of sharing the secret can also help you plan for the emergence of the secret (Imber-Black, 1993).

Sometimes the secret cannot be detoxified. Then you may need to work with the partners to develop the courage, trust, and conditions to share the secret. Helping them experience just how toxic holding a secret is, may help them see that the consequences of keeping the secret are worse than sharing the secret. For example, you may help the husband see that undisclosed financial problems are destructive to him, his wife, and the relationship and that secrecy is making the financial issues worse. You will likely also need to work on how to develop the courage to share the secret. Showing him that sharing requires strength, conviction, and caring is important. Helping him discover these qualities in himself is essential. Lerner (1993) suggests ways for clients to experiment with new behaviors that can lead to more honest ways of relating. She also describes ways of easing into bringing a secret out rather than confronting the secret in a way that produces defensiveness and resistance. Karpel (1980) suggests that the therapist can offer extra sessions to the secret holder to help prepare to disclose the secret.

You may help the partner with the secret to share gradually dip her toe into the water first before diving in. Bader and Pearson (2000) suggest, "Sometimes a couple may begin by using a small matter as a testing ground" (p. 117). If, for example, the client has secrets from her family of origin, you may suggest that she share some of the less upsetting secrets first to see how her partner reacts. Another way you can facilitate sharing is to speak for the client. You may say what she cannot with both partners in the room. This can open a discussion in which she then shares more and responds to her partner's concerns.

You can facilitate the secret's emerging by educating couples about issues related to the secret, which usually requires the secret holders' consent. For example, you may educate couples about ways to handle their finances or better ways to parent. This can create an opening for the secret holders to reveal issues they are hiding.

You may be able to provide an opportunity for partners to share a secret by involving other key people. If, for example, the mother is keeping a secret that the couple's daughter is gay and the daughter is afraid to let the mother share this with the father, you may want to meet with the daughter to help her talk through her fears about her father being informed.

A key way to provide an opportunity for a client to share a secret is by offering the client your support and counsel through the sharing process. This may be what the client needs to gain the courage to face the issues. The client's aloneness with the issue may be a main barrier to sharing.

Working on the Toxic Relationship Patterns

You may need to work on some of the toxic patterns in the relationship to pave the way for a secret to be shared. If, for example, a couple has a maximizer/minimizer pattern in which they become polarized into a dynamic where one exaggerates issues while the other downplays issues, they may not be prepared to handle the emergence of a secret. The couple therapy may involve changing this pattern of communication and reaction into a dynamic of sharing, listening, and understanding before a difficult secret can be shared.

Addressing Control Issues

Control issues may need to be addressed before a secret can be shared. As discussed, secrets give control and may be kept for that reason. A partner who needs control or fears losing control is not going to be ready to share a secret. You need to address the control issues first. This may involve facing some deeper personality issues, some family of origin issues, addiction issues, or any more serious psychological issues. The secret-holding partner will likely need individual therapy to work on these issues before any sharing can take place.

Facing the Secrecy and the Lying

One of the most powerful ways to face the lying involved in holding a secret is to directly confront it. This involves discussing the secret-holding partners' lying, the efforts involved in it, and the consequences of it. This is a tough love approach. As the therapist, you look the clients in the eye and clearly spell out the negative aspects of their lying. The goal is to shake the clients up, make them uncomfortable, and startle them into facing the situation and into action. You point out inconsistencies, thoughtlessness, control tactics, and hurts. You address necessary actions to rectify the situation. You should expect defensiveness, anger, and lashing out. To take this approach, you may need support and you must have good reason to think you will get through to the client. It is risky.

A gentler approach involves creating cognitive dissonance for the client. Hanna (2002) writes about how cognitive dissonance works:

> It begins with the presentation of incongruent, inconsistent or contradictory information concerning the self, beliefs, behaviors or lifestyle. This then produces a sense of anxiety in a person that is followed by a desire to resolve the incongruency and anxiety. (p. 202)

Show clients how lying 1) is undermining things they care about and value and 2) serves them in a limited, shortsighted way that will backfire. You then address how the secrecy is a strategy they learned in order to cope with a difficult situation, but is not working now. When the clients grasp these consequences, they may then be motivated to be more truthful.

To face the secrecy and lying, issues of power and control must be addressed. The goal here is to take away the power that the lying brings. This can be done by exposing the fallacies of the power of the lying, the temporariness of the power, and the hurtfulness of the power. As the therapist, you need to turn the power upside down. Secrecy is not ultimately power. It leads to isolation, distrust, more lies, shame, and self-loathing. This all needs to be exposed to the clients in a way that hits them where it hurts. You need to find that place of integrity inside, however well hidden it may be, and help bring it forward into their conscience. With partners with deeper personality issues, the best you may be able to do is to motivate them to change this behavior by showing them how the lying and secrecy hurts them and their lives.

Consequences of Revealing Secrets

"If I tell, will he leave me?" "What if she tells the neighborhood?" "Will she use the secret against me?"

Imber-Black (1993) describes how the aftermath of revealing a secret often involves the hard work of rebuilding and reconciling:

While the initial opening of a secret in therapy can have dramatic and positive effects on individual functioning and interpersonal relationships, much work generally remains to be done to restore reliability, heal broken trust, deal with anger and work on whatever issues may have been kept secret (p. 26).

There are a number of factors that need to be considered when a partner is thinking about whether to reveal a secret to his or her mate. Below is an outline of these considerations:

1. What are the consequences of revealing the secret?
   a. Decease or increase of pressure and emotions
   b. Increase or decrease of respectability
   c. External consequences: financial, professional, family, social
2. What are the consequences of not revealing the secret?

  a. Increased isolation
  b. Maintaining boundaries and privacy
  c. Increased or decreased sense of control
3. To whom would the secret be revealed?
  a. Is the person trustworthy?
  b. Would the person judge the revealer?
  c. Would the revealing change the relationship with the person told?
  d. Would the person told feel some obligation with regard to the secret?

Many of the consequences of revealing a secret have been discussed and illustrated in this chapter, particularly those related to items 1 and 2 above. The issues in item 3 warrant more discussion. One of the first considerations in deciding whether to reveal a secret to one's partner is whether the partner is viewed as trustworthy. Kelly (2002) discusses ways that people determine whether a partner is trustworthy or not. She writes that one indicative factor is whether after a revelation, "… the partner usually discloses very personal information in return" (p. 198).

Will the partner keep the confidence? Will he or she act responsibly with the secret? For example, will Dan go to June's boss to tell the boss that June has had an affair with a coworker? In addition to considering whether one's partner is trustworthy, the secret keeper needs to consider whether he or she is vindictive, strong enough to handle the secret, and willing to work through the issues that come with the secret. Usually the unknowing partner will have strong feelings about the secret once it is shared, and from these strong feelings may come judgments. The judgments may be devastating to the secret keeper and may lead to regrets about sharing the secret.

Another consideration for the secret keeper is how would revealing the secret affect the relationship? It is bound to have a strong effect, often a negative one. Would it raise the partner's suspicions in other areas? Would it alienate him or her? Would it cause the unknowing partner to leave? What kind of healing would be needed and how likely is it to happen? Revealing in and of itself can bring healing and more closeness, depending on the secret and how it is shared.

Secret keepers also need to consider whether the partner would feel some obligation with regard to the secret. For example, would they feel obligated to inform or warn someone else? Would they feel obligated to the partner in some way? Jim may not share that he has heart disease with his partner because he doesn't want him to stay in the relationship out of a sense of duty.

When Secrets Should or Should Not Be Revealed

Not all secrets should be revealed. It would seem that the goal of therapy is to bring issues out in the open. Yet some secrets, if revealed, can cause unnecessary harm and irreversible damage. I have already discussed how clients telling their partners that they are not attracted to their body can be hurtful. Telling a partner about feelings that may pass can damage the relationship. Yet, telling secrets can sometimes bring a couple closer together. How do we, as therapists, tell the difference? Much of the difference is relative to the individual and to the couple's relationship. However, there are a few guidelines therapists should follow. Secrets of feelings about something one's partner cannot control or change are often hurtful to reveal. Secrets about issues that may pass are often not helpful to reveal. Secrets that violate one's privacy if shared can be detrimental to one's sense of self. For example, Carmen may feel violated if she reveals that as she was growing up she had sexual feelings toward her cousin.

Sometimes the negative consequences of revealing a secret may outweigh the positive consequences. For Lauren to tell her husband Vijay that she was unfaithful to her high school boyfriend may create fear and jealousy in Vijay, particularly if he feels insecure about himself.

Lerner (1993) discusses how it may not be helpful to reveal truths when the truth teller is more interested in being honest than constructive. Tact and thoughtfulness are important in determining whether and when to reveal a secret.

When do secrets need to be revealed? As discussed earlier, secrets need to be revealed when they endanger the partner. They may need to be revealed if the couple cannot progress in the therapy because of the secret. Secrets may need to be revealed if they are creating distrust, isolation, or shame. Revealing can have many positive consequences including the following:

- More openness
- Better understanding
- Clarification of issues
- More closeness
- Lifting a weight or barrier

- More informed choices of response
- Better collaboration and cooperation
- Better sense of inclusion and specialness

Secrets may need to be revealed when they keep perpetuating more secrets, more lies, and more negative consequences. They need to be revealed to stem the tide of toxicity and destructiveness. And, of course, secrets likely need to be revealed when they are positive in nature. Thus surprises, promotions, pay increases, helpful deeds, celebrations, etc., that have been secret need to be revealed to bring the excitement and joy the secret keeper has been hiding to the unknowing partner (Roberts, 1993).

Case Study: Doreen and Larry

Something was off. I could feel it the minute they walked into the room. She was too calm. He was agitated. She was trying to appear put together, but there was a vagueness, a flatness underneath her measured engagement. I was alert right away, wondering and on guard. He was contained holding his energy in. Both were playing a role that revealed that their true selves were not in the room.

Doreen and Larry came into therapy ostensibly to work on their lack of intimacy. Larry complained about Doreen's withdrawal from him emotionally and physically. Doreen agreed that she had pulled back, yet claimed she did not know why. She professed carefully that she wanted to find the desire to be close again and that she would do whatever needed to be done. Larry kept expressing worry that she wouldn't try, she wouldn't work on it. His worry was tinged with accusation. Her assurance was calculated to seem real and to appease.

What, I wondered, is going on here? I had the feeling of walking on shifting ground, ground that was supposed to be solid, but indeed could move in some unknown direction at any time. I knew I had to move carefully. I could lose either of them at any time. Or something could break out at any time and disrupt the therapy. How would I get out the truths on the one hand and keep control at the helm so the boat wouldn't capsize? What was contained? What secrets were one or the other or both holding? Surely, there were numerous hidden issues.

Doreen was 52 and Larry 53. They had been married for two years and had known each other for five. Both had been married before and had grown children. Doreen worked as store manager and Larry was a buyer for an electronics store near her store in the same mall. Their lives were quite intertwined socially and professionally, yet she clearly wanted more separation from him.

We began the therapy working on the issue of intimacy as they requested. As the sessions progressed, it became clearer to me that this issue was a cover for much more, yet I was unable to make many inroads to deeper issues. I wanted to push. I didn't like my own uneasiness. I was uncomfortable with the covered up tension palpable in the room. I told myself to keep probing and to wait. Whew! The unknown secrets were unsettling.

Gradually details and stories emerged. Doreen spent many hours at home in bed watching TV. Perhaps this was the secret: She was depressed. Yet, I wasn't convinced. Perhaps this was a reaction to him. It became more evident that Larry was intrusive. He had inserted himself into a disagreement Doreen had with her sister. In fact, Larry had created an embarrassing scene that made Doreen's issues with her sister worse. When this emerged, he apologized in an angry way, clearly feeling hurt that she did not appreciate his "help." Perhaps the secret was his invasiveness.

As the therapy progressed, Doreen seemed intent on ascribing her lack of intimacy with Larry to a lack of attraction to him and to menopause. Was this it? Had she lost attraction? Was he not appealing to her? I was concerned for his feelings of rejection. Yet, Larry angrily rejected this notion. The more he rejected it, the more she focused on it as the central issue in the relationship. She claimed she just didn't have sexual feelings any more. He argued that they could do exercises to recapture the feelings. She didn't think so. He spoke of books he had read and things they could do to solve her issue. He wore her down. She retreated to her position that she would do whatever it took to work on the relationship.

What a bind. I knew this was not the real issue, but I was still getting only hints about what was true. I didn't want to play into their denial, yet where was I to go? I didn't want to side with Larry and yet opposing the exercises would expose her retreat. I decided that giving them exercises and homework could actually be a helpful way to get at underlying issues. The exercises would be diagnostic and would keep them engaged in the therapy. It was doubtful to me that the exercises would get anywhere, but I could see that they would likely bring out other issues. I was becoming particularly focused on what Doreen was withholding.

In fact, she did avoid doing any exercises. Larry became angrier. She began to reflect her discomfort with his anger. He seemed unaware of the intensity of his growing blame and impatience with her. Perhaps this was the secret: his anger and her fear of it. I began to probe for more stories of this dynamic. One of the first stories that emerged was about him flying off the handle one day when he discovered a note to Doreen from a male neighbor. He thought the note was overly friendly and he became suspicious. In the session he started accusing her of having an inappropriately close relationship with this neighbor. Doreen laughed. She minimized his concern and for once pushed back at him. He too easily backed off. Perhaps this was the secret. She was having an affair. Yet this issue died quickly.

I thought of having individual sessions to break the log jam. Yet, I was hesitant to do this. Was I ready to find out what was really happening? What if one of them, particularly Doreen, told me something that would put me in a bind? Yet, the therapy was not going anywhere and I needed to get at underlying issues. So I asked to meet with each of them individually. They were both more than willing to come alone. When Doreen came in the door, there was an urgency to her and a fragility that told me she needed this session. I explained my rules of confidentiality to her, particularly that if she was having an affair that I could not keep that a secret. She assured me that she was not having an affair. What did emerge was how beaten down she felt in the relationship. She described more incidents of Larry being controlling and explosive. Gradually I began to realize the secret, something I thought she herself was not completely admitting. She wanted out of the marriage and was afraid to leave.

I then met with Larry alone. I needed to find a way to bring out Larry's vulnerability and to get beneath his anger. Perhaps if he could open up and grow beyond his need for control, the relationship had a chance. I also wanted to explore if he had hidden issues with Doreen. Indeed, he too had a secret. He was terrified of her depression, something he had never told her. He had been married before to a woman who suffered severe depression and eventually left him. He had let the woman slip away and had felt helpless and ineffective. Larry vowed to himself that he would not let this happen to him again. He turned his grief and helplessness into anger and control.

So now, I knew. She wanted out and felt entrapped. He feared losing her and covered his fear with anger. If Larry let down his anger and showed his hurt, she might, in fact, leave the relationship feeling freed from his control. What a double bind. How to feel boxed in as a therapist. How was I to proceed? Was there any openness left in Doreen to hear Larry's pain?

The first step was for Larry to try opening up and see if Doreen could be receptive. He needed coaching about to how to share, how to avoid making himself too vulnerable, and how not to retreat into anger. We worked for a number of sessions for Larry to become more comfortable with his feelings. Meanwhile, Doreen worked on her fear and on learning how to stand up for herself. She explored how leaving would be a way to run from her fear. She came to understand that she needed to find her strength before leaving and then decide what to do.

After each had had several individual sessions, we resumed the couple work. Their interactions had already improved at home. Doreen was speaking up for herself more. Larry was stopping his anger and showing more vulnerability. These times were interspersed with falling back into their old anger–withdrawal patterns. Doreen had followed through on my referral to a psychiatrist who had prescribed the antidepressant medication Paxil.

In the couple sessions we worked on their basic anger–withdrawal pattern, replacing it with a new vulnerability–engagement interaction. Neither had told their secret yet. My work was to help them feel safe enough and trusting enough to share their deeper feelings. Larry could admit that he was scared when Doreen withdrew. Doreen admitted that she was afraid and left emotionally when Larry became angry. Slowly they began to make more connection. As I became more comfortable that Doreen was not going to leave and was more engaged in the relationship, I made more room for Larry to share his secret and his vow to himself. Doreen was quite moved by the depth of his experience. She had known of the circumstances of his ex-wife leaving, but did not know of his reaction and his vow to himself. This sharing became a significant point in a shift in their relationship. Larry was increasingly able to catch himself when he started to turn to anger and Doreen became more available and less self-protective.

Their work had begun. There was much more work in their couple therapy that came after this. Doreen did not share her secret mainly because she became more engaged. It was also clear that telling Larry that at one point she had wanted to leave the relationship would be too triggering for him. This was a secret that became obsolete and yet still had the power to hurt.

Summary

Chapter 8 has presented guidelines and strategies for the therapist in holding the secret, helping the secret to emerge, and helping clients face the secrecy and lying. Issues concerning the revealing of secrets and a case study were presented.

Dealing with secrets in couple therapy is enormously challenging. It requires careful balancing, emotional fortitude, and skillful boundary management by the couple therapist. Section III explores the many complexities and permutations of this work. The couple therapist must be able to delve into deep canyons of the human mind, walk a tightrope, brave tumultuous storms, reign in his or her own emotions, and carry heavy burdens. This work confronts a pervasive human dilemma: the boundary between self and intimate other.

Bibliography for Section II

Agnes, M. (Ed.). (2001). *Webster's New World College Dictionary* (4th ed.). Cleveland, OH: IDG Books Worldwide.

Bader, E. & Pearson, P.T. (2000). *Tell me no lies: How to face the truth and build a loving marriage.* New York: St. Martin's Press.

Baucom, D.H., Epstein, N., & LaTaillade, J.L. (2002). Cognitive-behavioral couple therapy. In A.S. Gurman & N. S. Jacobson, (Eds.), *The clinical handbook of couple therapy* (3rd ed., pp. 26–58). New York: Guilford Press.

Bok, S. (1982). *Secrets.* New York: Pantheon Books.

Bond, C. F., Jr., & DePaulo, B.M. (2008). Individual differences in judging deception: Accuracy and bias. *Psychological Bulletin, 134,* 477–493.

Bradshaw, J. (1995). *Family secrets: What you don't know can hurt you.* New York: Bantam Books.

Brown-Smith, N. (1998). Family secrets. *Journal of Family Issues, 19,* 20–42.

Casarjian, R. (1992). *Forgiveness: A bold choice for a peaceful heart.* New York: Bantam Books.

Ekman, P. (2001). *Telling lies.* New York: W.W. Norton.

Erikson, E.H. (1964). *Childhood and society.* Richmond, VA: Hogarth Press.

Ford, C.V. (1996). *Lies! lies! lies!: The psychology of deceit.* Washington, DC: American Psychiatric Press.

Gedimen, H.S. & Lieberman, J.S. (1996). *The many faces of deceit.* Northvale, NJ: Jason Aaronson.

Goldenberg, I. & Goldenberg, H. (2004). *Family therapy: An overview.* Pacific Grove, CA: Brooks/Cole.

Goleman, D. (1985). *Vital lies simple truths.* New York: Simon & Schuster.

Gottman, J. (1999). *The seven principles for making marriage work.* New York: The Three Rivers Press.

Hanna, F.J. (2005). *Therapy with difficult clients: Using the precursors method to awaken change.* Washington, DC: American Psychological Association.

Imber-Black, E. (1989). *The secret life of families.* New York: Bantam Books.

Imber-Black, E. (1993). Secrets in families and family therapy: An overview. In E. Imber-Black (Ed.), *Secrets in families and family therapy* (pp. 3–28). New York: W.W. Norton.

Imber-Black, E. (2000). The new triangle: Couples and technology. In P. Papp (Ed.), *Couples on the fault line* (pp. 48–62). New York: Guilford Press.

Karpel, M.A. (1994). *Evaluating couples.* New York: W.W. Norton.

Karpel, M. (1980). Family secrets: I Conceptual and ethical issues in the relational context. II Ethical and practical considerations in therapeutic management. *Family Process, 19,* 295–306.

Kelly, A. (2002). *The psychology of secrets.* New York: Kluwer Academic/Plenum.

Korelitz, A.Z. (1982). Dealing with sexual secrets in conjoint therapy. In A.S. Gurman (Ed.), *Questions and answers in the practice of family therapy, vol. 2* (pp. 105–107). New York: Brunner/Mazel.

Krestan, J. & Bepko, C. (1993). On lies, secrets and silence: The multiple levels of denial in addictive families. In E. Inmer-Black (Ed.), *Secrets in families and family therapy* (pp. 141–159). New York: W.W. Norton.

Lerner, H.G. (1993). *The dance of deception.* New York: HarperCollins.

Merriam-Webster's online dictionary. Retrieved October 1, 2008, from http:// www. merriam-webster.com/dictionary/privacy

Nyberg, D. (1993). *The varnished truth: Truth telling and deceiving in ordinary life.* Chicago: The University of Chicago Press.

Papp, P. (Ed.). (2000). *Couples on the fault line.* New York: Guilford Press.

Roberts, J. (1993). On trainees and training: Safety, secrets and revelation. In E. Imber-Black (Ed.), *Secrets in families and family therapy* (pp. 389–410). New York: W.W. Norton.

Rodriguez, N. & Ryave, A.L. (1992). The structural organization of everyday secret telling interactions. *Qualitative Sociology, 15,* 297–318.

Saarni, C. & Lewis, M. (1993). Deceit and illusion in human affairs. In M. Lewis & C. Saarni (Eds.), *Lying and deception in everyday life* (pp. 1–29). New York: Guilford Press.

Shlien, J.M. (1987). Secrets and the psychology of secrecy. In R.F. Levant & J.M. Shlien. (Eds.), *Client centered therapy and the person centered approach: New directions in theory, research and practice* (pp. 390–399). Westport, CT: Praeger.

Spinelli, E. (1989). *The interpreted world: An introduction to phenomenological psychology.* London: Sage Publications.

Spring, J.A. (1997). *After the affair: Healing the pain and rebuilding trust when a partner has been unfaithful.* New York: Harper Collins.

Vangelisti, A.L. (1994). Family secrets: Forms, functions and correlates. *Journal of Social and Personal Relationships, 11,* 113–135.

Webster, H. (1991). *Family secrets.* New York: Addison-Wesley.

Weeks, G.R., Odell, M., & Methven, S. (2005). *If only I had known: Avoiding common mistakes in couples therapy.* New York: W.W. Norton.

Welter-Enderlin, R. (1993.) Secrets of couples and couples' therapy. In E. Imber-Black (Ed.), *Secrets in families and family therapy* (pp. 47–65). New York: W.W. Norton.

Wikipedia. Retrieved October 1, 2008, from http://www.en.wikipedia.org/wiki

Section III

Dealing With a Partner Who Won't/Can't Change

9

The Dynamics of "Crossover" Issues in Couple Relationships

Introduction

> Justine and Mary struggle with Justine's lack of sexual drive. Mary tries to be supportive, seductive, and understanding sprinkled with outbursts of frustration, blaming, and tears. Justine reads books, buys erotic DVDs, and goes to her doctor, all the while feeling guilty, inadequate, and resentful. Nothing helps. Is Justine's lack of interest in sex biological or psychological?

One of the most perplexing and difficult issues in working with a couple is dealing with a couple member who doesn't change in some important way that affects the relationship. If that person doesn't change because she clearly "cannot," the path for working with the couple is more clear. Thus, for example, if a member of a couple has hearing loss, diabetes, is short, or comes from another culture, we know as therapists that these are aspects of the person that cannot change. The couple work is to deal with the limitations, effects, values, beliefs, and feelings that accompany the issue. On the other end of the spectrum are issues over which we would agree each member has or can learn to have some control: communication style, emotional expression, cognitive thought processes, etc., and in between are many gray areas.

One of these areas is what I call a "crossover" issue. A crossover issue has a combination of biological and psychological components. It is not clear which or both are the causes of the issue. Even if physical causes are primary, there are psychological factors that compound the issue.

In couple therapy the person with a crossover issue (from here on referred to as the "partner with a COI") often becomes stuck. It isn't clear how much the person won't or can't change. This person is facing a clear issue even if the issue is not yet understood. Examples of some crossover issues include the following:

- ADD
- Infertility
- Depression, Bipolar disorder
- Sexual drive
- Eating disorders
- Insomnia
- Sexual attraction
- Chronic headaches
- Erectile dysfunction
- Learning disabilities
- Addictions
- Fibromyalgia

Only issues that involve both a biological component and a psychological component are crossover issues. Many of the issues that couples bring into couple therapy are not crossover issues: for example, affairs, financial issues, child-rearing issues, expression of emotions, job issues, couple control issues, etc. Issues that, as far as we know, are solely physical in origin do not fit into this category either: for example, blindness, Lou Gehrig's disease, Lyme disease, scoliosis, etc.

This crossover category is fluid because we continue to learn more about the issues. Ten years ago this list would have looked very different and ten years from now it will undoubtedly be again different. Clinical depression is a good example of a crossover issue. We know there is a biological basis for clinical depression, plus we know that there can be a hereditary factor since depression runs in families. However, we also know that life events affect depression. A death, job loss, and divorce can all trigger depression. How much is biological and how much is psychological? How much control do the individuals with depression have over their symptoms? These are unanswered and troubling questions.

Chapter 9 explores characteristics of crossover issues including their common features, what we know about them, how they affect intimate relationships, and the emotions that accompany them. How crossover issues are viewed in general as well as by a couple with a partner with a crossover issue are discussed as well as partner issues and couple issues that contribute to crossover issues. The chapter concludes with a discussion of what the couple has done and what the outcomes of these efforts have been.

Characteristics of Crossover Issues

Crossover issues share some common features. Their main characteristic is a lack of clarity about the extent the person with the issue is responsible for both causing the issue and controlling the issue. Is the issue purely biological in origin and in manifestation? Can the person with the issue do anything to change the symptoms, behavior, or the underlying reason for the issue? How responsible is he or she for having the issue and for controlling the effects of the issue? In a couple relationship, the lack of clarity about how much responsibility the person with the crossover issue has can be a major bone of contention. The symptoms of the issue may greatly affect the other partner. In fact, the symptoms may necessitate that the non-symptomatic partner takes more responsibility for any number of aspects of life leading to resentment, anger, or guilt.

For example, John's ADD makes it difficult for him to be organized, complete tasks, remember appointments, and do his job thoroughly. Because of this, Becca runs the household, taking care of finances, appointments, vacations, and household duties. Even though they both know about John's ADD, Becca tends to feel burdened and resentful, blaming John for her greater load of responsibility. John in turn feels guilty about his symptoms and resentful toward Becca for her prodding, nagging, and judging of him. Where does biology leave off and psychology begin?

Edward Hallowell (1994), in his book *Driven to Distraction,* writes about the effects of ADD on a relationship:

> In couples where one or both partners have ADD, life can list and yaw from day to day. As one member of a couple said to me, "I never know what to expect. I can't rely on him for anything. It's really a circus." The syndrome can disrupt intimate relationships and leave each partner exhausted. (p. 107)

What is currently known about crossover issues? Knowledge about these issues is incomplete and changing. New information about them continually develops and emerges periodically. For example, at the time of this writing, a recent issue of *Newsweek* (Chavarro, Willett, & Sherrett, 2007) links infertility with diet. Does this mean that a woman who is infertile now has considerably more control over her situation than we thought? Think back to the evolution of what we know about and how we see alcoholism. We once thought it was a sign of moral depravity. Then it became a disease. Then it became genetically inherited. What will the next iteration of alcoholism be? O'Hare (2005) describes a multi-theoretical view of alcoholism (environmental, physiological, psychological, and interpersonal). Couples struggling with a crossover issue face confusion and uncertainty about what they are dealing with. Think about John and his wife Becca.

When ADD became a phenomenon with a name, there was often relief, an explanation, and some understanding. Then came the reports of over-diagnosis, inconclusive tests to prove the diagnosis, etc. So often the couple is left with not knowing what they are facing and not knowing what to believe. Health professionals don't even agree about low sexual desire as illustrated by the following discussion. Psychiatrists may not agree with endocrinologists. Psychologists may not agree with other psychologists. Social workers may have another point of view. Clinical nurses may not agree with any of the above.

Since knowledge about what causes the issues and what constitutes them is incomplete, certainly effective treatment for crossover issues is open for debate. And there is plenty of debate to be found. Does a woman with a low sexual drive need therapy to help with repressed sexuality? Does she need testosterone or estrogen? Does she need a partner who is a better lover? Does a person who is overweight need a diet, Weight Watchers, a conditioning program, a pill, or a more accepting culture? New programs are constantly emerging for many of these issues. New books are released and new reality TV programs show "miraculous" results. Celebrities overcome one of these issues and become even more famous with a latest self-revealing book about how they beat the problem. Beyond the popular culture, psychology and medicine continue to announce new programs, new experts, and new evidence. And so a couple sits in my office arguing about whether the partner with depression needs Prozac, shock therapy, a running program, graduate school, a trip to Bali, or hospitalization. Another couple argues about whether the partner with ADD has taken his or her meds, has called a coach to start sessions, or is getting away with being irresponsible.

In their book *Reclaiming Sexual Desire,* Andrew Goldstein and Marianne Brandon (2004) write that dealing with low sexual desire for women requires a holistic approach that integrates emotional, spiritual, physical, and intellectual approaches. Goldstein and Brandon (2004) write about the complexity of the issue of low desire in women and suggest some of the confusion that can result in determining how to deal with it:

Reviving your sex drive is a process that requires deliberate renewal of sexual awareness ... A woman with low libido may not realize that she has dissociated from her physical self and thus her sexuality. She must become reacquainted first with her body, then her sensuality, and finally with the sexual thoughts and feelings that she has rejected over time. (p. 49)

Goldstein and Brandon (2004) continue:

"A shortage of testosterone is a common factor in low libido" (p. 85).

They write further:

... "we've seen androgen supplementation make a dramatic difference for many women. In some cases, it's all that's necessary to restore a healthy sex drive" (p. 99).

Regarding the effectiveness of herbal treatments Goldstein and Brandon (2004) write:

"A woman who's taking ginkgo [an herb] may notice increased genital sensation and more vivid orgasms, along with sharper memory over a period of months" (p. 117).

So, what is a woman to do? Should she go to a therapist, a doctor, or an herbalist? A powerful characteristic of crossover issues is that they affect intimate relationships. They cause disruptions, disagreements, unfulfilled needs, fear, anger, and pain. They lead to miscommunication, misunderstandings, distance, and isolation.

Beach, Dreifus, Franklin, Kamen, and Gabriel (2008) cite research showing that depression in a partner can increase marital stress in various ways. One such study "... found that depression predicted greater negativity in support behavior toward the spouse which in turn predicted greater marital stress" (p. 546). Another study "highlighted the propensity for depressed persons to seek negative feedback, to engage in excessive reassurance seeking, to avoid conflict and to withdraw ... that lead to more stressful marital events"(p. 547).

One of the strongest ways that these issues play out in couple relationships is by creating a feeling of being out of control for one or both members of the couple. Each may feel like the victim. Each may feel helpless and confused. Each may go in and out of thinking that he or she knows the answer, only to be thrown back into confusion or to be rebutted by the other. Thus, the feeling of being out of control arises with regard to the cause of the issue, the symptoms, the actions, and the treatments. Control is often one of the primary issues for these couples when they come to therapy. Many of their issues will contain the following:

- Control debates
- Breakdowns
- Arguments
- New strategies
- Blaming

Because the partners with COIs can't in fact, control some or many of their symptoms, they often develop feelings of helplessness. This helplessness may be specific to the areas affected by the crossover issue or may generalize to other areas of their lives. The issue itself and the helpless feelings may lead to lack control of their behaviors.

In her book *Drinking,* Caroline Knapp (1996) describes her increasing lack of control over alcohol:

> I drank when I was happy and I drank when I was anxious and when I was bored and I drank when I was depressed, which was often … I'd gotten so drunk the night before, I almost passed out on the sofa … I'd done the drinking in secret, of course, stealing off to my bedroom every thirty minutes or so to take a slug off a bottle of Scotch I'd stashed in my bag … I was usually more careful than that, careful to walk the line between being drunk enough and too drunk … But I slipped up that time … (p. 2)

There are some common emotions couples experience in dealing with a crossover issue. The person with the COI often feels inadequate. Hallowell (1994) writes:

> The description of an adult with ADD as immature or selfish is not uncommon. People don't know how else to make sense of this behavior, so they attack it as beneath adult standards. They hope to shame the person into changing his ways. (p. 114)

The depth of the feeling of inadequacy depends on many factors, including how long the issue has been present, whether it started in childhood or adulthood, how the issue has been dealt with over time, and how the couple handles the issue. Many individuals with a COI have been through years of symptoms without knowing what was wrong and without help. As a result, they may have had many life struggles with school, relationships, jobs, and self-image. They may feel like damaged goods. They may have developed ways of compensating that have helped or made matters worse. Other individuals experience a crossover issue emerging in adulthood and are completely unprepared. They may feel overwhelmed, lost, and without the skills to cope well with the issue. Issues such as depression, infertility, or low sex drive can bring up these feelings.

Along with the feeling of inadequacy usually comes great guilt. People with the COI are all too painfully aware of the difficulties their issue causes, not only personally, but also with their partners as well. If they have weight issues, they may know that their partner finds them unattractive. If they have depression, they know they are not fulfilling their partners' needs. If they have ADD, they know their partner is carrying more of the load.

Feelings of inadequacy and guilt often increase the symptoms of the individual with the issue. If the person has ADD, inadequacy and guilt may lead to more procrastination and more disorganization. If the person has depression, these feelings may lead to more depressive symptoms, such as sleep issues, lack of motivation, and withdrawal. If the individual is overweight, the person may become less interested in intimacy and more afraid of judgment. It becomes even more difficult to ferret out what is biological and what is psychological.

At the same time, this individual may use denial as a way to cope with his or her issue. Denial works well to shield the person from the feelings of inadequacy, guilt, pain, and fear. Denial may take the form of "I don't have a problem" or "This is just the way I am." Denial may also be projected onto the partner; for example "You are too sensitive," "You want too much sex, " or "Nothing I do is right according to you."

Thus, denial becomes, "It's not my fault" or "It's your fault." Denial may come from years of living with the issue and not knowing any other reality. It may come from tremendous fear of facing all the emotions underlying the helplessness the person feels. Resignation also may lead to denial. Larry has lived with depression and resignation for so long that he denies that he is depressed to his partner Jason.

Epstein and McCrady (2002) write, "Resistance in its more subtle form is minimalization of the alcohol problem, often called 'denial' in traditional alcoholism treatment. It is not atypical … to hear some variation of the following: 'I don't think I have a drinking problem …'" (p. 609). Denial may be particularly effective if the partner is also in denial. Yet, usually denial drives the other partner crazy because he or she lives with the consequences of the issue daily.

Often denial leads this other partner to suggest, push, cajole, yell, cry, or threaten. The partner may read books, talk to friends, or go to doctors, etc. The couple often then becomes polarized, leading to communication breakdown and lack of intimacy. Ultimately, it may lead to a breakup.

The partner who does not have the COI often goes through a range of emotions. Early on, he or she may feel compassion and try to help and may be sympathetic and supportive. As time goes on, this often wears thin as he or she feels the impact of the symptoms and feels unable to make a difference. Then this partner may become angry and despairing. Emme and Phillip Aronson (2006) in their book *Morning Has Broken* give an example of Emme's reaction to her husband Phil's depression on a particular day:

> Anyway, I left the office on a kind of knife edge, with all that anger still very much at the surface, and I didn't have the patience for poor Phil at just that moment ... I took one look at my husband, slumped in that waiting room chair, looking all hang dog and defeated and so totally not like the man I'd married and I thought, *Oh great. Nothing's changed. Nothing's ever going to change.* (p. 17)

Often the couple does not know how to handle these emotions. Communication may break down. Resentments and arguments may build. Distance may grow. Each may feel unseen and unknown by the other (Whisman, 2001). Beach and Gupta (2003) describe how depression strains intimate relationships.

Hallowell (1994) describes how exasperating being the spouse of a partner with ADD can be: "The spouse often feels enraged and unheard. The more angry the spouse becomes, the more devaluing she becomes, and the more devaluing she becomes, the more her partner withdraws" (p. 111).

What do the nonsymptomatic partners do with these feelings? In some partnerships, they may become parental as a way to try to gain more control. Others may negatively enable the partners' COI by joining them. Joining in may consist of drinking too much with them, overeating with them, or giving up on their sexual relationship. Sometimes the other partners have their own complementary or similar issues. Thus, both partners may have addiction issues or one may have alcohol issues and the other clinical depression.

There are numerous ways that crossover issues are stressful for symptomatic individuals and for their partners. There is increasing research that indicates that stress is associated with "longer term down regulation of immune function" (Groth, Fehm-Wolfsdorf, & Hahlweg, 2000, p. 21). People who experience chronic stress, therefore, are a greater risk for health problems. This is likely to be particularly true for partners with crossover issues that are medical in nature, such as fibromyalgia. The stress of dealing with the disease negatively impacts the disease itself, which then creates more stress, etc.

How the Issue Is Seen

There are often many points of view about the crossover issue including the following:

- Cultural
- Medical
- Moral
- Legal
- Media
- Societal
- Mental health
- Historical

These viewpoints will have a powerful effect on the couple and how they deal with the crossover issue. Mario, who abuses alcohol, and Marcy, who does not, may live in a culture in which excessive drinking is accepted and joked about. Thus, Mario may think it is totally fine that he comes home at 4:00 in the morning and passes out on the couch and, although Marcy may feel resentment, she passes it off as something she has to accept. In another culture, Mario may be seen as irresponsible and a poor husband. Marcy may feel justified in yelling at him and blaming him for their problems. In yet another culture, Marcy may understand from what she has read and seen on television that Mario is physically addicted. With compassion and caring she may attempt to get him medical help. Mario may agree to go to detox to stop drinking. Thus, Mario's alcohol abuse may be viewed as culturally acceptable, as a personal weakness, or as a medical problem.

Infertility may be viewed as a sign that a woman is damaged and unworthy due to a medical problem or as due to a social issue related to poor health care. Obesity may be viewed as a sign of personal weakness and laziness, a medical condition, or as a sign of wealth and access to food. In the latter case, being overweight would not be considered an issue. Low sexual drive for a woman may be viewed as a sign of her being chaste and moral, as a personal rejection by her partner, or as a hormonal problem related to age.

For the person with the crossover issue, there are often conflicting views of the issue. The person may understand that there is a medical issue, yet feel socially unacceptable and morally unworthy. One may feel supported by friends, rejected by one's spouse, and judged by one's coworkers. Add to the mix that viewpoints about the issue are often changing.

Wincze, Bach, and Barlow (2008) write, "Over the last three decades, there have been dramatic shifts in beliefs about what causes sexual dysfunction" (p. 620). They go on to describe the swing from the 1970s when sexual dysfunction was considered psychological in etiology, to the 1980s when sexual dysfunction was considered biological, to the present when most professionals believe there to be both psychological and biological factors that cause sexual dysfunctions.

Papp (2000) describes the different views of depression developed by various therapy models. For example, cognitive therapy views depression as resulting from faulty cognitions whereas interpersonal therapy assumes that depression is caused by relationship difficulties.

Some crossover issues are now defined as illnesses: for example, bipolar disorder, alcoholism, and depression. Miklowitz (2008) writes about the resistance patients and their families may have to the concept of bipolar disorder as an illness. They may fear that this means they are unstable or powerless. They "…fear that their behavior will now be labeled as that of a crazy person [and]…the idea of having an illness feels like shackles" (p. 441).

How the issue is seen includes whether it is viewed as changeable or unchangeable. From some points of view the issue may be seen as a choice and from others as determined by an outside force such as biology, heredity, or gender. Suppose that Mario drinks because he just won't take hold of himself and buck up or Justine has low sex drive because she is furious at her partner and withholds sex. For them change is possible. Yet, if Mario drinks because "boys will be boys" and Justine has low sex drive because she is female, their behavior may be gender based and not changeable.

The issue may also be viewed as manageable or unmanageable. For example, ADD is seen in both ways. There are many ideas about how to work with the symptoms including medication, working with a coach, setting up charts, goals, reminders, etc. Yet, at the same time, it is believed that the symptoms cannot be completely controlled. How manageable ADD actually is varies from person to person. This leaves a lot of room for confusion, frustration, blame, and inadequacy. To make it more confusing, we hear stories daily of people who "conquer" their crossover issue and people who are taken over by it: Someone famous checks into rehab while another famous person miraculously loses 60 pounds.

Another concern about how a crossover issue is viewed involves whether it is seen as temporary, permanent, or cyclical. Issues like depression and weight tend to be cyclical: There are times when the depression is worse and times when it is better. People with weight issues tend to go up and down in both their efforts and their weight. Cyclical crossover issues can be particularly frustrating because during parts of the cycle they appear to be manageable and controllable. Yet at other times they appear out of control and difficult to manage. Partners seeing this up and down may believe that the symptomatic partner does have responsibility and really can manage his or her behavior. They may become more frustrated during a down cycle, thinking the partner is giving in or giving up. Miklowitz (2008) states, "Relatives of depressed patients are apt to see the disorder as willfully caused and not the product of biochemical imbalances" (p. 441).

Certainly if the crossover issue is seen as temporary, partners will be less stressed about it. If a significant weight gain is attributed to pregnancy and is expected to be resolved, the partner will be more forgiving. As the years go by and the weight doesn't go away, more issues will develop. If the crossover issue is seen as permanent, it may be more debilitating. It may feel like a life sentence. On the other hand, if the issue is a constant, it may feel like less of a moving target and may be something the couple can face more directly. People who join Alcoholics Anonymous and declare themselves to be an alcoholic come to know a way of dealing with their issue with structure, guidelines, a community, and an identity. People with learning disabilities may be given a diagnosis and a set of skills and guidelines for handling their particular disability.

How the Crossover Issue Is Viewed and Understood by the Couple

"Why doesn't she do something about her moods? Sometimes she is so easy and sweet. Then she comes out spitting nails. I don't buy her excuse that it is her depression."

How the crossover issue is viewed by the outside world may greatly affect the couple. How the couple themselves see the issue is also critical. A list of possibilities includes the following:

- Neither partner is knowledgeable, understands, or accepts the issue.
- One partner, but not the other, is knowledgeable, understands, and accepts the issue (either the person with the issue or the person without the issue).
- Both partners are knowledgeable about, understand, or accept the issue.

- The partner with the issue blames himself or herself, his or her partner, or both.
- The partner without the issue blames himself or herself, his or her partner, or both.
- Either partner blames a third party.

When the couple presents in therapy for treatment, it is very important for the therapist to understand what the partners see and understand about the crossover issue. It is common for the couple to be in difficulty and not know that they are dealing with a crossover issue. They may not realize that one of them has an addiction, ADD, low sex drive, lack of sexual attraction, etc. The therapist may be the first to surface the issue and to educate the couple about the issue as well as its possible causes and treatments. Psychoeducation is a critical part of couple therapy (Wells, 2005; Beach et al., 2008). Beach et al. write that in working with a couple with a depressed member, the therapist needs to "...provide psychoeducation on the symptomatology associated with depression" (p. 553).

The couple may know about the issue, but not understand or accept it. It may be that one partner in the couple is knowledgeable about and accepts the issue but the other does not. For example, Miguel may have read about fibromyalgia and believes Renata has it, but Renata herself just dismisses his ideas. Or vice versa, Renata may believe she has fibromyalgia and Miguel may believe she is just irresponsible and looking for an excuse for her issues. Three levels are important in this discussion: knowing, understanding, and accepting. A person may know he or she has clinical depression, but not understand or accept it; or she may know it and understand it, but not accept it; or she may know, understand, and accept it. Accepting is the hardest step because it involves dealing with the limitations, consequences, responsibility, and emotions about the crossover issue.

A critical concern here is whether the issue has been formally diagnosed. A partner may think he or she has ADD, but has never been diagnosed. A partner may think he or she has depression, but has not seen a psychiatrist for a diagnosis. Hallowell (1994) advocates "Make sure you have an accurate diagnosis. There are many conditions that look like ADD, from too much coffee to anxiety states to dissociative disorders to hyperthyroidism" (p. 120). Some issues such as obesity seem evident and don't need a formal diagnosis. Yet, consultation is still advised for accurate diagnosis and understanding of causes and treatment. To further complicate the issue, the individual with the crossover issue may have been incorrectly diagnosed as not having an issue or as having a different issue. It is even possible that the individual has had conflicting diagnoses. The source and the time period of the diagnosis are important since knowledge of these issues is ever changing.

How the partners view where the responsibility for the crossover lies is crucial. As discussed, this is one of the thorniest difficulties that crossover issues raise. How each person views the issue plays a big role in where he or she believes the responsibility lies. Each partner will be influenced by culture, history, personal history, available knowledge, and current opinions. Blame comes up often in couples struggling with a crossover issue (Wells, 2005). Emotions may take over and turn to blame. Blame from one person tends to evoke blame back. There can be an ever shifting view of responsibility. Even if Caitlin knows better because she understands Jacob's depression, she lives with the consequences. These consequences may overload her and lead her to see Jacob as responsible for his depression in a way that she doesn't really believe.

Partner Issues That Contribute to the Couple's Difficulties

Beach and Gupta (2003) discuss couple therapy when both partners are depressed. Partners may have any number of concerns that contribute to the difficulties of dealing with a crossover issue including the following:

1. Partners may have a crossover issue themselves.
2. Partners may be opposites. For example, one may have ADD and one may be compulsive.
3. Partners may have physical or emotional issues that exacerbate the crossover issue.
4. Partners may actually have issues that help the crossover issue.

If both partners have the same crossover issue, they may be supportive or enabling of each other. They may also project their symptoms onto each other. Having the same issue may make their lives particularly dysfunctional.

Opposites often initially attract and then repel. One wonders why Becca who is organized, thorough, and in control marries John who has ADD. Perhaps John's looseness, spontaneity, and expressiveness initially attracted Becca. However, once they have children, a house, and a mortgage, Becca finds John's ways enormously aggravating and irresponsible. She no longer gets the benefit of his loose ways because she is carrying a good deal of the responsibility. In couple therapy, the therapist needs to look for how the couples may initially pick each other to fulfill some need, but later in the relationship find that this backfires.

Sometimes partners have issues, either physical or psychological, that make the partner's COI worse. Beth may be a type A achiever married to Paul who has clinical depression. Sharon may have Crone's disease and be partnered with Mirella who has a food addiction. Mirella's constant eating and bringing home cakes and cookies drives Sharon crazy. Sometimes Sharon can't resist and eats the cakes, which aggravates her Crone's.

Then there are those occasions, probably less frequent, when a partner's issue actually helps the other partner with the COI. For example, Jason is very focused on exercise in a way that dominates other important parts of his life. Yet, Larry who has depression benefits from this because Jason gets him to come and work out with him. Denise gives to others more than she takes care of herself. This benefits her partner Ira who has learning disabilities. She reads all his reports and edits them for his job.

Couple Issues That Contribute to the Partner's Issue

In addition to individual partner issues that affect the partner with a COI, there can also be couple issues that contribute to that partner's struggles (Beach & Gupta, 2003). For example, if the couple has fights over money, this may affect how they deal with potential treatments for the partner's COI. If a couple is struggling with a parent's illness and aging this may affect how they manage one partner's depression or addiction. Wincze et al. (2008) describe how relationship factors such as poor communication and lack of attraction can affect a partner's sexual functioning. They write, "Patients who cannot communicate effectively with their partners may harbor anger, resentment, or other negative feelings that interfere with sexual functioning" (p. 626). Roberts and Linney (2000) cite studies that show the effects that relationship issues and partnership drinking have on the alcohol problems of one of the partners.

It is often difficult to tell if the couple's issues are factors unto themselves or are caused by the crossover issue. For example, poor communication can be a couple problem itself or it may result from the tension around the crossover issue. Sometimes the couple issues interfere with addressing the crossover issue. Epstein and McCrady (2002) write:

Acute couple distress can be manifested in session as excessive bickering, nasty comments, negative nonverbal behavior and/or references to separation or divorce. In these cases, the couple problems are too pressing to be deferred until treatment of alcohol problems is underway. (p. 610)

Fran has no interest in sex when she and Vince are fighting. When she feels blamed and hounded by Vince, she is even less likely to be interested in being sexual. Arguing, distancing, and blaming can exacerbate the symptoms of the partner's COI. As a therapist, it is often difficult to unravel how all these issues interact and what leads to what. Would better communication improve Fran's sex drive or would an increase in Fran's sex drive lead to better communication? Probably both, but which needs to be addressed first?

Approaches the Couple May Have Tried

"We went to the gym together and that didn't help. Medication made me spacey and nauseous. Joining a support group depressed me. Now what?"

Below is a list of scenarios describing how couples may have attempted to deal with the crossover issue before coming to couple therapy. This list describes who may have tried an approach and to what extent that person has tried an approach.

1. The partner with the COI has tried none/some/many ways of addressing the issue.
2. The partner without the COI has tried none/some/many ways of addressing the issue.
3. A third party, such as a family member, has tried none/some/many ways of addressing the issue.

The list below describes which approaches may have been tried and by whom. The list includes the typical approaches that each person may have tried. The treatments vary with the understood cause of the issue. Thus, some treatments are medical, some are psychological, some are a mix, some are community based, some require strong determination, and some require specific resources. Approaches attempted by the nonsymptomatic partner often take the form of support and education followed by pressure, upset, or distancing. Sometimes third parties become involved offering help, empathy, resources, or a planned intervention to push the person into treatment.

1. Possible approaches tried by partner with the COI:
   a. Specific program for this issue such as AA
   b. Medical treatment such as surgery or shock treatment
   c. Therapy: individual, couple, or group
   d. Church/temple counseling: working with a pastor or rabbi
   e. Medication, such as Ritalin for ADD or testosterone for low sexual desire
   f. Support group, such as a group for depression
   g. Health/exercise approach, such as running for depression
   h. Self-help, such as reading books about the crossover issue
2. Possible approaches tried by nonsymptomatic partner:
   a. Changing self, such as dieting in hopes of getting the partner to diet
   b. Changing environment, such as using sexual aids to enhance partner's desire
   c. Therapy to work on one's own frustration and anger about the crossover issue
   d. Helping partner by advising or strategizing to overcome the crossover issue
   e. Taking over, such as not allowing alcohol in the house
   f. Requests, threats, ultimatums to get the partner to stop the difficult behavior
   g. Distance or self-protection, such as withdrawing in order to avoid being hurt
   h. Secretive strategies, such as hiding food or alcohol
   I. Repression of self, such as shutting off one's own needs
   j. Joining the partner, such as drinking with the partner
3. Possible approaches tried by third parties:
   a. Financial help for treatment or living expenses
   b. Sharing common experience, such as discussing their own bipolar disorder
   c. An "Intervention": bringing together family members to confront the partner with the COI

The treatment possibilities for a given crossover issue may be either limited or overwhelming. More often, there are many options with many claims to success. Treatment options vary in terms of expense, invasiveness, degree of challenge, time needed, emotional involvement, and accessibility.

Possible Outcomes

Change efforts that the couple has made may have resulted in no change, significant change, and everything in between. Some of these efforts and their results include the following:

- No change
- More connection
- Some change
- New health issues
- Major change
- Sense of purpose
- Alienation
- Desire to help others
- Discouragement and helplessness
- Loss of job
- Anger and blame
- Holding onto a job
- Guilt or shame
- Increased symptoms
- Financial stress
- Increased or decreased anxiety
- Dependency

Birchler, Fals-Stewart, and O'Farrell (2008) describe the importance of dealing with prior failed attempts at sobriety in working with couples with a member with an alcohol problem. There may even be negative change resulting from discouragement, ineffective treatment, or poor treatment. When the treatments have resulted in no change or less change than hoped for, the partners will likely feel discouraged, helpless, or anxious. They may be more upset or angry at each other. There may be more blame thrown back and forth. The partner with the COI may feel guilt or even shame. The consequences of the crossover issue are likely to continue. The person's symptoms may even become worse. If the treatment has helped, the couple may feel hopeful and more connected. Chapter 10 examines the point where the couple and the individuals are stuck. Change has not happened or not enough change has happened.

Summary

Shame, frustration, helplessness, anger, relationship stress, misunder-standing—these are some of the common experiences of couples dealing with a partner with a COI. A crossover issue is defined as an issue that has a combination of biological and psychological components. There are often contradictory ways to view the issue. Couples have difficulty understanding and dealing with a partner who has a COI. There are many factors that contribute to dealing with a crossover issue, including issues of the other partner and other couple issues. Often couples have tried a myriad of approaches to handle the crossover issue with varying—often frustrating—results. So what does a couple do? Chapter 10 examines strategies for the therapist working with a couple with a partner with a COI.

10
Therapist Roles, Experiences, and Strategies

Introduction

Now what? Given all these concerns, it is daunting for a couple therapist to work with a couple with a COI. This chapter addresses the therapist's experiences, strategies, and traps in doing this work. The theoretical approach presented in the Introduction is reviewed as it applies to working with crossover issues with a couple. A prime focus of this chapter is dealing with becoming stuck, a common experience with a crossover issue in couple therapy. Strategies for dealing with many circumstances in couple therapy are given. Traps for the therapist are also explored. The chapter concludes with a case study.

Therapist's Experiences

Here comes that couple again. They are stuck. You are stuck. The room feels like the air has been sucked out of it. You start to feel helpless and immobilized—again. You've tried everything you know. You've pulled out the cognitive behavioral techniques, the strategic interventions, homework exercises, and role plays. Nothing. It feels like the therapy is in free fall with no landing in sight. You may feel strangely disconnected from the couple. Actually, you would like to fall asleep or scream. Following are some of the other signs that the couple is stuck and so are you:

- You have tried too many things to get the couple moving.
- You are taking too much responsibility for the therapy (Hanna, 2002).
- You feel incompetent, as if you don't know anything anymore.

- You wonder what happened to the smart, capable, clever therapist who used to be you. Hanna (2002) discusses difficult clients who seem to make a hobby out of cofounding and defeating therapists.
- The sessions drag on and you watch the clock.
- You want to avoid this couple and are relieved when they cancel.
- You feel irritated or angry with the couple or with one of the partners.
- You create artificial distance from the difficult client, "...unconsciously perceiving them as a threat to (your) sanity..." (Hanna, 2002, p. 172).

What do you do when you reach this point? Here are some preliminary pointers:

- Admit you don't know.
- Let go. You can't make it all work. See the limitations of what you can do.
- Find ways to reengage with the couple. You may need to chat with them at the beginning of the session about a sporting event or their vacation.
- Find ways to energize yourself, such as talking with a colleague for help or taking a walk before the session.

Working with a couple with a member with a COI pulls on all of your skills as a therapist. At the core of the work are several key therapeutic issues: change, acceptance, and responsibility. Before determining that a couple is indeed stuck, you need to use your knowledge and skills to help them move toward those changes that are possible and therapeutic. In the beginning of the therapy, your role is likely to be to educate and to lead the couple to possible resources such as doctors, support organizations, coaches, etc.

An important part of your role in this process is validating that there is a real issue. Couples may tend to diminish the issue, use it as a club over each other's heads, or ignore it. Giving support to the couple and at the same time holding them accountable is vital. They need to be responsible for the follow through and for how they interact about the crossover issue. Thus, in the couple therapy you will likely need to teach the couple management skills for handling both the issue and the couple dynamics. Communication skills, negotiation skills, emotional regulation, and mutual support are vital skills for the couple to learn. A critical part of this process is helping the couple to get on the same side. Often they are on opposite sides about the issue and making the issue more objective helps them to step aside from their dynamics and better address the issue.

As discussed earlier, it is critical to get a proper diagnosis of the crossover issue. As the therapist, you may be able to do the diagnosis yourself or you may need to refer to a specialist. McCarthy and Bodnar (2005) and McCarthy and Thestrup (2008) stress the importance of medical diagnosis with certain sexual dysfunctions such as erectile dysfunction and vaginal pain. There may be testing involved. Usually it is important for you to work with other professionals and to coordinate the follow through. This may involve you learning more about the issues yourself from the specialist, colleagues, research, and from the clients.

Theoretical Approach

The theoretical approach of this chapter and this book is phenomenological. (For fuller discussion see Introduction). The partners' experiences, perception, and meanings are explored in order to understand the dynamics of what they are going through right now in the therapy and in their relationship. Understanding the crossover issues requires awareness of what the partner with the COI is experiencing. The partner's experiences of the world and the meaning that he or she attaches to them may be quite different from the experiences and understandings of his or her partner. It is crucial that, as the therapist, you are free from bias and judgment. Spinelli (1989) writes:

> In order to assist clients in their investigation of their world-views as optimally as possible, it is necessary for phenomenological therapists to maintain empathy with and personal neutrality towards their clients' life experiences ... through neutrality, they are more able to bracket their own meanings and interpretations of the world so as to not make it their task to value, judge or criticize their clients' experience ... (p. 130)

Partners with a COI struggle with how their experiences can interfere with their ability to function and to feel fully successful in their worlds. Phenomenological therapy can be particularly helpful because "...phenomenological therapists strive to assist their clients in regaining greater control and mastery over their lives in order that they may experience a more authentic being-in the-world" (Spinelli, 1989, p. 127).

The couple may spend some time with you in couple therapy before they become stuck or they may come into therapy already stuck. Once you are at a stuck point, the therapy often shifts. This point in the therapy is a major focus of this chapter.

The strategies suggested for working with being stuck are influenced by the work of Fritz Perls (1992), Gestalt therapy, systems therapy, and cognitive behavioral therapy. These therapies are particularly helpful when a couple is stuck because they work with understanding what is happening and with discovering new behaviors. They also work well with a phenomenological approach because they are based in here-and-now experience and with understanding clients' reality.

Christensen, Wheeler, and Jacobson (2008) write of the development of integrative behavioral couple therapy (IBCT) in working with distressed couples. Three aspects of IBCT have made it more lasting and more successful in its outcome. These include (1) working with couples relational themes; (2) working with "contingency shaped" (p. 664) behaviors (behaviors that elicit desired responses); and (3) working on emotional acceptance. The techniques described in this chapter include these elements of IBCT.

It is important in this work to keep a systems approach to the couple work. Although the focus may be on the partner with the COI, the issues must be seen in the context of the couple's relationship. As the therapist, you need to keep the couple system balanced by bringing in the dynamics of the couple and the other partner. You need to understand the perceptions and experiences of the nonsymptomatic partner and the interplay between the two partners.

Becoming Stuck

There are a number of reasons partners with COIs become stuck including the following:

- They are unwilling to use treatment because they don't believe in it or they fear it.
- They have tried various treatments that have not helped.
- They don't like the side effects of treatment.
- There are emotional issues blocking them from progressing forward with the issue.
- They claim they have accepted how they are and don't want to change.
- Physical issues prevent the change.
- They are unable to use the treatment because of interfering variables such as other medical issues, inadequate financial resources, or religious prohibitions.
- The treatment helps, but something else undermines its effects.

Young, Rygh, Weinberger, and Beck (2008) write about various reasons for lack of progress in working with patients with depression. For example, they describe such issues as the high risk of relapse, premature termination of medication, the need for long term treatment and inadequate care (pp. 251–254). Epstein and McCrady (2002) discuss a number of factors that may interfere in the therapy with a couple with an alcoholic member. For example, the client with the alcohol issue may have significant ambivalence about changing or he or she may have significant cognitive deficits in abstracting and problem solving.

A most important question at this point is this: Is the person stuck because he or she *won't* change or because he or she *can't* change? Is there something else that can be done to address the issue?

This leads to the central issue for the therapist and therefore the couple: When do you accept that the issue, its symptoms, and its consequences are not going to change? As the therapist, it is your responsibility to go as far as you can to help the couple make progress with the issue. It is also crucial to recognize when you have reached a limit and to then move into a different therapy mode either dealing with the impasse or dealing with acceptance. Of course, it is rarely so clear-cut. Usually we need to be interlacing working on progress with the issue and on acceptance. There is a danger in focusing only on progress. What if the limit of progress has been reached and you are still pushing ahead?

You can lose the partner with the COI if you are primarily pushing toward progress. He or she may be yearning for acceptance. You may indeed be playing into the other partner's issues of blaming, frustration, and unmet needs.

This point is a troubling dilemma for us as therapists. We may be up against the limits of our own knowledge as well as currently available knowledge. We are potentially in a place of great influence in the couple's relationship. We are faced with dealing with our own beliefs about the nature of change and about our role as an agent of change. We are also up against our own frustrations in our ability to do our jobs. The first issue for us is our own ability to perceive what is happening when the couple is stuck.

Challenges for the Therapist: What to Do When the Couple Is Stuck

Following is a list of possible challenges and strategies for the therapist when the couple becomes stuck:

1. Recognize when there is still the possibility of change
2. Push the partner with the issue to take more responsibility

3. Recognize when the partner with the COI is reacting to the other partner and becoming more symptomatic
4. Work with the nonsymptomatic partner's issues that add to the stuckness
5. Recognize when the relationship system increases the symptoms of the partner with the COI
6. Focus on the impasse
7. Recognize when no change is likely
8. Work on acceptance of the issue
9. Know when acceptance may be avoidance of responsibility

1. Recognize when there is still the possibility of change

Although the partners may be stuck, you may still see the possibility for further change. You may see room for more understanding, treatment, or management techniques that the individual and the couple could try. It may be that the most distressing issue has not yet been uncovered (Young et al., 2008). What can you do? You can attempt to further educate, you can address resistances, and you can help the couple work through obstacles to growth. This may feel like more of the same. Yet, there may still be a new angle or a new approach you haven't tried. After all, we know that we can't think of and do everything. It may be that, indeed, you don't know enough about the crossover issue and you may need to gain additional knowledge, input, or training yourself. This may be an important time to request feedback from other professionals. Perhaps they can see something that you don't. Perhaps they can think of approaches that you can't. Pope, Sonne, and Greene (2006) advocate regular consultations with a variety of colleagues as a way to handle therapy impasses. Another option may be to have a consultation with another professional directly. This professional might join you and the couple for a session or see the couple alone for a consultation. This may be especially appropriate if the professional is a specialist in the crossover issue. For example, you may want to refer Miguel and Renata to a specialist for a consultation for fibromyalgia.

You may also need to dig into your own bag of therapy approaches and take a completely different tack. For example, you might bring in a more strategic approach or a more cognitive behavioral approach. You may need to explore new approaches. Pope et al. (2006) suggest:

> When stuck, it is almost always worth conducting a literature search or using some other means to find out whether there are new theoretical contributions, research findings, or practical innovations or guidelines that might be helpful in understanding how we arrived at an impasse, how we might find a way to move beyond … (p. 151)

Sometimes you may need to push yourself outside of your usual way of being. You may not be a confronting therapist, but you may need to become more confronting for this couple. This may push you to act outside your comfort zone and help you to grow as a therapist. Baucom, Epstein, and LaTaillade (2002) write about the importance of couple therapists being flexible and taking on multiple roles. They emphasize that couple therapists attend to many factors including: couple interactive processes, individual factors, environmental factors, couple development, gender and ethnic background. Epstein and McCrady (2002) write:

> Working with couples with drinking problems requires the ability to be flexible and to respond to the unexpected. The therapist may be supportive, empathic and encouraging in one session, and limit setting and confrontational in the next. (p. 607)

It may be helpful or even crucial to ask the couple what they think they need to help them get unstuck. They might, in fact, have some ideas that they have not yet raised. Being stuck could help them move outside of their comfort zones to consider new approaches. You also might ask them what they need from you. Sometimes a member of a couple will be able to say, for example, that they need you to push them or to be more regular in checking up on their therapy homework.

One of the dangers is that by this point you may be too immersed with the couple. You may feel too responsible. You may, in fact, be working harder than your clients. This may be because you have become invested in them, because you don't want to face how stuck they are or because your sense of success has become wedded to their progress. We are supposed to help. Our clients come to us for help. Is not stuckness an indication that we are not doing our job, that we are not quite competent? Even if we know better, it is hard to avoid feeling these doubts. In fact, it is important to check to make sure that we haven't missed something or that maybe the clients are stuck because of our limitations.

2. Push the partner with the issue to take more responsibility

The partners with COIs may be stuck because they are not taking enough responsibility for their issues. Since the issues have psychological components, they may be able to

- Take more control
- Face difficult blocks
- Come to terms with parts of themselves that give up
- Gain more courage
- Face deeper issues of self-esteem

This is one of the critical points in the couple therapy. How do we as therapists know when this partner needs to be pushed? Miklowitz and Morris (2003) write of patients with bipolar disorder:

> Part of the repair of the family or couple relationships involves clarifying that at least some of the patient's behavior is biologically based and is not intended to hurt the caregiving partner...at the same time, the bipolar partner is not taken off the hook...(p. 118)

The nonsymptomatic partners will usually believe that their partner can do more, should do more, and better do more. There may be a kind of learned helplessness that symptomatic partners are experiencing. They may be avoiding, denying, or running away. We need to assess if these partners need a push, a shove, a wake-up call, or straight talk. Perhaps they don't understand the seriousness of their issues. Perhaps they have been clever at avoiding taking responsibility. These partners may need tough love, detox, or AA. Wells (2005) writes of the importance of partners with ADD taking personal responsibility for changing. Stark (1994) describes how the clients need to recognize that the issues they acquired are not their fault, yet it is their responsibility now to deal with what to do about them from here. It may be that, as the therapist, you need to be the one who spells out the stakes and gives the tough talk. This may be quite tricky. How can you be firm, tough, and supportive? How do you keep allied with these clients? There are many ways to give the partners with a COI a push.

Spell Out the Consequences of the Clients not Taking Responsibility
This may be one of the most powerful interventions. Leticia may lose her job. Amit may lose his marriage. Partners with the COI often avoid looking at the consequences of not taking responsibility for their issues. It is too painful and overwhelming. This is why talking about the consequences may wake up the person. The emotional impact may be strong because the consequences are so undesirable. The partner may be startled and shaken.

Consequences are objective. They don't directly involve judgments or assumptions of the person's character or behaviors. As the therapist, it is vital to point out the consequences that can startle and mobilize clients rather than the consequences that don't matter or increase their stuckness. Point out consequences that need addressing right away. Then it is crucial to look at what to do about these consequences and how to address them. Further examples of critical consequences that can startle and mobilize are harm to one's child or harm to one's health. Long-term consequences that won't be felt for awhile are not mobilizing.

See Clients Individually and Work to Get at Their Resistances and Defenses
John is scared to death that he is making a mess of his life. He fears that he is damaging his children. He can't admit these feelings to Becca. His resistance is his defense against knowing the truth about himself. It is also the "tension between yes and no" (Stark, 1994. p. 2) that pulls the part of him that wants to get better against the part that clings to the past. So far the work in the therapy may have been primarily with the couple. It may now be time for some individual sessions with John. The goal is not to do individual therapy or to increase the focus on this partner as the identified patient (though this is a danger). The goal is to give John space to look at himself to voice feelings and concerns that may not be emerging in the couple therapy, and to get beyond his defenses and resistances. Often seeing these partners alone allows them to open up and discover important feelings, perspectives, and beliefs that may be blocking both the couple therapy and their progress with their COI.

As another example of the value of individual therapy, Larry could explore more of his feelings and symptoms of depression in some individual sessions. Without his partner Jason in the room Larry may be able to make important disclosures and discoveries and find new directions.

These results can be carefully brought back into the couple therapy to help the couple move forward.

Goldstein and Brandon (2004) describe how women who feel self-conscious about their bodies may develop ingenious ways to avoid being seen naked. Women's negative feelings about their bodies can contribute to low sexual desire. They suggest ways women can work individually in therapy to cultivate a healthy body image in order to increase their level of desire.

Help the Client Recognize When Medication is Appropriate
A number of crossover issues can be greatly aided by medication. For example, Miklowitz (2008) asserts that medication can be of significant help in managing bipolar disorder:

> Some of these drugs not only control the acute episodes of the illness, but also have "prophylactic value," meaning that they help prevent future episodes or minimize the duration or the severity of the episodes that do occur. (p. 424)

However, clients will often resist the idea of medication. Clients with ADD will often report that they don't feel like themselves on medication. They don't like the idea of taking medication because it makes them feel like something is wrong with them. As the therapist, you may need to spend a good amount of time educating the couple about medication, helping them work through their resistances to considering drug therapy, and checking on the crossover partner's compliance with using medication.

Tell the Partner Stories About People Who Have or Have Not Faced Their Issue
In individual sessions or in the couple therapy it may be helpful to tell the partner(s) about others who have and have not faced the crossover issue. These stories should be poignant in order to make a strong point about taking steps forward. They need to be striking and motivating. These stories can come from the therapist's experience with other clients (with appropriate confidentiality), with people the therapist knows (with appropriate boundaries), or from books or articles. Clients are often moved and inspired by such stories.

*Put the Partners in Touch With Others Who Have the Issue
and Will Help Them Face Their Lack of Responsibility*
Sometimes the partner with the COI needs to have contact with others with the issue in order to face taking more responsibility. Support groups such as Weight Watchers and Overeaters Anonymous provide contact

with others who know the ins and outs of denial and avoidance. These group members can "call the person out" most effectively. They are often more knowledgeable and credible than most others. They can help lead the way for the stuck partner.

Refer the Partners to Another Therapist or Program that Will Address Their Issues
Sometimes it may not be appropriate to see the partner with the COI yourself. It would possibly unbalance the couple therapy or focus too much on this partner as the identified patient. It may also be that another therapist, group, or program that focuses on the crossover issue would be more helpful to the individual (Birchler, Fals-Stewart, & O'Farrell, 2005). For example, maybe Mario needs to join AA or Mirella needs to see a therapist who specializes in eating disorders. During this time the couple therapy may be suspended or the other partner may also see a therapist or be part of a group such as Al-Anon. Birchler, Fals-Stewart and O'Farrell (2008) emphasize that couple therapy for a couple with a partner with substance abuse is typically not successful without other supportive treatment.

Make a Contract for Specific Follow-Through to Address the Issue
Hector will call his friend Leroy to take him to an AA meeting. Shawn will make an appointment with a primary care doctor for a referral for medication for depression. Another approach to the couple therapy becoming stuck is to develop a specific plan with follow through as part of the therapy. This involves you, the therapist, getting into a role of planner, monitor, and facilitator. The advantages of taking this role include (1) it is needed and you are already involved; (2) you will be able to see the issues that arise regarding the follow through; (3) you can be objective and take the heat off the partners by being a neutral party; and (4) you can help make something happen. The disadvantages include (1) you becoming too involved in the plan; (2) you becoming the cop; (3) you appearing to side with the nonsymptomatic partner; (4) the plan and the follow through becoming too much a focus of the therapy; and (5) the plan doesn't work. Thus, you need to weigh and balance this role before taking it on. Birchler et al. (2008) describe behavioral contracting in the treatment of substance abuse:

> Written behavioral contracts to promote abstinence have a number of useful common elements. The substance use behavior is made explicit. Specific

behaviors of each spouse to help achieve this goal are detailed. The contract provides alternative behaviors to negative interactions about substance abuse. (p. 532)

Discuss Ending the Therapy If the Partner Does Not Take Some Specific Steps
The goal here is not to threaten the partner or the couple. It is to show them that the couple therapy will not progress unless the partner with the COI takes some steps forward. It is often useful to use the analogy of a roadblock. Couple therapy is like a journey along a road. From time to time there will be blocks along the road that prevent progress. Right now the crossover issue is a roadblock. It doesn't mean that this issue is the only significant issue in the couple therapy. It means that right now it prevents movement. At other times in the therapy other issues, including those of the other partner, will or have blocked progress.

If either partner or the couple does elect to stop therapy, it is critical to frame the ending in a nonblaming way, to have a good termination, to look at alternative steps, and to keep the door open to returning. Sometimes it is helpful to frame the stopping as a break from therapy. Stopping could actually be a planned break with a check-in time or a schedule to resume later.

3. Recognize when the partner with the issue is reacting to the other partner and becoming more symptomatic

Justine's sex drive may stay stuck or even decrease because of pressure to change from her partner Mary. Justine's stuckness may be a way to assert herself against Mary's control.

Perhaps the partner with the COI is stuck because that person is reacting to the other partner. The partners may be polarizing each other. In this case, each person's reaction to the other pushes the other further into his or her issues and behaviors. Thus, partners with the COI may be stuck in reaction to pressure or judgment by their partners. The focus of the therapy may need to be on how the partners with the COI need to work on their reaction to their partners in order to move forward.

4. Work with the nonsymptomatic partner's issues that add to the stuckness

Becca's need for control may be playing a role in the couple being stuck. She becomes rigid making lists, schedules, and plans. John feels choked by her control.

It may be that the nonsymptomatic partner's issues and behaviors contribute to the stuckness. Usually the other partner is contributing to the couple being stuck in some way. It is critical to identify this contribution. There may be a need for a period of the therapy in which the other partner's issues are the focus of the work. This may be tricky because this partner may be too frustrated with the other partner's issues to be willing to see his or her own. Nonsymptomatic partners may also think that focusing on themselves is wasting time because their partners' COIs are the real issues. As the therapist, you need to help nonsymptomatic partners see how their issues play into the couple issues without making them feel that you are turning on them or are letting the partner with the COI off the hook. It is important to keep a systems approach to the couple work (O'Hare, 2005).

5. Recognize when the relationship system increases the symptoms of the partner with the COI

The relationship itself may also contribute to the couples' stuckness. It may not be just the partners' issues individually that contribute. The dynamic between the two may foster the impasse. The focus of the therapy now would be on the couple's system, not individual partner issues. Thus, as the therapist, you need to focus on improving the dynamics between the couple in order to get the therapy unstuck. O'Hare (2005) emphasizes the importance of treating depression in a relational interpersonal model.

6. Focus on the impasse

Dealing with an impasse in therapy is one of the more uncomfortable experiences of our work. An impasse may mean failure. Therapists are not always trained to recognize that impasse is a phenomenon in itself. It is not just the absence of something. Fritz Perls (1992), in his book *Gestalt Therapy Verbatim*, describes the importance of the impasse. Something is happening in the impasse and the clients and therapist need to recognize it, sit with it, and experience it. When clients let themselves experience the impasse, something will emerge. Perls writes, "But if you really get in contact with the emptiness, something begins to happen—the desert begins to bloom" (p. 284). Further understanding or feelings about the impasse may emerge. Emotions may develop and lead to an inner push to move forward that would be missed if the impasse were not faced. Your job as the therapist is to help the couple acknowledge and fully experience this impasse. One of Perls's techniques was to have the client exaggerate the impasse in order to fully see it and know it. Applied to a crossover issue in a couple, perhaps Mirella, who overeats and frustrates Sharon with her weight gain, needs to overeat more to truly own her overeating and feel its consequences. Perhaps Becca needs to harp on John's irresponsibility more for her to see how disruptive she can be and for John to see how frustrating he can be.

Another aspect of focusing on the impasse may be doing less as the therapist and putting more responsibility on the couple to face the impasse. There can be some very uncomfortable moments in doing less. It is important to explain to the couple what you are doing and why or they may not understand and benefit from being in the impasse together.

7. Recognize when no change is likely

This may be one of the hardest parts of doing couple therapy. How do you know whether this means the therapy has not helped? In fact, seeing that no change is likely may be the needed breakthrough. It is not fun to knock your head against a brick wall—not for your clients or for you. Acknowledging that no change is likely can be upsetting, frustrating, and scary, yet it may also be a relief. What tells you that you are at this point?

a. You have run out of options.
b. You have been working on the issue for a long time and are now stuck.
c. More evidence has emerged that the issue is physical and difficult to change.
d. The person with the COI has had this issue for a long time, perhaps all his or her life.

e. The person with the COI has been stuck in this same place in other past relationships that have not worked.

f. The couple is missing sessions, coming late, or working less in their sessions.

g. The relationship is becoming more unstable. The nonsymptomatic partner is beginning to give up on the symptomatic partner or the relationship.

h. After a period of making progress, the progress has stopped.

i. The partner with the COI is defending himself and is less interested in help or change.

j. You know that many people with this crossover issue get stuck in similar ways.

k. An outside reliable source, such as a specialist, tells you there is not likely to be further change.

Getting to a point where change is unlikely is different from being at an impasse. An impasse is dynamic. There are feelings and experiences that are hidden. However, when no change is likely, there is no movement. The direction of the therapy needs to be changed altogether.

For you, as the therapist, this point can be the most frustrating, tiring, and frightening. You may recognize that you've reached this point before the couple does. Or it is possible that the couple is ahead of you and already knows that change is unlikely, while you are still working hard for change. Facing that change is unlikely is facing a loss. You may have put months of work into helping the couple to move forward. Has it been wasted? It is important to see this as a step in the process and to know that you have done as much as you can. For the couple and the therapist this is a tricky place. It can be, but doesn't have to be, the end of therapy. Hopefully it signals switching gears to a new direction: acceptance. Yet the couple has to go through a loss of hoped for change. In the process, they may want to give up on the therapy or their relationship. It is critical how you as the therapist help the couple face that change is unlikely. With some couples, you need to face this directly. With others, it is important to start the process of working on acceptance before facing that change is unlikely in order to give them hope and direction. The couple may need this more gradual transition.

What is the loss that the couple is facing? It is often the loss of a hope that the crossover issue will go away. For example, John's ADD is treated and the symptoms are gone. He becomes more responsible, thorough and reliable. Justine's sex drive increases and the couple's sexual relationship greatly improves. Larry's depression lifts and he is able to participate in more activities with Jason. Giving up these dreams may be devastating. Hopefully the couple has already come to more acceptance of how things are. Yet, facing that further change is unlikely can be a huge blow. Each member of the couple may have held onto dreams and fantasies. Hallowell (1994) writes about the importance of couples facing the realities of ADD and its effect on their lives. Couples need to deal with the symptoms, the limitations, and the disappointments of ADD and other crossover issues. At the same time one or both may feel relief. They may have had a growing sense of the limits of change. Now they can possibly admit what is true and let go of efforts that aren't helping. They can focus instead on accepting, managing, and adjusting.

8. Work on acceptance of the issue

What is acceptance? There are many aspects to acceptance. It does not mean giving up, resignation, or compromise. Acceptance means

- Coming to terms with something
- Letting go of the fight
- Seeing a way to live with the issue
- Finding compensating aspects of the situation
- Making the issues less important
- Finding coping skills

Lawrence, Eldridge, Christensen, and Jacobson (1999) give numerous couple therapy strategies for partners to develop acceptance. A key aspect of accepting is redefining and reformulating the issue. Reformulating sheds a different light, shows the issue in a new or larger context, and shows other ways to assign meaning to the issue (Christensen et al., 2008). For example, if Miguel can attribute Renata's need to rest and not clean the house to her fibromyalgia rather than as a thoughtless act of defiance, he will be more accepting because he will see her resting as a necessity and less personal.

As couples interact over the years, their behaviors tend to become shaped by how they interpret and give meaning to each other's behaviors. They often develop distortions of meaning that can be realigned in therapy. When partner one sees how partner two defines partner one's behavior as negative, partner one can help by explaining his or her true intentions or by being sensitive to how his behavior triggers partner two. Finding a new meaning to behavior tends to affect the emotions that follow from the meaning. Thus, Becca is less likely to be angry with John when she finds a different and less personal meaning to his lack of follow through.

In a reverse sequence, working through emotions can open up a different perspective, allowing a new meaning to emerge. For example, if Becca can find an appropriate way to vent her frustration (perhaps to a friend or therapist), she can then see things in better perspective.

Edward Hallowell (1994) writes about the importance of how understanding ADD is a critical tool in coming to acceptance:

> In Mary's case the single most useful tool was knowing about ADD. Before she knew what ADD was and that Sam had it, she was left with explanations like "selfish" or "narcissistic" to explain what she didn't like about Sam. Once she understood what ADD was, and once she understood that it was a neurological condition, she was much better able to forgive Sam his shortcomings and work on finding solutions. (p. 111)

Part of acceptance may involve reprioritizing values and needs. Once a couple is faced with letting go of their fantasies of life without the crossover issues, once they understand that the issue in some form is here to stay, they may need help seeing the issue as it relates to other aspects of their life and their being together. For example, Mary thought she would leave Justine if her interest in sex did not increase. When she faced that Justine's interest in being sexual was not going to change substantially, Mary looked again at whether to leave the relationship. She came to see that there were many important things she was getting from the relationship. Given her upbringing, Mary came to see that what she was getting were things she did not get as a child. Frequency of sexual activity then seemed less critical.

An important aspect of acceptance for couples is finding coping skills. Miklowitz (2008) describes problem-solving skills training as an important part of couple and family therapy with a member with bipolar disorder. As the therapist, you have likely been helping the couple gain coping skills throughout the therapy. This work is particularly important at this point. If Caitlin is to accept that Jacob's depression means the family will have less money because he can't hold a high-powered job, she needs help planning the finances. She may have been holding off getting a higher level job herself hoping Jacob would get well enough to change. Seeing that this won't happen, she may decide to take a higher salaried job. Or she may decide to figure out how to live more frugally. To make these kinds of adjustments she may need help seeing the compensation for doing so. For example, she may need to see how Jacob can help out more at home while she works longer hours at her job. Unless she can find some compensation for her sacrifice, Caitlin is likely to be bitter, resigned, or distant. The compensation may also take the form of her feeling more fulfilled at her new higher level job.

Hallowell (1994) writes of a couple coping with ADD:

> Let the one who is the better organizer take on the job of organization ... If you can't do the checkbook, don't do the checkbook. If you can't do the kids' clothes shopping, don't do the kids' clothes shopping. ... You have another person to help out. However, the job the other person does instead of you must be adequately appreciated, noticed and reciprocated. (pp. 124–125).

A significant aspect of coping with accepting a crossover issue is identifying and handling the needs of each partner. If Bianca's depression requires her to have rest and a nap regularly, perhaps Aaron, who wants to be more active, can seek out friends with whom he can do his activities. Perhaps one way of Mary and Justine's handling Mary's higher sex drive is for both of them to accept that it is OK for Mary to look at pornography and masturbate more often.

Finding a support group may also be a way of partners coming to acceptance of a crossover issue. For example, there are support groups both for people with depression and for family members of people with depression. There are AA and Al-Anon. Support groups serve a number of functions. They provide an outlet for emotions and they normalize experiences. Other group members often have helpful advice, resources, and experiences. Primarily they provide community and help for learning how to understand and live with the crossover issue.

An important part of acceptance is for each partner to come to understand the reasons the nonsymptomatic partner chose the symptomatic partner. There may be two reasons for the choice: (1) The symptomatic partner may have characteristics that the nonsymptomatic partner appreciates, needs, or admires, or (2) the nonsymptomatic partner may have chosen the symptomatic partner because the troublesome symptoms fit with needs of his or her own. For example, Becca may need John's spontaneity and outgoing personality. Miguel may admire Renata's sensitivity to other's needs, which has developed out of her own struggles. Perhaps the nonsymptomatic partner is used to the symptoms and is comfortable with them having grown up with a family member with similar symptoms. The nonsymptomatic partner may get benefits from being with his or her symptomatic partner. Marcy chooses Mario who drinks too much because Marcy defines her own being by Mario's drinking and by taking care of

Mario. This is co-dependency. Perhaps Mary's focusing on Justine's sex drive allows Mary to avoid facing some of her own issues about sexuality. An important part of the healing work that leads to acceptance involves the partner with the COI taking responsibility for the effects of his or her issue. This partner most likely avoids this responsibility because facing these effects is painful and brings up feelings of inadequacy. Taking responsibility involves developing a part of oneself that can step aside from one's symptoms and see the crossover issue more objectively. The symptomatic partner needs to own the issue, recognize its effects, and discover ways to handle the effects. In her book, *The Fibromyalgia Advocate*, Devin Starlanyl (1998) describes a partner with fibromyalgia (FMS) telling her nonsymptomatic partner what she needs. The partner with FMS is also taking responsibility to do her part in dealing with her symptoms. Starlanyl (1998) writes:

> I do need a companion. I also need a partner. I need you to be understanding and willing to travel this confusing path with me. Neither of us invited FMS …into our marriage/partnership, but they're here all the same. They won't go away if we ignore them. I'll try to do everything I can to reduce the pain, fatigue and other symptoms they have brought. … I know I get moody but please let me know when I do. (pp. 255–256)

Forgiveness

A crucial part of acceptance is forgiveness. When a couple comes to the point when further change on the crossover issue is unlikely, they need to address forgiving each other and themselves for past judgments, blaming, hurts, resistances, and rejections. They will likely need to forgive each other for not being the person each wanted the other to be. The partner with the COI is not going to be thin if he or she has an eating disorder, is not going to be organized and efficient if he or she has ADD, is not going to be bright and energetic if he or she has depression. The nonsymptomatic partner is not going to be continuously understanding, sympathetic, and supportive. Each has already (and will again) let the other down. How do partners handle their disappointments and come to forgiveness?

In her book *Forgiveness: A Bold Choice for a Peaceful Heart*, Robin Casarjian (1992) describes the process of forgiveness. The primary aspect of forgiveness is coming to see that the person you need to forgive is a human being who is more than his or her hurtful behaviors. You need to acknowledge and relate to the other's essential Self (e.g., the wise and reasonable nature in him or her). You need to let go of your idealized expectations of your partner. Further, you need to see your partner from your heart and see what is fundamentally good and innocent in him or her. Doing this affirms your own essential Self. This does not mean condoning hurtful acts. You need to set appropriate boundaries and consequences for unacceptable behaviors.

Part of the process of forgiveness involves acknowledging the truth about your thoughts and feelings and working through the anger, fear, and hurt that you feel. You may also need to address the guilt that you feel for your own part in what has not worked in the relationship. Forgiveness involves those who have done the hurting recognizing their responsibility, understanding the effects of their behavior, and making amends. If Jacob can recognize how his depression has affected Caitlin, can express his concern for her, and can make amends, Caitlin is more likely to be able to let go of her resentment and be forgiving. Making amends may be more difficult because of the limitations of the crossover issue. Jacob is not able to make amends by becoming more lively and happy. He perhaps can make amends by, for example, helping Caitlin with some area in which he has skills and she needs some help and support. Justine could recognize that her low sex drive leads to a feeling of rejection in her partner Mary. Taking responsibility for these effects might include showing love to Mary in other ways.

Often the effects of the crossover issue can give rise to feelings of rejection and loneliness in the nonsymptomatic partners. It is the partners' responsibility to deal with their own reactions. At the same time, when their partners can see and help with these feelings and be responsible for their contribution to them, the couple is far more likely to develop forgiveness. Hallowell (2004) writes that forgiveness requires wisdom, guts, and strength. Most importantly forgiveness sets us free. This is essential in a relationship in order to move on from the past.

When a couple faces that change is unlikely to happen, they may be freed up to consider alternative ways of dealing with the issue, ways that they hadn't or wouldn't or couldn't consider before. The couple facing infertility may decide to adopt. The couple facing one partner's depression may decide to move to a better environment. Hoping the symptoms will change may obscure considering changes that are hidden. That hope may also obscure getting the type of help that is needed for the symptoms.

Once a couple has started to face the reality of the crossover issue, they may decide to focus their energy on helping others with the issue. They may join an organization devoted to the crossover issue. They may redefine their lives to include helping find better solutions for the issue. For example, Jacob may write about his depression and Caitlin may join an organization that is devoted to research for depression.

9. Know when acceptance may be avoidance of responsibility.

It is possible that either of the partners may move to acceptance in order to avoid the partner with the crossover issue having to face responsibility for his or her stuckness.

If avoidance is involved, the acceptance is not full acceptance although it may look like acceptance. As the therapist, you need to be able to tell the difference. The partner may go through the steps of acceptance, yet there is something missing. Underneath there may still be resignation, resentment, and lack of energy. Or there may be some remaining distance. True acceptance involves finding a new way of being, finding new energy and connection.

Traps for Therapists

There are many traps for you, the therapist, in working with couples with a partner with a COI. Some have already been discussed throughout this chapter and include the following:

1. Do you recognize the issue?
2. Can you stay neutral and not take sides?
3. Given the potentially volatile nature of the issues, are you experiencing countertransference?
4. Do you recognize the stage the couple is in in addressing the crossover issue? If not, do you take inappropriate steps in the therapy?
5. Do you get caught in the crossfire between the partners and become ineffective?
6. Do you stay focused on the couple system and not take a stand about the crossover issue when needed?
7. How well can you work with the other professionals who may be involved in the therapy?
8. Are you able to play the various types of roles that may be needed in the couple therapy: supporter, confronter, resource gatherer, monitor?

We cannot be fully educated on all the issues that are crossover issues. Thus, as a therapist, you may not recognize the partner's crossover issue. Some are easier to miss than others. For example, ADD and low sex drive may not be clear or may be masked by couple issues. It is important to talk with other professionals about your work and stay up to date as much as possible.

Couples who are dealing with one member who has a COI can get quite polarized. It is a challenge as a therapist to stay neutral as the couple argues and particularly as the couple becomes stuck. You may well have an opinion or feel frustration about what is going on in the couple relationship. Since this work involves confronting either or both of the partners, you can slip into taking sides or appearing to take sides. Birchler et al. (2008) write about the challenge of managing alliances in working with a couple in which there is a partner with depression:

> On the one hand, it may be tempting for the therapist to side with the nondepressed spouse, seeing this partner as the long suffering and aggrieved partner in the relationship. On the other hand, it may be tempting to side with the depressed partner, seeing him or her as the victim of spousal insensitivity. (p. 553)

Thus, this couple work can evoke countertransference of your own feelings. You need to be aware of how the crossover issue may exist in some way in your own life. For example, if you have a sister who has untreated depression that is affecting her marriage, you may be ripe for some countertransference on to your couple.

As the therapist, feelings of your own may be evoked by the partner with the COI behavior. McCrady (2008) describes working with clients who abuse alcohol:

> Working with a client with an alcohol use disorder often is difficult, both because of the client's behavior during treatment and because of his or her history of drinking-related behaviors that the therapist might find repugnant or upsetting. The client may lie about or minimize drinking during treatment. (p. 526)

This work involves subtle steps in moving forward in the couple relationship. The work can be a delicate dance. If you do not see where the couple is in their process, you may act inappropriately. For example, if the couple is at the point where no change is likely, but you perceive that the partner with the COI needs to step up and take more responsibility, you may make interventions that will lead to increased frustration in the couple's relationship. The couple work requires careful tracking and constant attentiveness on your part. You need to be able to see the dynamics in the room and know what they indicate about where the partners and the relationship are in their work.

Another danger in this work is that you become ineffective in the midst of the conflict in the relationship. You may get overwhelmed. You may not know how to direct the couple. You may spend too much time attempting to get them to communicate more effectively and not address underlying issues. It can be easy to get bogged down with the couple in their polarization or in their confusion about the crossover issue.

Most of us who work with couples have a systems approach to the work. It is an essential part of training for doing couple work. Yet, when dealing with a crossover issue, there are times when you will need to take a stand, offer an opinion, advise a direction, or confront one of the partners, particularly the one with the COI. This may put you outside of your comfort zone. It may also create an imbalance in the couple system. This imbalance may be necessary temporarily in order to get past a roadblock.

Often in this work, you will need to consult with other professionals: doctors, group leaders, other therapists, etc. Some of these professionals will be very helpful and others will not. It can be difficult and wearing to consult with someone with whom you disagree or don't respect. You may need to give the couple advice that contradicts other professionals' advice. This can be tricky to do and maintain your professionalism and the couple's trust.

Finally, this work requires you to play various roles, which may stretch you beyond your expertise or comfort zone. You may need to get some supervision or additional learning to be helpful to the couple. If you can't or don't want to do this, you need to recognize your limits and deal appropriately with the couple. You may need to refer them to another professional.

Case Study: Ian and Danny

Ian and Danny came into therapy very stuck. Ian was completely fed up with Danny. Danny had a history of depression and headaches that had profound effects on Ian and him. There were days that Danny could barely make it through. He managed to carry on at work, but would then come home and go to bed, leaving Ian alone for the evening. Ian had taken to playing guitar and had become very involved with a band. This required hours of his time, something Danny resented. When Danny was available, Ian was not. In fact, Ian was very vocal about his resentment that Danny did not participate in their relationship and could not be counted on to do things together. Ian took Danny's depression very personally, feeling totally rejected. As a result he refused to be close and intimate.

They had been together seven years. It was just before they met that Danny's depression had begun to surface. They were 33 and 34 years old. Danny worked as a chemical researcher and Ian was a manager at a start-up company. Early in the relationship, Danny's depression and headaches did not interfere strongly in the relationship. They often went out with friends to clubs and dinners. They enjoyed sports events and movies. Danny loved that Ian was quite a character with a great sense of humor and an iconoclastic sense of life. Ian was attracted to Danny's seeming stability and responsibility. As Danny's depression increased, Ian felt cheated and abandoned. Given his own history of a mother who paid little to no attention to him and a brother who was emotionally unstable and volatile, Ian had little tolerance for or understanding of Danny's increasing withdrawal and lethargy. In fact, Danny was often left on his own to figure out what to do about his depression and headaches. Strangely, every so often Ian would be comforting, offering to give Danny head rubs. Ian was also quite loyal to Danny despite Ian's friend urging him to find a side lover. Ian had seen his mother have affairs and was determined not to be like her.

Danny had tried a veritable cocktail of medications for his depression and headaches. For several years, he had been on and off different medications working with a psychiatrist. At the point they entered therapy he had settled into a somewhat successful regimen of medication. Danny was in individual therapy to work on how to manage his depression. He was, in fact, in a period in which his depression was better, but his headaches still caused him periods of severe pain and withdrawal.

The couple therapy began with each of them expressing their frustrations about their life and each other. The sessions often became quite volatile with each venting anger and blaming the other. For the sessions to be of help, we had to address their communication process immediately. I worked with them on how to express their anger without attacking and blaming. As they learned these skills, they were better able to hear each other and to gain understanding of the difficulty of each of their positions.

Mixed in with this work was education about depression. They were quite polarized in their views of Danny's depression. Ian was convinced that Danny's depression was purely psychological. He also believed that Danny's depression resulted from "screwed up" dynamics in Danny's family. Danny, on the other hand, saw his depression as purely medical. He could track other family member's depression and see the same pattern in his own. Given his work in research, he tended to see things literally.

I gave them material to read on depression and directed them to support groups. Ian would have nothing to do with groups, but Danny joined a depression support group. Ian dismissed the material on depression. They remained polarized.

At the same time, I worked with them to reengage with each other. They agreed to plan some time to go out together. They enjoyed these outings and felt some sense of their old selves together. However, Ian would become frustrated when they had a plan and Danny could not go because he had a debilitating headache.

Danny and Ian were deeply stuck. Strategies were helping only a little. Their attitudes were entrenched. Their relationship dynamics improved, but their intimacy did not. They tried many techniques including medication, education, behavioral interventions, and support group referrals. What was going to break the log jam? I felt the burden of responsibility for their being stuck. Although neither of them blamed me or questioned the therapy, I did question whether I was of any substantive help to them. When a couple becomes stuck, it is easy as the couple therapist to become stuck with them. Their communication had improved, but their level of understanding and compassion toward each other had not. I told myself to keep going, to keep looking for helpful steps forward, and to wait for an opening. Meanwhile I often agonized about what to do. The sessions were dragging and I felt heavy and bogged down.

The break came from an unexpected place. I asked Ian if he knew anyone else who had depression. He immediately said, "No." Then several sessions later he told me he had a buddy, Curt, with whom he had grown up who also had depression. He had infrequent contact with this buddy. Yet, Ian remained loyal to him because they had been through a lot together in high school. Both were star athletes who had gotten hurt and been unable to continue in sports. They hung out together and supported one another through devastating losses of status, college scholarships, and friends. I suggested Ian call Curt and talk with him about his depression. After much resistance, Ian did call. His friend was thrilled and grateful for the chance to reconnect. In fact, Curt told Ian about how he had coped with his roller coaster ride with depression. Through this contact, Ian became more open to seeing depression more objectively and compassionately. As he softened his approach to Danny and shared his friend's experience, Danny became more open to seeing the psychological aspects of depression. Eventually the three of them got together. This was a breakthrough for all. In fact, Danny and Curt began talking by phone sharing experiences and resources. I suggested at this point that Danny and Ian have some individual sessions to explore some of their own issues that contributed to the relationship difficulties. Danny's sessions helped him to become more open to his family dynamics that had contributed to his depression. Ian's sessions helped him to see how his own family

history had created intolerance, fear, and strong self-protection that pre-
vented him from accepting the consequences of Danny's depression and
headaches. In response to Danny accepting feedback from Ian about how
Danny's family dynamics could have contributed to his depression, Ian
was able to become less rigid in his response to Danny's difficulties.

Danny continued to have days of not functioning well and withdrawing. Ian continued to feel rejected. They were, however, better able to be
understanding and to use skills they were learning to make contact and
address each other's needs.

Summary

Chapter 10 explores the therapist's roles and experiences in working with
a partner with a COI. The theoretical approach for working with couples
with a partner with a COI is discussed. The main focus of the chapter
is on strategies for what to do when the partner with the COI and the
couple therapy becomes stuck. There are many emotional traps for the
therapist in this work. The chapter concludes with a case study.

There is much written in Section III that applies to doing couple therapy in general. Certainly getting stuck, acceptance, forgiveness, etc., are
important aspects of most couple therapy. This section focuses on working with a couple with a partner who has an issue that is known to have
both biological and psychological components. This combination creates
particular dilemmas about causes, treatments, and responsibility for the
crossover issue. One of the central dilemmas for the couple therapy is what
to do when the couple becomes stuck primarily as a result of the presence of the crossover issue. This can be one of the most difficult challenges
of doing couple therapy. When do you push forward and when do you
work on acceptance because further change is unlikely? Acceptance and
forgiveness go hand in hand. When the time has come to work on acceptance, the couple may in fact be freed to move to another level of relating.
The dance changes and the partners need to learn new steps.

Bibliography for Section III

Aronson, E. & Aronson, P. (2006). *Morning has broken*. New York: New American Library.

Baucom, D.H., Epstein, N., & LaTaillade, J.L. (2002). Cognitive-behavioral couple therapy. In A.S. Gurman & N.S. Jacobson (Eds.), *The clinical handbook of couple therapy* (3rd ed., pp. 26–58). New York: Guilford Press.

Beach, S.R.H., Dreifus, J.A., Franklin, K.J., Kamen, C., & Gabriel, B. (2008). Couple therapy and the treatment of depression. In. A.S. Gurman (Ed.), *The clinical handbook of couple therapy* (4th ed., pp. 545–566). New York: Guilford Press.

Beach, S.R.H. & Gupta, M. (2003). Depression. In D.K. Snyder & M.A. Whisman (Eds.), *Treating difficult couples* (pp. 88–113). New York: Guilford Press.

Birchler, G.R., Fals-Stewart, W., & O'Farrell, T.J. (2005). Couples therapy for alcoholism and drug abuse. In J.L. Lebow (Ed.), *Handbook of clinical family therapy* (pp. 251–280). Hoboken, NJ: John Wiley & Sons.

Birchler, G.R., Fals-Stewart, W., & O'Farrell, T.J. (2008). Couples therapy for alcoholism and drug abuse. In A.S. Gurman (Ed.), *The clinical handbook of couple therapy* (4th ed., pp. 523–544). New York: Guilford Press.

Casarjian, R. (1992). *Forgiveness: A bold choice for a peaceful heart*. New York: Bantam Books.

Chavarro, J.E., Willett, W.C., & Sherrett, P.J. (December 10, 2007). Fat, carbs and the science of conception. *Newsweek*, pp. 54–62.

Christensen, A.C., Wheeler, J.G., & Jacobson, N.S. (2008). Couple distress. In D.H. Barlow (Ed.), *Clinical handbook of psychological disorders*, (4th ed., pp. 662–689). New York: Guilford Press.

Epstein, E.E. & McCrady, B.S. (2002). Couple therapy in the treatment of alcohol problems. In A.S. Gurman & N.S. Jacobson (Eds.), *The clinical handbook of couple therapy* (3rd ed., pp. 597–628). New York: Guilford Press.

Goldstein, A. & Brandon, M. (2004). *Reclaiming desire*. Emmaus, PA: Rodale.

Groth, T., Fehm-Wolfsdorf, G., & Hahlweg, K. (2000). Basic research on the psychobiology of intimate relationships. In K.B. Schmaling & T. Goldman Sher (Eds.), *The psychology of couples and illness: Theory, research and practice* (pp. 13–42). Washington, DC: American Psychological Association.

Hallowell, E.M. (1994). *Driven to distraction*. New York: Random House.

Hallowell, E.M. (2004). *Dare to forgive*. Deerfield Beach, FL: Health Communications, Inc.

Hanna, F.J. (2002). *Therapy with difficult clients: Using the precursors method to awaken change*. Washington, DC: American Psychological Association.

Knapp, C. (1996). *Drinking*. New York: Bantam Doubleday Dell Publishing Group.

Lawrence, E., Eldridge, K., Christensen, A., & Jacobson, N.S. (1999). Integrative couple therapy. In J.M. Donovan (Ed.), *Short-term couple therapy* (pp. 226–261). New York: Guilford Press.

Maltz, W. *The Porn Trap: The Essential Guide to Overcoming Problems Caused by Pornography* (HarperCollins, 2008).

Maltz, W. *The Sexual Healing Journey: A Guide for Survivors of Sexual Abuse* (HarperCollins, 2001).

McCarthy, B.W. & Bodnar, L.E. (2005). Couple sex therapy: Assessment, treatment and relapse prevention. In J.L. Lebow (Ed.), *Handbook of clinical family therapy* (pp.464–493). Hoboken, NJ: John Wiley & Sons.

McCarthy, B.W. & Thestrup, M (2008). Couple therapy and the treatment of sexual dysfunction. In A.S. Gurman (Ed.), *The clinical handbook of couple therapy* (4th ed., pp. 591–617). New York: Guilford Press.

McCrady, B.S. (2008). Alcohol use disorders. In D.H. Barlow (Ed.), *Clinical handbook of psychological disorders* (4th ed., pp. 492–546). New York: Guilford Press.

Miklowitz, D.J. (2008). Bipolar disorder. In. D.H. Barlow (Ed.), *Clinical handbook of psychological disorders* (4th ed., pp.421–462). New York: Guilford Press.

Miklowitz, D.J. & Morris, C.D. (2003). Bipolar disorder. In D.K. Snyder & M.A. Whisman (Eds.), *Treating difficult couples* (pp. 114–136). New York: Guilford Press.

O'Hare, T. (2005). *Evidence based practices for social workers.* Chicago: Lyceum Books.

Papp, P. (2000). Gender differences in depression. In P. Papp (Ed.), *Couples on the fault line* (pp. 132–151). New York: Guilford Press.

Perls, F. (1992). *Gestalt therapy verbatim.* Highland, NY: The Gestalt Journal.

Pope, K.S., Sonne, J.L., & Greene, B. (2006). *What therapists don't talk about and why: Understanding taboos that hurt us and our clients.* Washington, DC: Amercian Psychological Association.

Roberts, L.J. & Linney, K.D. (2000). Alcohol problems and couples: Drinking in an intimate context. In K.B. Schmaling & T. Goldman Sher (Eds.), *The psychology of couples and illness: Theory, research and practice* (pp. 269–310). Washington, DC: American Psychological Association.

Spinelli, E. (1989). *The interpreted world: An introduction to phenomenological psychology.* London: Sage Publications.

Stark, M. (1994). *Working with resistance.* Northvale, NJ: Jason Aronson.

Starlanyl, D., M.D. (1998). *The fibromyalgia advocate.* Oakland, CA: New Harbinger Publications.

Wells, K.C. (2005). Family therapy for attention-deficit/hyperactivity disorder (ADHD). In J.L. Lebow (Ed.), *Handbook of clinical family therapy* (pp. 42–72). Hoboken, NJ: John Wiley & Sons.

Whisman, M.A. (2001). The association between depression and marital dissatisfaction. In S.R.H. Beach (Ed.), *Marital and family processes in depression: A scientific foundation for clinical practice* (pp. 3–24). Washington, DC: American Psychological Association.

Wincze, J.P., Bach, A.K., & Barlow, D.H. (2008). Sexual dysfunction. In D.H. Barlow (Ed.), *Clinical handbook of psychological disorders* (4th ed., pp. 615–651). New York: Guilford Press.

Young, J.E., Rygh, J.L., Weinberger, A.D., & Beck, A.T. (2008). Cognitive therapy for depression. In D.H. Barlow (Ed.), *Clinical handbook of psychological disorders* (4th ed., pp. 250–305). New York: Guilford Press.

Section IV

The Breakup of a Couple Relationship

11

The Dynamics of a Breakup

Introduction

"We're going to break up." These words from a couple in therapy begin a difficult and wrenching journey. They usually come after a time of struggle and turmoil. How can you, the therapist, most effectively help this couple? What are the effects of the breakup on you and the work you do with the couple? The phrase "I don't want to be in the relationship any more" can be even more devastating. When the decision to break up is not mutual, the upheaval can be even greater. The couple therapy can be more treacherous.

Section IV is about couples breaking up and about the couple therapy that can help them. It is about the (1) dynamics of a breakup; (2) the role that the therapist can most effectively play during and after the breakup; (3) the experiences and feelings of the therapist; and (4) the stages of breaking up. Walsh, Jacob, and Simons (1995) write that therapy during divorce usually brings greater clarity, decreased tension, mutual understanding, and shared ownership of the divorce process. Thus, the role of the couple therapist during a breakup can make a significant difference for the couple.

Chapter 11 addresses issues prior to a breakup, four common types of breakups, and factors that contribute to a breakup. These factors include how the breakup happens, when the breakup happens, and previous loss.

Chapter 12 examines the stages of breaking up. These stages developed from my work with couples going through a breakup. The couples taught me the stages by sharing their feelings, their perceptions, and their reality as they were living it. For 15 years, several times a year, I ran a one-day workshop for people going through a breakup. These stages emerged in the pain, agony, and healing the participants were experiencing.

The theoretical approach to working with couples breaking up comes from phenomenological psychology and Gestalt therapy. (For a fuller discussion see Introduction.) That is, I look at what the couple and the individuals perceive and experience and what meaning they are making out of these experiences. Spinelli (1989) writes, "The Gestalt therapist ...urges the deeper exploration of this [the client's current] experience" (p. 161). He further explains, "...the aims of Gestalt therapy—the encouragement of acknowledging responsibility of one's subjective experience, self-acceptance and reintegration—are essentially the same as those of phenomenological therapies" (p. 162). For partners working through the breakup of a relationship, their subjective experience dominates their lives. Finding meaning in what they are going through is crucial to their healing and "reintegration." Thus, this theoretical approach is particularly suited for the therapist's work with a couple breaking up.

The therapy techniques suggested through these stages are influenced by Gestalt therapy, systems therapy, and cognitive behavioral therapy, all of which fit well with a phenomenological approach (see Introduction). These approaches are particularly suited to working with a couple going through the breakup of a relationship because they are active, problem oriented, and focused on the issues and meanings the couple is struggling with in the present. Throughout the stages of break up, attention is drawn to what is happening in the situation and to the couple's immediate experience.

Family systems therapy looks at how a family or a couple functions and how it is structured. I examine issues such as communication patterns, boundaries, power structures, and problem-solving abilities. During the breakup of a couple relationship, many aspects of the couple system are falling apart. In therapy a family systems approach can help a couple see the crumbling of their couple structures and ways of functioning. From this they can learn to let go, heal, and be better prepared to be in an intimate relationship without repeating the destructive patterns.

Kraslow (1987) writes about the application of family systems therapy to understanding a couple going through a divorce, "Invariably I work from the theoretical stance of a family system perspective ...I believe that is the most comprehensive and illuminating perspective for the divorce therapist" (p. 29).

Dealing with a couple breaking up can be one of the most difficult and draining challenges of doing couple therapy. The sessions are usually quite emotional and demanding. The couple's world is breaking apart and turning upside down. They bring this energy and the resulting issues into the room. You are there to keep chaos from erupting, to help the members of the couple make sense of what is happening, and to guide them forward through a thick and overwhelming forest. The journey is all the more difficult if the couple is one with whom you have worked for some time, attempting to help them heal and stay together. You may indeed have an investment in their working things out together. You may be upset and sad along with them. A breakup can challenge your own feelings of effectiveness. Inevitably, memories and feelings of your own losses and possible breakups awaken. This chapter addresses these dilemmas and provides guidelines for the therapist working with a couple breaking up. This is tough work. It is an inevitable, but unwelcome, part of doing couple therapy. Judith Wallerstein describes the intense feelings of anxiety, grief, and fear of abandonment that working with a divorcing couple can evoke in the therapist. She writes:

> Moreover, the clinician most surely has had personal experiences that bear directly on these concerns. Observing the unhappy couples can evoke childhood memories of conflicts between the clinician's own parents. It can inflame fresher wounds, closely related to the client's experience in the present … (Wallerstein, 1990, Counter Transference to the Marital Breakdown Para. 4).

Therapy for a couple breaking up can help them go through the process with support and guidance. It can make an enormous difference in how each person makes it through, heals, and moves on. For children, couple therapy for the parents can be crucial in the children's ability to adjust to their new life. In view of the great benefits that breakup therapy can bring, it is surprising that as of this writing there are no studies on the effects of divorce therapy (Lebow, 2008).

Prior to the Breakup

Most couples come in to couple therapy hoping to improve and save their relationships. Even those on the brink of breaking up usually have some hope of working things out. Occasionally, as therapists, we have couples who come in knowing they are going to break up and are looking for help with the process. This is unusual.

As couple therapists then, we set about to help these couples heal and work through issues in their relationship. What is our goal? Is it to keep the relationship together? Is it to help each individual grow and become his or her own person? It is my belief that our job is not to keep the relationship together or to push them apart, but to help the couple learn the skills to be a healthy couple. These skills include better communication and understanding of each other and of the relationship. Our job is to teach, guide, facilitate, and support. We don't know and can't know what the outcome is going to be. If we become invested in a certain outcome, we will be biased and blinded. Sometimes we may, in fact, become invested in a couple relationship breaking up because we see how destructive the relationship is. What a trap if we were to guide such a couple to break up! The decision about whether to stay together or break up must be the couple's. This decision is not our responsibility. Our responsibility is to help heal. Thus, in most cases we need to work with the couple to help them understand and work through their issues. The tools we give them will help them with whatever direction they take.

Emery and Sbarra (2002) write that the goal in couple therapy is to help couple communication and mutual understanding increase rather than to save the relationship. A couple therapist is there to provide a container within which they can open up, struggle, learn, and grow. David Schnarch (1991) describes the couple therapist's role as being a crucible, which he defines as "… a highly nonreactive ('refractory') vessel in which a transfiguring reaction takes place" (p. 158). We need to hold the relationship while the members explore, wrestle, face truths, learn new tools, and find new ways of relating. To do this we must be ever watchful of our role and our own reactions to what is happening in the couple. Couple therapy demands our utmost attention and self-awareness. Whatever issues we as therapists have lurking within us will be touched upon particularly in dealing with a breakup.

Judith Wallerstein (1997) describes how the intense emotions that a couple is experiencing at this time, such as love, hate, loneliness, and jealousy, are likely to stir up the therapist's strong emotions. We need to know what our issues are and how to appropriately deal with them so they don't interfere in the couple's work. This is no small feat. If ever we need to be a crucible, it is now when we are helping a couple through a breakup.

At some point in working with a couple that eventually separates, we will get the first hints of a possible breakup. These hints may hit us over the head or slowly seep into our awareness. The couple may or may not be aware of a possible breakup themselves. Many couples who do not break up also give these hints. How do we know when the hints are real possibilities and when they are just passing feelings, thoughts, or ideas? We don't. I have had couples that I was sure could not possibly stay together end up doing great work and developing a strong relationship. Remember that couple who yelled and screamed at each other in the first session such that you wished they would just go home? I have seen them make remarkable turnarounds. Remember the couple who learned to communicate so thoughtfully, had such respect for each other, worked well on their issues, and then broke up? How could they? More than once I have been stunned. Most of the time I am not surprised.

John Gottman (1999) believes he can predict with 91% accuracy when a couple is going to break up. I refer readers to Gottman's important work to learn more about these predictors. He has found that there are reliable predictors for most couples who will end up breaking up. Yet, because there are those couples that defy the odds, we need to be ready to be surprised. That is part of what is amazing in this work.

Gottman (1999) writes about the presence of a number of predictors of divorce. In his book *The Seven Principles for Making Marriage Work*, Gottman describes the following six crucial predictors:

1. Harsh Startup: A discussion that starts off with accusations, criticism and contempt.
2. The Four Horsemen: Criticism, contempt, defensiveness, and stonewalling.
3. Flooding: "Flooding means that your spouse's negativity...is so overwhelming, and so sudden, that it leaves you shell-shocked. You feel so defenseless against this sniper attack that you learn to do anything to avoid a replay" (p. 34).
4. Body Language: Physical distress and flooding including increased heart rate, increased blood pressure, and hormonal changes.
5. Failed Repair Attempts: Failed efforts to deescalate tension and prevent flooding.
6. Bad Memories: A negative view of the history of the relationship.

When we encounter these predictors, we need to identify them to the couple and help the partners learn skills to work through them. For example, we need to teach them how to be respectful rather then contemptuous. At the same time, we need to begin to think about the possibility of the relationship breaking up and what this would mean for the couple. As predictors increase and efforts to help the couple don't work, we begin to think about what a breakup might entail and how we can begin to prepare the couple. We may, for example, include in the couple work an emphasis on each partner developing his or her sense of self more strongly. We may encourage each to build or strengthen a social support network. These areas could help the individuals if they stay together or break up, and they are essential if they do break up.

Since this chapter is about couples who are breaking up rather than couples who might break up, I will focus on the stages of breaking up rather than on the earlier predictors. These stages are ones that I have developed out of my work both as a couple therapist and as the leader of the one-day workshops I mentioned previously. The stages are chronological, yet people do not necessarily go through them in order. They may skip around to different stages, they may circle back into prior stages, or they may be in several stages at once. Add to this that each individual in the couple may be in a different stage or stages than the other person. I will describe each stage and then look at the role and the experiences of the therapist in working with the couple going through the stage.

Some aspects of the therapist's role are similar in different stages through out the process. For example, normalizing is a critical role in all the stages. I will focus primarily on the stages couples are likely to go through while in couple therapy. At a certain point, couple therapy is no longer desirable or appropriate. Yet, the partners continue to go through more stages of loss and recovery. I will describe briefly these stages of breakup after the couple therapy usually ends.

Many writers and therapists have developed stages of breaking up. Rollie and Duck (2006) review many stage models of the breakup of a relationship. One excellent book for couples is *Crazy Times* by Abigail Trafford (1992). The stages I developed focus on the sequential phases that take place during a breakup. In each stage I discuss the emotions that are involved. Trafford's stages are a combination of events, emotions, and issues. There is overlap between her stages and mine. For example, we both describe the stage of Shock. Her stages of confrontation and separation are similar to my stage of Decision. I refer the reader to her work for an excellent in-depth description of the process of breaking up. She captures well the emotional turmoil of the process and the issues that come up for couples. Her book is for the couples going through the breakup, whereas this book is for couple therapists.

Before describing the stages, I will discuss various other aspects of a breakup that affect the stages. These aspects include types of breakups, factors that contribute to a breakup, ways of breaking up, when in the couple therapy the breakup happens, and previous loss.

Common Types of Breakups

Not all breakups are alike. The most common type of breakup that presents in many clinical practices is the hostile breakup: the partners are hurt, angry, distrustful, accusing, and deeply disappointed. They often feel let down by their partner in some fundamental way. There may be deceit and distrust. For example, breakups precipitated by an affair fall into this category.

Isaac and Reba were in constant conflict. Each felt disrespected by the other. She saw him as ungiving, uncaring, and self-centered. He saw her as cold, accusing, and unsupportive. Neither trusted the other. Each believed that the other could be having an affair. Each kept information from the other.

Another type of breakup is the disengaged breakup: the couple has grown apart and shares little emotionally or spiritually. They often live separate lives. In some sense they have been broken up for some time. The actual breakup may be carried out dispassionately with a sense of regret and relief. Sometimes a breakup in a disengaged couple will bring out repressed emotions and disappointments and they will enter into a hostile breakup.

Sharon and Jed lived essentially separate lives. He felt he couldn't open up his feelings to her. She was a survivor: someone who soldiered on and worked hard. She focused on the children and her job. Jed worked three days a week in another city where he had good friends. Sharon felt more and more closed out by Jed's absence and his greater emotional engagement with people in the other city.

A few breakups are amicable: the couple mutually accepts that breaking up is inevitable or just makes sense. They understand what happened and do not blame each other. They may even remain friends.

Eileen and Seth worked hard on their relationship for several years. They worked through some key issues learning to communicate more openly, spend more time together, and respect each other's needs. Yet, in the end they had very different goals for their lives. Seth was focused primarily on his work and could not put more time into the relationship. Eileen wanted a life that was more relationship focused. Despite the progress they had made, they had not achieved more intimacy or a better sexual relationship. They decided to go their separate ways.

Yet another type of breakup is the one-sided breakup (Lebow, 2008): one person wants to break up and the other does not. One feels done or is unhappy or sees no future. The other still cares for the partner, fears being alone, or sees hope (Mowatt, 1987). These types of breakup are often filled with tears, guilt, resentment, appeals to try, feelings of rejection, etc. Walsh et al. (1995) discuss the difficulty when one partner wants to break up and the other does not. A variation of the one-sided breakup is the "have to" breakup. One partner feels she has to leave because of the other's drinking, affair, irresponsibility, abuse, etc. Yet another variation of the one-sided breakup occurs when one person feels he or she has outgrown the other and sees the other partner as unwilling or unable to grow further. In this case, the one who leaves may be feeling stifled or trapped while the other partner may feel judged, lost, or abandoned. The partner who wants to leave may see the other partner as unwilling to be intimate or to face his or her obstacles to intimacy.

For example, Barbara was no longer attracted to Amanda. She saw Amanda as dependent on her and as lacking confidence. Amanda had put on weight, whereas Barbara worked out regularly bicycling. Barbara found herself attracted to other women and worried about having an affair. The couple had two children born to Amanda. Barbara found herself less and less engaged with the children. Eventually Barbara decided to leave the relationship. Amanda was devastated.

Each of these couples will be explored further in Chapter 12 in the discussion of the stages of breakup.

Ahrons and Rodgers (1987) describe a number of types of couple interactions that often emerge during divorce. Two of them are similar to two of the above types of breakups: "Angry Associates" and "Perfect Pals" (p. 115). "Angry Associates" is similar to couples in a hostile breakup in that anger and heated battles are the defining characteristics of the couple's dynamic. "Perfect Pals" is similar to couples in an amicable breakup in that the couple gets along and often remains friendly.

Factors That Contribute to a Breakup

There are many reasons couples break up. Some of the most common reasons include the following:

- Violation of the relationship by one or both partners
- Lack of intimacy or attachment
- Breakdown of intimacy associated with increased time pressures and time spent apart
- Incompatibility of beliefs, needs, lifestyles
- Individual psychological issues that interfere in the relationship: addictions, mental illness, trauma history
- Breakdown of trust
- Death of a child
- Financial stress

- Lack of respect for the other
- Too many irresolvable issues
- A major irresolvable issue such as whether to have children
- An affair
- Contempt for each other
- Lack of communication and negotiation skills
- Significant unmet needs
- Violence

Many of these issues by themselves will not necessarily lead to divorce. Each may contribute stress to the relationship and, in combination with other issues, lead to divorce.

Whisman, Dixon, and Johnson (1997) surveyed practicing therapists and found the following five issues are the most important problems in couple therapy: affairs, power struggles, communication issues, unrealistic expectations, and lack of loving feelings. Janus and Janus (1993) report that 45% of divorced men and 40% of divorced women admit to having extramarital sexual affairs. Emery and Sbarra (2002) cite various studies showing the prevalence of physical violence in couples to be over 40% (Holtzworth-Munroe, Waltz, Jacobson, Monaco, Fehrenbach, & Gottman, 1992; O'Leary, Vivian, & Malone, 1992). They further describe that physical violence may well play a role in divorce.

Walsh et al. (1995) discuss references indicating that issues such as financial strain, loss of a child, affairs, and emotional detachment can contribute to marital breakup. Roberts and Linney (2000) review the research on alcohol abuse as a cause of marital breakup. Although many studies support that alcohol abuse does lead to marital dissolution, other studies are not conclusive, plus there are methodological issues in such studies that make a conclusion difficult.

Usually there is more than one reason for a breakup. Looking at the list, one can see how one issue can lead to a number of the other issues. Breakups usually involve a sticky web of feelings, issues, experiences, and history that become tangled together.

Ways of Breaking Up

Couples may drift into, explode into, fall into, or be pushed into a breakup. The breakup may just evolve out of increased distance and dissatisfaction. It may erupt out of a crisis such as an affair or a bankruptcy. One person may tell the other it's over. One person may create a situation where the other decides to leave. Both partners may calmly decide together that this is it. An everyday negative incident may be the last straw for one or both. One may give the other an ultimatum that isn't met. The children may grow up and leave home, exposing the emptiness in the relationship. One may announce in therapy that he or she is done.

When in Therapy Does the Breakup Happen?

There are several scenarios during couple therapy when a breakup can happen:

1. The couple has worked in couple therapy for quite awhile. They have even made progress. Then things come apart and they break up.
2. The couple has worked in couple therapy for awhile without making significant progress. The therapy has been difficult and the couple breaks up.
3. The couple comes to therapy in a crisis that could lead to a breakup.
4. The couple has decided to break up and comes for help to move through the process.
5. One partner brings the other into therapy in order to be able to break up (Lebow, 2008). In addition, this first partner tells the other partner during the therapy session in order to make sure that the other partner has the support of the therapist (Emery, 1999).
6. One partner is in individual therapy with you and then brings in the other partner for couple help. The breakup then happens while you are seeing them both.

How the therapy proceeds will depend in part on which of these scenarios is present.

Previous Loss

Breakups are traumatic losses and often bring up other losses the partners have experienced. These other losses can compound the issues, stages, and intensity of the breakup process for the partners. Except for those partners who had continuously been only with each other, all partners have been through breakups before. Those who experienced previous traumatic breakups are likely to have the current loss trigger old feelings from the previous losses. Whatever unfinished business the partners had from before may come screaming into the present. They may be dealing with "grieving for a lost relationship, lost roles or lost ideals" (Appell, 2006, pp. 99–100).

Losses from growing up may also be triggered. These losses may consist of important deaths, lack of approval and love, neglect, or abuse. For example, Mowatt (1987) writes:

> A client who has lost a parent in childhood through death or divorce may experience exaggerated dependency when the new loss triggers feelings similar to those of the earlier loss, especially if the client was never able to complete mourning for the lost parent. (p. 82)

As the therapist, it is often crucial to check with each of the partners to learn if other prior losses are affecting this current loss. You may want to recommend to either or both of the partners that they seek individual therapy while going through this loss. If either partner is seeing an individual therapist, it is important to be in contact with that therapist to coordinate the work in each therapy.

Summary

Breaking up is devastating. It is walking into the valley of death. We are becoming more aware of the factors that lead up to and contribute to a breakup of an intimate relationship. There are different types of breakups and breakups can happen in any number of ways. Previous loss can affect partners during a breakup. This chapter explored these issues while also addressing the emotional upheaval breaking up brings to the couple and to the therapist.

12

The Stages of Breakup, Therapy Strategies, and the Therapist's Roles and Experiences

Introduction

Is there a way to make sense of such a chaotic time in a couple's life? Once they decide to break up, isn't that the end of couple therapy? In fact, breakup or divorce therapy can be crucial for the health of the individuals who are parting and certainly for their children. The six stages of breakup described in this chapter developed from many workshops I led on the breakup of a relationship plus my work for over 35 years as a couple therapist. Chapter 12 examines each stage and gives therapy strategies for helping couples through each stage. The therapist's intense experiences doing this work are explored. Further stages after the couple therapy are also described. The chapter concludes with a case study.

The Stages of Breakup

Disintegration

Couples in this stage are frequently headed for a breakup. It is, however, the one stage in the breakup process in which couples are more likely to recover their relationship with a lot of hard and dedicated work. Actually, couples can recover their relationship at any stage even after divorce, but the likelihood of recovery decreases dramatically as they progress to each stage.

Markman, Stanley, and Blumberg (2001) found in their research that there is a turning point when couple conflicts often increase and become more intense. Partners begin to experience being together as painful and stressful rather than as comforting and positive.

The hallmark characteristic of the Disintegration stage is that the partners are increasingly living in two different realities. This is particularly devastating in one area: The person each partner believes himself or herself to be is not who the other partner believes him or her to be. The partners' perceptions of reality, in phenomenological terms, are extremely different. Thus, one partner may believe the other to be ungiving and argumentative, whereas the other partner may believe himself or herself to be cooperative, helpful, and forthright. This difference becomes unbearable. To have the person with whom you share your intimate life see you as someone other than who you see yourself is crazy making. You then may fight for who you think you are, doubt who you really are, feel terribly misunderstood and alone, or withdraw. At the same time, you may need to see your partner as wrong to hold on to your sense of self.

Your partner is the person who probably knows you best and who you want most to love you. To see him or her as wrong puts you in the bind of distrusting the person whom you trust (or want to trust). As a result, you then want your partner to be wrong, yet you also don't want him or her to be wrong. Since survival of your sense of self may be at stake, you want to be right, yet you want to be wrong to be able to stay in the relationship. Staying in the relationship then becomes increasingly harder.

This living in different realities extends beyond this core issue. Other aspects of the couple's life can be in dispute about what is real. One partner may believe that the couple is in financial trouble while the other thinks they are doing fine. One may believe that they have no sex life and the other believes they have sex often. The list goes on. As a result, each person feels more and more unsafe. Trust breaks down. The partners may feel like they are losing their sense of self. Basic needs are not being met. Cooperation on the daily tasks of living often breaks down. One or both are becoming more critical and trying to change the other. Issues become more about who is right and who is wrong. Daily concerns become magnified into major meltdowns and then become referendums on each other's character.

The experience for the couple going through Disintegration is somewhat like talking on a cell phone in an area of poor reception. You try to communicate, but you can't understand each other. Your conversation keeps getting interrupted with static and fuzziness. Often you say, "Can you hear me?" or "Did you hear that?" Sometimes you get through and often you don't. Then you feel frustrated and try again. Then you get angry and swear at the phone. Then you give up.

During the Disintegration phase, a number of Gottman's (1999) signs of probable divorce show up frequently: harsh start-up, the Four Horsemen, failed repair attempts, and flooding (see Chapter 11 for further discussion of Gottman's signs). Repair attempts are efforts by the couple to lower the tension between them. When repair attempts fail, the tension remains or increases and flooding results.

Whitfield, Markman, Stanley, and Blumberg (2001) in their research on couples found four patterns that destroy relationships: (1) escalation (one upping the other's negative behavior); (2) invalidation (putting down the other); (3) withdrawal and avoidance (unwillingness to be involved); and (4) negative interpretation (believing the other's motives to be more negative than they are). These patterns are similar to Gottman's and are present in the Disintegration phase.

In emotionally distant couples the same dynamics are often happening, yet the couple is withdrawing and closing down rather than arguing. They are becoming increasingly disconnected because they don't feel seen, known, or understood. Their day-to-day lives have less and less to do with each other. They cease to know who each other really is and what each other feels. The disintegration is not necessarily hostile. In fact, it can be eerily unspoken and quiet. The relationship is becoming dead. Hackney and Bernard (1990) describe the process of alienation during a breakup as distancing from oneself and the marriage.

Disintegration for the couple who part amicably usually lacks hostility and deadness. The two members of the couple may be pulling apart and living in more separate realities. These realities may not clash and, in fact, the couple may stay friendly. This does not mean, however, that one or both of them are without pain. Coming apart hurts even when you understand.

The disintegration that is happening may not be perceived by both members of the couple. In a one-sided breakup, one partner may be experiencing growing apart while the other still feels connected. One may be becoming more hopeless while the other, not realizing the extent of his or her partner's dissatisfaction, has more hope.

The Therapist's Role
As the relationship disintegrates, a critical job for you, as the therapist, is to tell the couple what is happening. You need to describe the phenomenon of this disintegration with the two different realities each person is experiencing. It is important to define the reality that each person sees for the following reasons: (1) it surfaces and focuses what may be hidden; (2) it validates each person's experience; and (3) it shows the couple system that has developed and the role that the two different realities play. In a hostile breakup, each person is often lost in his or her own picture

of what is happening and doesn't even see that the other has a different picture. Feeling isolated and attacked, each person tends to hunker down into an increasingly strong fortress that defines what is true and keeps the individual safe. Even as each is blaming the other, one or both may be building an increasingly negative image of himself or herself both from the partner's images and from how he or she is in fact acting. The partners may well be acting in ways that make them not feel good about themselves. Isolating, attacking, judging, and fighting are not behaviors people are proud of in themselves. Each person may, in fact, be becoming someone he or she doesn't like. Each person's self-confidence is being eroded.

This tense dynamic often triggers old issues for each partner. There may be issues from past relationships or from each person's family growing up. Chances are each has lived in this dynamic before. Otherwise, how could they each know their part so well?

Since the partners are struggling for survival and see each other as the problem, it is difficult to get them to reach out to each other. The first place to appeal to them to break out of this dynamic is to help them see that they need to act differently in order to feel better about themselves. I often tell couples that a relationship is not worth behaving in ways that make you disrespect and dislike yourself. You need to act in ways that you can feel good about. You need to feel good about yourself first. If this helps the relationship, great. If not, go out with dignity and self-respect rather than feeling like a victim or an abusive person.

Often partners at this stage of a hostile breakup use each other's negative behavior as permission to act badly themselves. Each is in a bind where one lashes out at the other because the other lashed out at him or her. Each thinks it's OK to act badly because the partner acted badly. Thus, each is using the other's behavior to define his or her own behavior and then feeling justified and righteous.

For example, Isaac and Reba spent most of their therapy criticizing each other. Each gave examples of the other's despicable behavior in the prior week. Each used the other's behavior as justification for his or her own attacking behavior. In such a couple, eventually each partner may become what the other partner describes: attacking, angry, and uncaring. Thus, a goal at this point is for individuals to become more consistent in having their behavior match who they see themselves to be. The appeal here is to the individual's sense of self-respect.

Another way to appeal to the individuals is to show them how their negative behaviors affect them in many different ways. Not only does it potentially make them not like themselves, but it can also trigger feelings of depression and hopelessness. Acting in negative ways creates stress. If the couple has children, this behavior is undoubtedly hurting the children even if the couple is sure the children don't hear it. Children pick up tension and suppressed negative feelings. Also, the negativity may be hard to shut off outside the home and may spill over into other relationships and work. In addition, if partners don't learn to act differently, they are likely to carry the behaviors into their next relationship. How many of us as therapists have seen clients in new relationships acting just as they did in the last relationship while still blaming the other who is now the new partner.

Beyond appealing to the individuals to take responsibility for their contribution to the destructive dynamic, the therapist also needs to help the couple see the larger picture of the relationship system. This may not be possible if the couple is determined to break up and sees the other as the problem. However, seeing the relationship system that they have created together can help them move to some healing whether or not they stay together. The work at this stage is to help the couple to see how they mutually reinforce each other's negative views of themselves, each other, and the relationship. This negative view has developed from a cycle of interactions that push each other into a rut of more negative behaviors. This rut develops a life of its own and takes over. Each could write the script of what they both will say.

Many researchers have found that destructive patterns of communication can contribute to marital breakdown and divorce (Kayser & Rao, 2006). Lebow (2008) describes the case of a high-conflict couple. As the therapist he writes: "At the systems level, there was a need to calm the frequent crises and break the circular chain of accusations and counteraccusations that were being unleashed" (p. 473).

The Therapist's Role in an Emotionally Distant Breakup
I have described disintegration in a hostile breakup. In an emotionally distant breakup the same dynamics can be occurring, yet they are underground. One doesn't reach out because the other doesn't reach out. One acts uninterested in the other because the other doesn't act interested in one. Gradually they pull apart, eventually not even remembering this earlier dynamic. Now they live separate lives either emotionally or physically. In couple therapy, the negative behaviors that each partner needs to own include the internal blaming and the withdrawal. Each needs to recognize how distancing can be a way of protecting oneself, hurting the other, or punishing the other.

When the couple can see the rut they have created, they can possibly move to the next step, which is to develop some understanding of each other's view of reality. For example, Jed may be able to come to understand that because he is away several days a week, Sharon feels closed off by him. This then leads to Sharon's feeling that Jed doesn't care about and value her. Sharon may be able to see how her independence and lack of emotional openness leads Jed to share more with his friends in the other city than with her. If the relationship is indeed going to break up, this understanding will help the couple leave the relationship with more compassion and sense of personal responsibility for what went wrong. This is crucial for their children. It is also crucial for each person's future growth in new relationships.

The Therapist's Role in an Amicable Breakup

When the couple is in the Disintegration stage in an amicable breakup, the main work they need to do is to see the disintegration that is happening and to understand the effects it is having on the relationship and themselves. There may even be difficult feelings of hurt and anger that need to be owned and discussed. Eileen and Seth recognized that their relationship was unraveling, yet neither wanted to address what was happening. Neither wanted to lose the friendship that they had in their relationship. Yet, neither was satisfied with their lack of intimacy and sexuality.

The Therapist's Role in a One-Sided Breakup

Working with a couple in a one-sided breakup at this stage can be particularly difficult. Fisher and Calhoun (1989) and Jurich (1989) write of the potential for the therapist to become caught in the couple's issues. When one person wants in and the other wants out, there is "… the potential for the therapist to be triangulated into the couple's dilemma" (Fisher & Calhoun, 1989, p. 41). When one person wants in and the other wants out, each member of the couple may pull on the therapist to support his or her position.

Those who are headed for breaking up the relationship may not want to be honest about what they see ahead and how they are is feeling. As the therapist, you may need to help the other partner gradually recognize how the relationship is disintegrating and build some reserves to be able to handle what may come. Or you may need to help this person learn constructive behaviors in order to avoid wreaking havoc when the breakup comes. When Barbara tells Amanda that she wants to leave, Amanda may get angry, become depressed, or put the kids in the middle. She may need help before she can handle what is coming.

How do you, as the therapist, handle such a situation? If you know that Barbara is going to leave, but Amanda does not know, it can be very tricky. The dangers include the following: it may look like you are holding a secret, you may seem to be colluding with Barbara, or you may seem to be enabling Barbara to leave. In this situation, it may be difficult for you to continue to be the couple therapist because you are holding secret information that will hurt Amanda. You may need to refer the couple to someone else. The more likely situation is that you haven't been told by Barbara, but you can tell where she is and where things are headed. Then you need to continue to work with the couple toward healing the relationship while looking to what will help Amanda and Barbara individually. (See Chapter 7, The Challenge of Working With Secrets in Couple Therapy.)

Effects on the Therapist
Working with a couple in the Disintegration stage of a breakup is very demanding and taxing work. As the therapist, you need to be tracking the couple interactions carefully. It can be easy to become overwhelmed by the complexity and the intensity of what is happening in the room. It is like standing on the fulcrum of a seesaw trying to keep it balanced. These sessions are often exhausting.

Rice and Rice (1986) describe the difficulties the therapist may experience at this pre-divorce stage: loss of objectivity, impatience, and evoking of one's personal conflicts. They write, "The therapist can become impatient dealing with the couple's ambivalence...but can also allow values, personal conflicts and/or countertransference to influence the couple's decision negatively" (p. 153).

Stuck

Stuck is the stage of a breakup in which nothing is changing. The couple may be treading water, repeating efforts, trying new efforts to improve the relationship, or working on themselves individually, yet the relationship is not changing. The couple may be becoming quite frustrated or they may be staying stuck because it is safe. One individual may be facing the issues and trying to get the other to join him or her. The other may be unwilling or unable to move beyond where he or she is stuck. The couple may be going around and around in predictable loops of discussion, accusation, and argument.

Appell (2006) refers to the repetitive and automatic responses in which couples get entrenched at this stage of stuckness. There is no movement even if there is a lot of commotion. Sometimes commotion can hide the lack of movement. It appears there is a lot going on, but it is the same interaction over and over with different content. Alternatively, the couple may have reached a standoff in which they don't deal with issues because they don't get anywhere. Or they may be emotionally shut down and barricaded for self-protection.

This stage of being Stuck is like trying to get an older car to start. You keep going out to try to start the car. Nothing happens. You push the accelerator more and fiddle with the key in the ignition. Nothing happens. You consider whether it is the battery that needs charging or the starter motor that needs replacing. You try fixing these things. They don't help. You begin to wonder if you should take the car in for major repair or give up on it.

At this Stuck stage the couple and you may be becoming increasingly frustrated. The lack of movement becomes more painful and draining. Inertia starts to develop. Appointments are cancelled. The couple may begin to blame you for not helping them. Insights aren't helping. Homework exercises are not helping or are not being done. You may be working too hard. You may be tired, bored, and starting to feel incompetent. Even external efforts the couple makes to create change such as going on vacation or buying a new house aren't having any real impact.

In this Stuck stage a couple facing a hostile breakup will often act out their conflicts more repeatedly and intensively, yet without change. The disengaged couple may become more lifeless. The amicable couple will often keep trying to find answers. Finally, the one-sided couple may be in a lull as the person who initiates the breakup gets ready to tell the other. The therapist's role may vary somewhat with each type of couple, yet the central tasks of therapy at this stage remain the same.

The Therapist's Role
One of the most important interventions at this point is for the therapist to acknowledge that the couple and the therapy are stuck. This may be hard to do because the couple is expecting you to change something. As the therapist, you need to be willing and able to sit in this stuckness with them. They need to experience this phenomenon. This can be very uncomfortable. Stuckness is a deadening place. The couple needs to own that they are stuck. They need to stop using the ways they find to hide from how they are stuck. It is important to look at the ways they are stuck and to see

how this is affecting both the couple and the individual. Sometimes seeing that they are stuck and being aware of how this feels can generate some energy to move to a different place. Sometimes they flee and leave therapy. One of them may decide the therapy is making things in the relationship worse. As the therapist, you need to look at this possibility. At the same time, the therapy may be revealing what is there that the couple does not want to see.

Another step the therapist can introduce is to evaluate the therapy together with the couple. Does the therapy need to change? Does the couple, in fact, need a break from therapy? Would it be more helpful for one or both of the individuals to do some sessions alone? Individual therapy may be important so that one or both can look at their own feelings and concerns without the other person in the room. This may work well if the individuals have their own therapists. The decision about whether to see one or both alone yourself is tricky. There can be a clear bind if you become privy to information from one that compromises your role as the couple therapist. (See reference to confidentiality in Chapter 7.)

If you see one partner and not the other, the couple therapy can become unbalanced. On the other hand, you are in a unique position of knowing both people. You may be able to provide some coaching to one or both people individually that helps the couple. You may be able to help one or both face some issues that are blocking the couple therapy. Generally, it is best if you are going to see one member individually to also see the other in order to keep balanced. This balance may be important not only for the clients, but also for you. You may need to hear both sides so that you don't get caught up in one person's perspective.

Part of facing being stuck may be recognizing when no change is likely. The couple has gone over and over the issues. They have tried many things to change the relationship. They continue to be unhappy and there is no more movement. The reader is referred to the Chapter 10 "Therapist Roles, Experiences, and Strategies" for further discussion about being stuck and how to deal with it.

An important decision at this point is whether to bring up the "B" word: breakup. One of the couple members may well bring it up himself or herself. If not, then you, as the therapist, need to weigh the benefits and drawbacks of raising it. It could scare the couple such that they flee. It could further immobilize them. It could launch a crisis or an avalanche of fighting.

On the other hand it may get the couple to face how serious their situation is. It may scare them into attempting some new steps to help the relationship. It may also help them toward an inevitable breakup. Sometimes it is helpful to not only bring up a possible breakup, but have them "walk" through it and to think through how it would happen, how they would handle it, and who would go where. This process is usually very sobering. Wherever it will take them, it often helps to move the couple along. As therapists, we need to remember that our job is to help them heal, not to keep them together or break them apart. Breaking up may bring more healing than staying together or vice versa. Certainly, facing the truth of where they are is a key step.

Jed and Sharon, the disengaged couple, were stuck in their therapy. Because they were so disconnected and were living separate lives, it seemed that they could go on living this way with no change. Attempts at opening up the relationship and working through issues had helped to some small extent. As the therapist, I brought up the possibility of breaking up. The effect was positive in that each worked harder to create more intimacy.

Decision

The decision to break up begins when it first enters one partner's mind. Many partners think of breaking up at some point, but these thoughts don't go anywhere. For couples who do actually break up, the first thought may be this fleeting. Yet, as time goes on, the possibility of breaking up becomes more real. There is a point at which there is a shift in reality. One or both partners begin to think of their lives alone without the other. For many this is terrifying, depressing, unfathomable, and horribly painful. Reality begins to turn upside down. Before considering breaking up, life is about being a couple and sharing one's life. When breaking up is a serious consideration, life becomes about loss, turmoil, financial disruption, and aloneness. It seems as if nothing will be the same.

For some this change may seem like escape and relief. Yet, even for those people there will be loss and upheaval. Facing ending a relationship may feel like standing on the edge of a cliff knowing that what is about to happen is frightening and unknown. There is nothing quite like going through a breakup. It can tear you apart and scatter you about in pieces. Mowatt (1987) states, "The decision is often drawn out and painful ... To pull out of a commitment, to untangle oneself from a shared life, to leave a familiar routine is like facing the prospect of expensive surgery with no assurance that it will succeed" (p. 9).

For many couples the decision comes in waves. There is much backing and filling. It is like getting up the courage to run out into a downpour and then turning to run for cover. But once you have run out in it, you are drenched. Once you have begun to consider breaking up, insecurity sets in. The thought may be scary enough that you decide to stay in the relationship whether or not staying is a good idea. For most people approaching breaking up happens gradually. As the possibility becomes more real, the feelings become more intense.

If the decision is eventually mutual, the couple is likely to go in and out of phases of approaching breaking up. They may be in different places at different times. One may be in a time of hopelessness while the other is working hard to salvage the relationship. When both feel hopeless over a long period of time, breakup may be imminent.

If one person decides to end the relationship and the other wants the relationship to go on, the two people will be in very different places. Fisher and Calhoun (1989) write that the disparity in such a couple "… almost always involves ongoing issues of power, hurt, abandonment and unilateral decision making…" (p. 23). The one who wants to break up will often be far ahead of the other in facing the issues and feelings about breaking up. The one who wants the relationship to last will often be faced with dealing with the issues and feelings of ending condensed together all at once. He or she will often have multiple stages of breaking up to deal with, one on top of the other. This partner often will feel like the victim. He or she has been left behind! Critical to this partner's healing will be coming to a place where he or she too decides this breakup was best. That can be a long way off.

The Therapist's Role
The therapist's role during the beginning of the Decision phase of a breakup often depends upon how the decision comes about. Following is a discussion of three possibilities:

1. The Therapist Helps Facilitate the Emergence of the Decision.   In this situation, the couple is heading toward breaking up, but they don't see it. You, as the therapist, need to name and describe what is happening: the disintegration, the stuckness, and the sense of direction that is emerging. It is important when you are playing this role that you give breaking up as one option among several possible options. As mentioned before, it is not the therapist's role to promote breaking up.

2. One Member of the Couple Decides to End the Relationship   Lebow (2008) writes about clients who "...enter marital therapy with the explicit purpose of utilizing this venue as a step in the process of leaving their partners" (p. 459). There are two possible scenarios here: (1) the partners say they want to break up or (2) they do not express their desire to break up. If they say they want to break up, your role will be different than if they are not saying it but you "know" it. If it has not been said, then you have time to help the couple to be more prepared for the decision when it comes out. Clearly, this is tricky because you don't want to look like you are preparing the other partner for the breakup.

For example, before Barbara told Amanda that she wanted to leave, Barbara evaded Amanda's statements that she sensed Barbara wanted out. As the therapist, it was clear to me that Barbara was hedging. She wanted Amanda to gain strength before hearing that she wanted to leave. In the couple therapy we focused on how each could feel better and more confident in herself whether the relationship stayed together or came apart. When Barbara did tell Amanda that she wanted to leave, Amanda was heartbroken. Yet, the time each had spent gaining a stronger sense of self helped each of them when Barbara did tell.

3. The Couple Decides Together to Break Up   The relationship may be becoming so dissatisfying to both partners that they both decide they want to break up. They may talk about it for some time, or it may seem to emerge suddenly. The couple may be so disengaged that both have already left. Clearly, the process of breaking up can be easier if both people own the decision to end the relationship. There tends to be less blaming and more acceptance of the decision. In a high-conflict couple, however, the blaming and arguing may continue even when both want out.

Once a couple enters the Decision stage, the breakup is under way. Whether the couple's breakup is hostile, disengaged, amicable, or one-sided, the therapist's tasks often are similar. One reason for this is that the process of breaking up has a driving force of its own that often outweighs the dynamics of the couple. Certainly in a hostile breakup the dynamics are exaggerated, whereas in an amicable breakup the dynamics are quieter and smoother. In a hostile breakup the therapist may need to control and slow down the process, whereas in a disengaged couple the therapist may need to help the process to emerge. The following tasks of the therapist need to be addressed in most kinds of breakups at the Decision stage.

As the couple stands on the edge of the precipice and starts to topple over the edge, you, as the therapist, play a critical role. This is potentially the most difficult time in the breakup process because it is a time of high emotion, tearing apart, and changing realities. One of your main jobs is to hold the two people who feel that their world is crumbling. They need you and you need to let them need you and lean on you. You need broad shoulders, deep compassion, and wisdom to carry them through the process. Holding the couple involves a number of important roles including the following:

- Hearing them and being there in the starkness of this loss, pain, and anger
- Being able to bear the emotions that they cannot
- Being accessible for emergencies, extra sessions, and advice on little things that they cannot handle

You must to be able to tolerate what they cannot. Your ability to do this becomes a beacon for them. They need to leave some of their unbearable burden with you. This demands a lot of stamina, depth, and wisdom from you. At times, this can be overwhelming and exhausting. The sessions at this stage can be among the hardest to leave at the office. You will likely need friends and colleagues yourself for venting and support.

For example, Eileen eventually brought up that she wanted to separate. Seth agreed. Despite the breakup being amicable, they each went through a difficult time as they faced this decision. They needed help coming to terms with losing their best friend. The sessions focused on the grief that they each felt. The grief encompassed the loss of each other, the loss of their partnership, the loss of their home together, and the loss of their activities that they shared. The sessions were heart wrenching. They knew the loss of their partnership also meant the loss of their friendship.

Another critical part of your job during the Decision phase is to lead the way through the breakup chaos. You need to tell the couple about the jungle ahead, the tigers hiding in the bushes, and the monsoon season they are entering. You need to warn them and give them guidelines and tools for making it through. This may be uncharted territory for them (unless they have been through a significant breakup before). They need to feel confident that you know how to navigate through this jungle and will guide them. You need to give them perspective and to normalize their experiences. Knowing that others go through what they are experiencing and that they are not crazy is so very important. Because they may break down in the middle of a meeting at work, yell at a grocery clerk, or wake up in the middle of the night crying, they often feel crazy.

Another important facet of your role as the therapist is to begin to provide meaning for what is happening. This involves the members of the couple beginning to see the breakup in a larger context: "What happened?" "How did we get here?" "What part did we each play?" "What role did our past experience play in getting to this point?"

These are some of the questions with which couples need to grapple. Johnston and Campbell (1988) discuss the importance of couples making meaning of the failure of their relationship. Many couples at the Decision phase are too overwhelmed to begin to look at this larger meaning and primarily need crisis management. Yet, for some, looking at the larger meaning helps them feel less chaotic, less lost, and less overwhelmed. This may be particularly true for a couple in which one person is initiating the breakup. Looking at the larger picture may help both partners better understand their differences. Mowatt (1987) writes, "After a couple has finally decided to end their marriage there will be less stress if each party can sort out, verbalize, and accept what happened in the marriage so that the past can be laid to rest" (p. 29).

Once the big decision to break up has been made, there are many subsequent decisions: "Who goes where? How is money dealt with? What do we say to the children and when?" Walsh et al. (1995) describe how emotionally overwhelming these decisions can be. A critical role for you as the therapist is to help the couple figure out which decisions must be made and which can be delayed. It is usually better to delay noncritical decisions because neither partner may be thinking clearly enough to make decisions. There may be a tendency for the couple to rush into decisions because making some decisions gives them a feeling of some control and some grasp on reality. The decisions they must make usually need guidance from you because the couple often does not know what is best. You need to advise; something we as therapists don't often do. Yet, this is a time for advice.

Gray (1996) argues for the importance of the therapist working from the expert-consultant or advice-giving model. Lack of advice from you may lead to disastrous behaviors such as putting the children in the middle. You need to advise the couple as objectively as possible, showing them the negative and positive consequences of their behavior. The areas in which advice is often needed include moving, telling others, handling the children, and managing the couple's emotions. Barth (1988) writes of the importance of the therapist's role in strengthening decision-making abilities of divorcing couples to help them get through the divorce and to help them grow as people.

There are many roles the therapist plays at this stage. Baucom, Epstein, and LaTaillade (2002) describe the different roles a cognitive behavioral couples therapist needs to play to be helpful. These roles include director, teacher, advocate, and facilitator. The couple therapist needs to be flexible and adapt to the situation and the needs of the couple. Even though the relationship is breaking down, the couple therapist needs to maintain a collaborative alliance with each partner to be effective. Many schools of therapy stress the importance of this collaborative role throughout the therapy (Johnson, 2007; Lebow, 2008).

The Decision stage can go on for some time. Partners and couples can make and unmake the decision to break up. This is clearly nerve-racking for everyone. Yet, it may take time to be clear about whether breaking up is the best option. It is important to help partners understand the difference between making the decision and accepting the decision. After making the decision comes accepting the decision. The two can be mixed up and the phase of "accepting the decision" can be mistaken as "not having made the decision." How are they different? Making the decision involves a period of not knowing, debating, and going back and forth and trying to decide what to do. When the decision is made, it is followed by many emotions including loss, fear, anger, and pain (Barth 1988). Accepting the decision means going through these emotions and coming to terms with the decision that has been made. Accepting involves absorbing the reality of the decision. To help clients figure out the difference, you can ask if the partners are having trouble making the decision, or whether they know what the decision is, but they are having trouble accepting it and all the emotions and ramifications that go with it. Most people can usually tell which dilemma they are facing when asked. If one partner has made but has not accepted the decision and the other partner does not want to break up, the second partner may take signs of the first partner not accepting the decision as not having really decided. As the therapist, you need to help the second person make this distinction so he or she doesn't build false hopes. You may also need to help the partner who has already decided not give out mixed signals.

If the couple has children, it is critical to address issues about the children at every phase of the breakup process. During the Decision stage, the partners will likely be very concerned about how this decision will affect the children. They may have read about the damage breakups and divorces have on children. They fear the worst. Most couples at some point think of staying together for the children. Telling the children that they are breaking

up is probably the most wrenching part of the whole process. As the therapist, one of your most important roles is to help guide the couple through
the process of dealing with their children. When to tell them? What to say?
How to deal with their reactions or lack of reaction? How to be good parents at a time when they feel like they are failing their children?

Guidelines for Dealing With Children in a Breakup

Don't Put the Children in the Middle.   This includes not bad-mouthing
the other parent, not making the children have to choose between the parents and not giving the children responsibility for making arrangements
when they are too young.

Talk to the Children Together.   Explain the breakup in words and concepts
that are age appropriate. For example, for younger children: "Mommy and
Daddy aren't happy together any more" or "Mommy and Daddy don't love
each other any more."

*Assure the Children that the Breakup Is Not Their Fault and That You Both
Love Them Very Much.*   Tell them that each of you will still be their parents and will see them and spend time with them.

Tell the Children What Is Going to Happen.   Explain to the children who
will live where and what their schedule will be. Assure them about what
will remain the same (e.g., school, activities, neighbors)

*Allow the Children to Have Their Feelings or to Not Be Ready to Address
Their Feelings.*   Some children will cry, some will ask questions and
some will ask "what's for dinner." If they express emotions, it's important to acknowledge their feelings and not push them away. This may
be very hard because their feelings will likely trigger strong feelings for
you. If they don't express emotions, it is helpful to tell them they can
talk to you anytime feelings do come up.

Tell the Children Before Anyone Moves, but Not Too Far Ahead.   Telling
young children a few weeks ahead of the move usually works best but
teenagers may need longer. It is often helpful for the children to see where
the moving parent will live before he or she moves.

Emery (1999) and Lebow (2008) give a summary of the research on how divorce affects children and the role parents play in how children fare. For example, Emery discusses issues that influence children's adjustment to divorce, such as a good relationship with the residential and nonresidential parent, low parental conflict, and financial stability.

Some married couples head straight for divorce once the decision to break up has been made. Many are not ready to deal with whether to divorce. They separate the decision to break up from the decision to divorce. As the couple therapist, you need to consider whether to encourage the couple to seek mediation (Folberg, Milne, & Salem, 2004) or legal counsel. If the couple starts talking about possible divorce, it is wise to explain their options to them including mediation, collaborative law (in some states), divorce coaching (Portnoy, 2006), and divorce options. Lebow (2008) reports studies that show positive outcomes from mediation. He cites research that shows that, "The success of mediation in promoting positive outcomes in divorce for both parents and children has been well established" (p. 463).

It is important that you know the basics about the legal aspects of a marital breakup. You are likely to be the first person the couple talks to about divorce. You also need to be very clear about the limits of your knowledge and expertise regarding divorce. Gray (1996) presents a model of clinicians working together with mediators and attorneys through the divorce process.

Shock

Shock comes during and after the decision to break up. It is the direct result of facing a world turned upside down: "How can this be? How can I face this?" So much is about to change that the partners become overwhelmed. Shock involves being disoriented and disbelieving as well as feeling stunned, immobilized, and flooded. The phenomenon of being in Shock can take over all else. The partners may well feel out of control and/or they may act in out of control ways. It is not uncommon for partners to have accidents, forget important things, get sick, lose direction, and have difficulty getting things done.

Edvard Munch's famous painting "The Scream" shows a person in Shock. The woman is stunned, fearful, and screaming. At the same time, she is immobilized and stiff. Often partners going through the Shock stage of a breakup feel much like the woman in the painting. If they could scream, it would help them release some of the fear and helplessness they feel.

One hallmark of being in Shock is not knowing what is real: Is this really happening? A woman may think, "This is my husband...but he isn't any more, but we're still married, but he's leaving, but we have to go to a school meeting together, but I don't want to sit next to him." If the wife in the couple was the one to decide to leave, she may have already been through this Shock while her husband is just entering this phase. Seeing the husband in Shock can evoke guilt, fear, and frustration. The wife who decided to leave may be ready to make other decisions that her partner can't fathom. The husband in Shock may need some protection so that his wife doesn't take advantage of this vulnerable state.

The Therapist's Role
During the time of Shock, your primary role as the therapist is one of grounding, focusing, warning, directing, and reassuring. Grounding involves helping the partners who are in Shock figure out what they need to do to function most effectively. This may mean focusing on doing the basics of living; doing the things that bring tangible results and doing the things that help them know who they are. Grounding may mean focusing on getting the laundry done, the driveway plowed, and the meals prepared. It may mean taking walks to make contact with nature and letting others who care for them be helpful.

Focusing involves deciding on doing the things that sustain their life, their children, their job, and their health. As the therapist, you may need to help the partners set specific achievable goals during this time. Partners will also need to decide what to set aside for now. Johnston and Campbell (1988) describe clients' need for help and direction in managing their lives at this stage of psychological shock. The therapist's role is often one of support and guidance.

When it became clear that Isaac and Reba, the hostile couple, were going to separate, their lives became more chaotic. Each became even more uncooperative and angry. The hostility turned from arguing into iciness. Each was in Shock. A major focus of their sessions became how to function together as a family during this time. The basics of their life were falling apart, including their schedule, arrangements about their children, and preparing meals. They needed grounding to keep things functioning. For example, in couple therapy they spent time discussing who was going to be home for their children after school each day.

You need to alert partners to possible dangers during this time. They will need to drive carefully, make sure the stove is turned off, do things to stay healthy, make sure they eat enough but not too much. Sleep often suffers. Partners drop things, cut themselves, and bang into things because their attention is absorbed and distracted. When a wave of Shock hits, partners need to sit down, breathe, or take a nap. They should not drink alcohol, drive long distances, or get into arguments with others.

Reassurance is very comforting and grounding during this time. Partners in Shock need this regularly from you. The greatest reassurance is that this behavior and distraction are normal and is part of what people go through when breaking up. When partners are in the throes of Shock or many of the other stages, they often feel like they are the only ones who have ever experienced this chaos. This is part of the isolation that comes with breaking up. Reassurance helps partners begin to thaw out from Shock. They also need reassurance from others who care or have been through this process themselves.

As the therapist working with a couple in Shock, you will likely feel a strong sense of responsibility. You may worry about one or both partners. They need you right now. You are likely to feel a heaviness and vigilance for them. You may want to tell them to call you if they are having trouble functioning.

If the couple is amicable at this point, they can help each other through the Shock by watching out for each other. Sometimes the person who has made the decision can watch out for the partner who doesn't want the relationship to break up. When the breakup is one-sided, the partner who does not want the breakup is likely to be in greater Shock than the other partner. He or she will need more of your guidance and support. Because you must stay neutral, you may need to refer this client to an individual therapist.

Disengaged partners may not even realize they are going through Shock because they are too shut down. You may need to alert them to being in Shock to warn them to be careful and to get the support they need. When Jed and Sharon decided to break up, Sharon carried on as before, not showing much reaction. Yet, inside she was devastated—something she had difficulty admitting to herself. Jed, too, carried on, but was quite disoriented. For example, he missed an important meeting at work because he went to the wrong building.

Limbo

Limbo is a period of the breakup in which the decision to split has been made, but the couple is still together. Much is changing on the inside, but little has changed on the outside. In day-to-day life, the partners are still a couple. The old reality is crumbling, but the new reality isn't here yet.

Everything is different, and yet everything is the same. As the new reality begins to set in, the partners are confronted regularly with the old reality. Life is a yo-yo: "We're splitting, but we're together. We're not a couple, but we are a couple."

In this place of Limbo, hope may keep reemerging, particularly for a partner who doesn't want the breakup. Partners may forget for a second that they are breaking up. Then the cruel reality hits them again, and then again. This can be a wrenching and volatile time. New boundaries are needed but are not in place. Some of the questions partners may ask themselves during Limbo include "Do we sleep in the same bed together?"; "What about the holidays?"; "Do we tell each other where we are going each day?"; "Do we keep the same schedule?"

All day long the partners are faced with ambiguity about who they are and what to do. It can be exhausting. There is often quite a bit of tension in the couple relationship. This may result in outbursts, last ditch attempts to make the relationship work, and behaviors that are uncharacteristic of the partners. Lebow (2008) writes about the negative effects that result from couples continuing to live in the same house while divorcing.

Couples who are breaking up but don't live together may have a different experience of the Limbo stage. There is much less to break apart externally. In fact, for these couples, the breakup may seem quite abrupt because they suddenly don't see each other or share their lives together anymore. They may skip much of the Limbo stage and go right to Splitting. The Limbo stage provides some time to get used to the breakup even though it can also be excruciating. Without much of a Limbo stage, the partners may feel suddenly adrift, abandoned, and alone. The only time they see each other may be in your office.

There is a dance called the Limbo in which the dancer bends backward to go under an increasingly lowered bar. If the dancer touches the bar, he or she is out. To not touch the bar as it lowers, the dancer must get into an increasingly uncomfortable, crunched up, and out of balance position. Being in the Limbo stage of a breakup often feels similar in its discomfort, its lack of balance, its torturous movement, and in the knowledge that eventually you are going to lose.

The Therapist's Role
One of your central roles as the therapist is to help the couple get through this Limbo time. Sessions often involve talking about the week and looking at ways of coping with the tensions and the ambiguities. Gray (1996) describes the role of the therapist in these early stages as one of

expert-consultant. Your role as a therapist is often one of giving the couple behavioral coping skills, such as how to deal with a blowup or how to handle social events. The couple needs to define new boundaries. You need to help them come apart and create more separation. Thus, you may be helping them negotiate how to avoid being in the house at the same time or how to stop sharing intimate details of their lives. This can be very painful for the couple and even for you as the therapist. You may well absorb the stress of the couple. As you feel terrible guiding the couple apart and seeing their pain, you need to remember the overall goal, which is to help them get through this constructively and to heal.

Limbo was a particularly difficult time for Barbara and Amanda. Amanda, who still wanted the relationship, kept looking for signs that Barbara would change her mind. Each time the reality of breaking up confronted her, she would get upset. Amanda needed help facing the new reality and Barbara needed help handling her guilt. She felt like the bad guy constantly rubbing Amanda's nose in the breakup. As the therapist, an important part of my role was to provide direction and coping skills for coming apart while they were still together.

Jed and Sharon, the disengaged couple, had difficulty deciding where Jed would stay when he came home from his job in the other city. Since they were still together and they hadn't worked out how to separate, they thought it would make sense for Jed to stay at the house. On the other hand, both felt awkward about continuing to act as if nothing had changed. We negotiated that Jed would sleep in a different room and sometimes stay at a friend's during this time.

As you help the couple come apart, you need to provide the framework for what is happening. Help them understand Limbo and the difficulty of living in two different realities. This can normalize their experience and prepare them for the tension and unpredictability of this period. For example, if a couple knows that one of them might suddenly act uncharacteristically, they will be more prepared to handle the circumstances should this happen.

Another important role as therapist during this period is to help the couple not get too far ahead of themselves. In each person's need to get some control, one or both may push forward to address issues that they are not ready to handle. For example, one may want to address money issues or custody issues while the couple is still getting used to the idea of breaking up. When one person has decided to leave the relationship, he or she is likely to be ahead of both the other partner and the relationship. This person may want to get on with issues that the other partner can hardly begin to contemplate. As the therapist, it is important to remember that your client is the couple. Thus, you need to help the couple find the pace of breaking up that works best for the couple and not necessarily for one or the other partner. You may need to set the pace and the accompanying boundaries. Since the partners are functioning less and less as a couple, your role in guiding them as a couple is critical.

Splitting

Splitting is the stage of breakup in which the couple comes apart. The focus of the couple is on separating their lives and becoming single. Appell (2006) describes a number of options couples can consider at this stage including a trial separation and a pre-divorce separation. The separation involves all of the following: house, finances, time, friends and family, belongings, schedule, and children. It is a time of disorganization and restructuring. Splitting includes many decisions (Rice & Rice, 1986). Ahrons and Rodgers (1987) state, "There are immediate tasks which demand attention. These range from the minute to the highly complex" (p. 67). It can seem to the partners that their lives are consumed by decisions. There is constant negotiating and boundary setting. The couple's reality is changing daily. There is plenty of room for anger, rejection, outrage, and devastation. Either partner may feel that he or she is being turned inside out, ripped apart, and carved into pieces. Every day can seem like an auctioning off of one's life. Any small issue can cause a major wound or argument. For example, splitting up the CD collection may elicit a major firestorm. One's heart and soul may be tied up in those CDs. Each person may feel like he or she is fighting for his or her soul. Also, each may be fighting for a sense of fairness and justice: "I'm not going to be jilted out of my rightful portion of the CDs." This may be a way of standing up for one's sense of self.

The stage of Splitting is somewhat like a piece of wood split by an ax: The ripping apart is sharp and everything cracks open. The partners feel raw and vulnerable. They end up with less than they started with. They usually feel like something was done to them. It somehow feels violent. Ahrons and Rodgers write, "This early stage of separation plunges the individual into an intense state of emotional social anomie, literally normlessness. Old roles have disappeared, but new ones have not yet developed" (p. 64).

Splitting makes it real that the breakup is happening. Denial becomes harder to maintain. Unresolved feelings from the relationship can easily be played out in the decisions that are being made. Years of lack of fulfillment and dissatisfaction can rear up. The grief and anger can be overwhelming. The process of splitting can be quite consuming and draining. For some, however, it can be liberating as the individuals break free from a debilitating relationship. Some partners will begin to experience a sense of freedom. As the couple spends more time apart, one or both partners may see a new world opening up and hope appearing. This is more likely to be true for someone who has initiated the breakup or for a couple who have mutually decided to break up.

For couples who do not live together, splitting may occur relatively quickly. It may involve returning items that were in each other's homes. How involved the partners' lives were with each other in the physical and financial world usually determines how much splitting needs to be done. Like the Limbo stage, Splitting may happen too quickly, leaving one or the other partner feeling bereft and abandoned. Sometimes you may need to help the couple complete the Splitting stage emotionally by suggesting a ritual that acknowledges the split.

The Therapist's Role
Your primary roles in the Splitting stage are navigator and referee. A navigator helps guide the ship through rough waters. A referee keeps the game from falling into chaos by keeping the players on the field, by requiring fair play, and by focusing on the goal. As the therapist, you can help the couple make decisions and handle their emotions in appropriate ways. Appell (2006) writes that therapists during divorce counseling may need to help clients look at achieving a sane, peaceful result rather than taking certain actions that may only meet their immediate emotional needs. At this stage there may be mediators or lawyers who are central to the negotiations. If not, you may need to recommend that the couple get this help, particularly if they are married. If the couple is not married, you may be the only negotiator they have.

You can help them navigate through some decisions such as who lives where, how to handle the children, and how to deal with families. Appell (2006) writes of the importance of helping a couple keep a fair balance of power in going through a divorce. As a therapist during the Splitting stage, your role is in part to help the couple make decisions that keep some balance of control and power. Decisions that involve financial and legal issues should be dealt with by other professionals.

As navigator and referee you are a voice of balance and reason. When the couple is lost in emotions, you need to bring them back to the decisions that must be made. Sometimes to get to those decisions, you will need to help them deal with their emotions first. Yet, the goal at this point is not emotional resolution so much as appropriate channeling of emotions.

The couple is no longer working toward resolving their issues with each other. They are working toward a breakup that is fair and possibly healing. The scope of your role has become limited. The couple may have difficulty even being in the room with one another. It is important, as the therapist, to recognize and accept the limitations of your role. During the Splitting stage, you may have your own opinions about the decisions being made. It is difficult to stay balanced. You may think the CDs should be split a certain way or that one partner should get the house. This part of dealing with a breakup taxes your ability to stay objective.

Isaac and Reba's sessions during Splitting were icy and angry. All trust had broken down. My role was to keep the breakup from spiraling out of control. I became the bands around the boxing ring and the referee inside. My role was to help them navigate through the breakup without destroying each other. We dealt with such issues as who would move out, time with their children, and temporary financial arrangements. The two things that kept them moving forward were their concern for their children and my role as the referee.

As navigator, an important part of your role is to keep the process on course. Often neither one of the partners can move forward in any way that makes sense. They are likely to be all over the place. The sessions can easily veer off over a cliff or into the woods. You need to keep them moving forward. This can be a grueling and morose task. It can feel like a slow killing and dismembering.

Another important aspect of your role is to be the voice of realism. You need to keep the partners from having unrealistic expectations about this stage in their breakup. One partner still may wish to get back together. Another may wish to take the other partner to the cleaners for vengeance. Still another may wish for the couple to remain best friends. Yet another partner may wish to show the children how awful their father or mother is and how he or she screwed up the marriage. Your role is to help show how these wishes are fantasies or destructive ideas.

Part of your role is to be witness. Your presence gives reality to what is happening. As witness, you listen, notice, and give support. When the couple agrees to something in front of you, they are more likely to stick to it because you are there. Being a witness helps them to focus and keep more control.

An important issue that often arises in this stage is whether to see either or both of the partners individually. Seeing either of them individually is generally not a good idea because you may lose your role as impartial helper. When partners see you by themselves, they are there for themselves, not for the relationship. You can't be in the role of helping the partners individually if that conflicts with your role as the couple therapist. However, there are times when seeing the partners individually can help the couple move toward making the decisions they need to make. You and they need to be clear about the limits of your role. You need to be clear that you are there to help the breakup process not to support one individual at the expense of the other.

In a hostile breakup the partners usually cannot be understanding or helpful to one another. You, as the therapist, can offer understanding to them for what they are going through. This can help them feel supported and cared for at a time they are losing the primary person in their lives. If you offer support to one, you need to be sure to offer support to the other.

In an amicable breakup the couple may be congenial during the Splitting stage without acknowledging the tension and loss that is happening. You may need to bring these feelings out in order for them to fully go through the process of Splitting. Seth and Eileen were quite civil and friendly during the time that Seth was moving out. Yet, Seth was having a very difficult time, often crying by himself. He felt the burden of being the one who had to make the most changes. In the couple therapy he was able to express these feelings with my encouragement. We were able to negotiate ways for Eileen to help him that felt appropriate for both of them.

During the Splitting stage in a one-sided breakup, the partner who does not want to break up may come to realize that the breakup is really happening. This may open the dam of that partner's emotions as his or her hopes are dashed. The couple will likely need help recognizing that they are at different stages of the breakup process. Your role as therapist may be to help them find ways to navigate the very different waters they are in.

A word needs to be said about divorce. Breakups that involve a divorce are almost always more intense and messy than nonmarital breakups. The process of divorce has its own difficult, expensive, and complicated course (Appell, 2006). It tends to draw out this Splitting stage, especially when the partners can't agree on such issues as assets, child support, and alimony. Chances are that once a couple enters a divorce process, you will not be seeing them together regularly. You may be only called upon to help with important decisions such as how to handle the children.

Beyond Splitting: Friendship?

After the Splitting stage, couple therapy is usually over. Those few couples who are going through an amicable breakup may continue with sessions in order to gain more understanding about their relationship ending. Such a couple may also want to try to transition to a friendship. Many couples want to have a friendship after breaking up, but few can achieve it. If there is a chance for friendship, there usually needs to be a period of separation with little or no contact. This allows the partners to grieve, pull apart, and see if they can have a relationship on new terms. In the gay and lesbian communities it is much more common for couples to be friends after breaking up. The couple is often part of a community of people who know each other. They are more apt to be in social situations together. Men and women are less apt to have friendships with each other than are women and women and men and men. Thus, it may be easier for people of the same sex to be friends after breaking up. Perhaps gay and lesbian couples have stronger friendships within their couple relationship before they break up. Marvin and Miller (2000) describe how lesbian ex-partners have a strong need to stay close and often stay in the same social network.

Individual Therapy

As the couple therapist, it does not usually work to see one or both members of the couple after couple therapy ends. Certainly if there is a legal process of divorce, it is advisable that you don't see either person individually. You may put yourself in a position of conflict of interest. There are, however, some situations in which you might see one of the clients individually (Lebow, 2008). Lebow stresses that the therapist needs to fully consider the ethics of the situation and that, "It is always wise to obtain the partner's consent to this transition before making it" (p. 471).

If you started as one of the client's individual therapist and then worked with the couple for a while, it may make sense for you to remain the individual therapist for the person with whom you started. In this case, there needs to be the understanding that you were always primarily the therapist for that person even when you were doing couple therapy. The couple therapy was an adjunct to the individual therapy. If, however, your role switches to being the couple therapist, you may not be able to resume the role of individual therapist.

If the person who initiates the breakup wants you to see the other partner individually and the other partner wants to see you, it may be possible. Perhaps the partner leaving wants the other partner to get support and help. Perhaps he or she wants to feel less guilty. As the therapist, you need to be sure that switching roles won't compromise your role as either the former couple's therapist or as the individual therapist for the partner.

Eileen had an individual therapist. Although she and Seth were going through an amicable breakup, she was concerned about how difficult the process was for Seth, who did not have a therapist. Eileen encouraged Seth to see me individually to help him get through the breakup. Given that the breakup was amicable and that both wanted Seth to see me, I agreed. His individual therapy became vital for him and helped Eileen to feel less responsible for him. The focus of his therapy was on his own journey and not on Eileen's issues.

Sometimes you may do conjoint couple therapy with the individual therapist for one of the partners. You may be the therapist for the other partner. In this case it may well work for you to remain the therapist for the person you are seeing after the breakup. In such a situation, you are not the sole couple therapist. You probably maintained your role as one of the partner's individual therapist during the couple therapy.

Sometimes years after the breakup one of the partners may call you for help with a new partnership. Usually you cannot see the person for the above mentioned reasons.

When a couple breaks up, I sometimes offer each of them a postmortem session. The purpose of this session is to help them on their way through the breakup. In the session, we discuss how they are doing, what they need to do from here, and what they can learn from what has happened. It is important to stay away from any reflections about the other partner or any judgments about the breakup. Often these sessions are very welcome and meaningful for the individuals. I would not offer such sessions to a high-conflict couple because each partner will most likely spend the time complaining about the other and looking for my agreement.

Further Stages of Breakup Beyond Couple Therapy

Many of us see people in individual therapy who have gone through a breakup. As mentioned, we may also see one partner after the couple therapy is over and the couple has broken up. For these reasons, I will next outline the stages of breakup after Splitting. I will describe each stage, but will not go into the role of the therapist since the therapy is not couple therapy at this point. Various authors (Mowatt, 1987; Appell, 2006) describe stages that individuals experience after the breakup.

Recuperation

This is the stage when healing often starts. The previous stages are about the couple coming apart. Now begins the recuperation for the individual. One of my clients announced one day, "I'm back." She felt that she had begun to click back into place with herself. This is the time when the person can begin to get some strength back. He or she is finally able to attend to some basic things that haven't been addressed—doing the laundry, cleaning the house, going to the dentist. The person can catch his or her breath and can feel mending starting. Breakup recuperation is like flu recuperation: If the person does too much too fast, he or she may have a setback.

Pacing is important at this stage. This is an important time to get support and take care of oneself. This is a time to balance being alone and getting oneself out. There are still wounds to lick even as strengthening begins. This corresponds to Hackney and Bernard's (1990) stage of Reality when a person going through a divorce can focus on the present and accommodate to the realities of divorce.

Settling In

Settling In involves developing routines and some sense of normalcy. A feeling of control begins to come back to the person's life. New habits are found and a new schedule begins to settle in. Adjustments are made as the person is getting used to life apart from the former partner. Now the individual can figure out the bills without help. The person knows how to cook some decent meals and figures out how the heating system in the house works.

Forgiveness

To heal from a breakup, one needs to go through forgiving the former partner and oneself. Forgiving the other is primarily an internal process and is usually not shared with the former partner. Many partners hold onto their anger and hurt as a way of justifying their wounds and as a way of punishing the other partner. To be freed from these feelings and connections to the former partner, the person needs to find a way of forgiving. As discussed in Chapter 10 "Therapist Roles, Experiences, and Strategies," forgiveness involves (1) understanding the contribution that each partner has made to the relationship issues and the breakup; (2) taking responsibility for one's contribution; (3) seeing that the former partner is more than his or her hurtful behaviors; (4) working through one's own anger and hurt; and (5) forgiving the former partner and oneself for not being the people that one wanted each to be.

New Life

This is a time of rejuvenation. Hackney and Bernard (1990) call this the stage of Renewal, a time for hope and growth. Mowatt (1987) states, "The old way of life is gone, yet now there is the possibility of making a new life with different kinds of satisfying options" (p. 119). It is a time to reclaim old parts of the self that were lost in the relationship. Perhaps the person goes back to playing music or starts going to ball games again. Maybe one reconnects with friends who got lost along the way. It is also a time to discover new parts of oneself. Maybe it is time to join a chorus or start biking with a club.

"The next step might be to take an inventory of assets. Making a list of abilities and accomplishments may help a person view himself [herself] in a positive light " (Mowatt, 1987, p. 121). New Life is a time to break from old patterns and focus on self-development. This is a time to gain a sense of personal power and to look at new possibilities. In the process there will likely be fears to be faced. There will be slipping back into old patterns. Thus, an important part of this period is to continue to understand what went wrong in the relationship and how each person contributed to the breakup. One needs to know what one contributed in order not to repeat the behaviors in a new relationship. One also needs to know what the partner contributed in order to watch out for picking a similar person the next time around. This is an opportunity to make desired changes in one's life. It is a time to look at the options. For heterosexuals this may be an important time to meet members of the opposite gender as friends in order to get to know them better before embarking on a new romantic relationship.

One Year

The anniversary of a breakup and the beginning of a new year are significant. The individual made it through a whole year! Often people don't believe they can make it through this awful time. Most people are doing better after a year. From then on, looking back to a year ago, they are looking back to a time when they were alone. They are no longer solely looking back to memories of being a couple. The one-year anniversary can be a time to look back over what they have come through and see the changes they have made. It can be a time of integrating what has happened and who they have become. It can also be a very difficult time. Feelings and memories of a year ago can come flooding back. Sometimes they may be even stronger because they were held at bay while the individuals were focusing on surviving. Many cultures designate a year of mourning after a death. When the year is over, the grieving can possibly recede from center stage.

New Relationship

Starting a new relationship after a breakup is usually a scary experience. The person often worries, "Will I make a mistake again? Will I be hurt? Will I be rejected"? Meeting someone new and becoming interested in him or her can bring back excitement, terror, dread, and hope. Mowatt (1987) describes the fear of rejection that both men and women may feel as they attempt to meet new partners. People need to go slowly and honor their wounds. Old issues will likely resurface.

Our clients need time to look at themselves and the new person with new eyes and with the learning that, hopefully, has taken place since the breakup. Rice and Rice (1986) describe the experience of rebonding. Some people rush into a new relationship, have a relationship waiting, or are already deeply in a new relationship when they leave. These relationships often don't work. The person isn't ready and doesn't know how to make different choices.

A key step before entering a new relationship is to learn from the old relationship. There needs to be a "… period of questioning, reworking, redefining, analyzing or 'feeling' the separation or dissolution …" (Rice & Rice, 1986, p. 199). The individual needs to know how to choose differently, how to experience oneself differently, and how to behave differently. This takes considerable introspection and ownership of one's issues. Without these the person will often be doomed to repeat his or her mistakes.

Case Study: Pauline and Rachel

Pauline and Rachel argued ferociously with blaming, defending, and accusing. Rachel became like a chastising parent. As she started to get wound up at Pauline, she gathered more and more steam and volume. She barraged Pauline until Pauline said, "Stop, I can't take it. Stop yelling." This was very upsetting to Rachel. She then said things such as, "I can't be who I am ... These are my true feelings."

Rachel had difficulty with boundaries. Her understanding of an open relationship was one in which you can say what you want. As Pauline started to withdraw, Rachel would intensify like a gathering thunderstorm ready to unleash. Pauline then often became like a child digging in her heels, feeling entitled to a number of acting out behaviors that Rachel didn't like such as eating junk food, watching TV, and refusing to be sociable with Rachel's friends. Pauline then became detached as if she had been slapped. No matter: Rachel rained down with chapter and verse about Pauline's many ills.

My role for many months was to interrupt this pattern, to explain the destructive dynamics, to insist on being heard, and then to raise my voice above Rachel's to stop the deluge. Then, in the pause before Rachel started up again, I showed them how they each played a role in the dynamic of pursuer–distancer. I explained how they were using each other's behavior to justify their own negative responses. Gradually they grew to understand the destructiveness of their pattern of blaming and withholding. Eventually they began to discuss real issues in a meaningful way.

Yet, clearly, they were in the Disintegration phase of their relationship. Each lived in a separate reality. Neither saw herself as the other saw her. To Rachel, Pauline was irresponsible and acting like a rebellious child. To Pauline, Rachel was a controlling "mother" with impossible expectations. On the other hand, Rachel viewed herself as conscientious and highly responsible. She worked as the director of the special needs department of a local school system. Pauline viewed herself as stressed and under great demands in her work as a city firefighter with no time to relax and no energy to socialize. They were caught in an intertwined mesh of unfulfilled expectations and needs. They cared deeply for one another, but their caring was suffocated by each woman's inability to see beyond her own triggers and underlying deprivation.

Pauline was 47 and Rachel was 52. They had been together for eight years and lived together in Rachel's apartment. Another presenting issue for Rachel and Pauline was intimacy. Rachel liked to talk, touch, cuddle, and be sexual. In the beginning of their relationship, their intimate and sexual life was open and exciting. Both were thrilled, particularly Pauline who had not had satisfying sexual or emotional relationships in the past.

When Pauline moved in with Rachel, their closeness began to diminish. Pauline began to withdraw physically. Gradually over time she became more and more shut down until she lost interest in cuddling, touching, playing, and being sexual. Rachel had become increasingly frustrated. Both felt that this tension contributed significantly to their stress with each other.

Rachel was very frustrated that Pauline had health issues that she wouldn't face. Pauline often complained of abdominal and bowel pains. She sometimes couldn't go to work because she would have diarrhea. She would take various over-the-counter medications that sometimes helped. Rachel wondered if Pauline had colitis or some other bowel disorder. She knew Pauline's diet was wreaking havoc with her system. Yet, Pauline would not see a doctor. Rachel also believed that Pauline's health issues were interfering with their sexual life.

In spite of their conflicts, it was obvious Pauline and Rachel were very connected to each other. They felt a deep bond that kept them together through this difficult time. In the third month of their relationship, Rachel lost her brother to leukemia. Pauline comforted Rachel through her loss and subsequent depression. Throughout their relationship, each had been through difficult times during which the other was quite present and nurturing. Both wanted their relationship to work. They were willing to work hard.

During the Disintegration phase of their relationship, my main role was referee. I thought at times that I should wear stripes and bring a whistle. I introduced a talking stone to the sessions: Only the partner with the talking stone could speak. This helped Rachel to stop, to gulp down her ferocity, and to listen. It helped Pauline to have space to find her feelings, to know herself, and to speak out loud.

The couple made remarkable progress through many ups and downs. At times they seemed close to a decision to break up, yet they pulled back from the edge as they learned about themselves and each other. My role through this time expanded from referee to educator and supporter. For each I was, at times, a lifeline. The women became better friends.

And yet, they broke up. Why? Ultimately it was Rachel who made the decision to break up. She recognized that, in spite of the couple's progress, they were stuck in a parent–child dynamic. The focus of her reason for breaking up was Pauline's refusal to take responsibility for her health, especially given Rachel's experience with her own brother. In some clear way it was also Pauline's decision to end the relationship because she knew her lack of responsibility was not tolerable to Rachel. Pauline was not ready to face her issues about her health. Under Rachel's constant scrutiny she could not find the space to become her own person. Even as Rachel learned to speak more appropriately, to own her feelings, and to see the origin of her anger, and Pauline learned to speak her feelings and to know her own mind, Pauline still could not come out of the shadow of Rachel's control.

My role in the Decision phase was teacher, guard, and protector. At times, I focused on each woman for a number of sessions, probing into her history and helping her to face demons that swept her into excruciating aloneness and neediness. I was the connector helping them reach out and find the other during these moments despite their fears and judgments. These sessions helped, but they were not enough to keep the relationship together.

The Decision phase was ironically more painful for Rachel than for Pauline. Rachel had had hope. Rachel had a focus and had drawn a line in the sand. She believed that if Pauline would face her health issues and her irresponsibility, she would grow up and they could remain together. Pauline became more relieved as the line in the sand was drawn. She knew she couldn't meet Rachel's criterion. At times she was defiant. Ultimately, she needed to come out from what felt like Rachel's vise-like grip to find herself.

I, too, at times felt Rachel's frustration with Pauline. If only Pauline would face herself and deal with her health. They had come so far. How could she let the relationship go? Then I would see how Pauline needed to find herself on her own terms. My role was primarily guide and supporter, helping each to understand her own path at this point in her life. I pushed Pauline to go to a doctor and to get some help. She refused. Rachel's pain was wrenching. Her sense of loss was profound and her loneliness was intense. Both still cared about the other. This was at once a hostile breakup, an amicable breakup, a one-sided breakup, and a mutual breakup.

The couple was stuck. My role was to name the stuckness and be clear that no further change was occurring. It was as if they kept trying to get a car to start and it would not. Rachel kept going out once more to try to turn the motor over. Nothing. Pauline merely watched, waiting for the inevitable. We all sat in the excruciating place where there was no air, no movement. Rachel came closer and closer to realizing that they had crossed the line in the sand. She had to make the call. It was over.

The Limbo stage was quick—almost too quick. Since they lived in Rachel's apartment, Pauline moved out. There was no legal process since they weren't married and had no children. The main issue was Pauline finding an apartment she could afford. Rachel participated in this process and helped Pauline financially. In fact, Rachel did much of the work, plunging them back into their parent–child dynamic. These sessions consisted of my tightly balancing their dynamics in order to move forward and not regress into blaming and withdrawal. I kept bringing them back to what they had learned, helping them to find specific ways to stay out of their old roles. The pain of breaking apart and their fears of aloneness kept pushing them into regressive patterns. I was the referee, the navigator, and the crucible.

Splitting was extremely rocky. Pauline moved into an apartment alone. She panicked. Her health deteriorated. She often called Rachel for help. There was a visit to the emergency room when Pauline had rectal bleeding. They continued to meet with me as a couple with my role being primarily supporting each of them and helping them define boundaries. In some ways as they separated, they became more enmeshed. Both understood that Rachel needed to *not* rescue Pauline, yet Pauline was in real trouble. She was slipping.

This was also the phase of Shock, which usually comes after the Decision phase. Each was struggling to function. Each was highly disoriented and vulnerable. They were being torn apart inside and outside. My role was to help each of them function and move ahead. I often gave them support, empathy, and coping skills. I took on more responsibility to help Pauline to allow Rachel move forward on her own. I saw Pauline for several individual sessions and helped her find her own supports.

Eventually, facing how much she was struggling, she agreed to see a doctor and an individual therapist. Rachel continued to work intensively with her own individual therapist. I communicated regularly with each therapist.

And so they went apart! And so the couple therapy ended. So often this is where we are left as therapists when a couple breaks up. What happened to each of them? Did the couple therapy help? I felt drained and suspended. What was I to do with my own grief, my concern, my caring, my desire to know what happened? Sometimes, but not often, the clients will let us know. Sometimes we can learn some basics from the individual therapists. In this case (unlike most), I was fortunate to learn what had happened.

Some years later Rachel asked her individual therapist to tell me (with Pauline's blessings) that she and Pauline had indeed become good friends and that Pauline had finally sought medical help. She had colitis, which was being treated and was under control. Both were in new relationships.

Rachel wanted me to know how much the couple therapy had helped them. Whew!

Summary

Chapter 12 presented six stages that a couple goes through in the breakup of a relationship. The focus was on what the couple experiences as well as on strategies, experiences, and roles of the therapist. Further stages of a breakup that usually occur after couple therapy were explored. The chapter concluded with a case study.

One of the difficulties of doing therapy with a couple that is breaking up is that you also are left. Most often you stop seeing the couple as they split up. You are left with not knowing what happened, how they made it through, and what happened to each of them. You don't get to experience with them their stages of recuperation, new life, etc. You are left with the immense sadness of two people who had hopes and dreams that fell apart. You can hope that your work helped them through this difficult time in their lives in a way that helped them heal and move forward with more understanding. When you do get to see positive results from your work, you can be heartened by the importance of having been the crucible during the couple's difficult journey.

When a couple who is breaking up terminates, it is important that you, too, do your own healing and affirm your courage in going through this chaotic and wrenching time with your clients. You have carried part of the burden for the partners. You are a healer.

Bibliography for Section IV

Ahrons, C.R. & Rodgers, R.H. (1987). *Divorced families: Meeting the challenge of divorce and remarriage.* New York: W.W. Norton.

Appell, J. (2006). *Divorce doesn't have to be that way: A handbook for the helping professional.* Atascadero, CA: Impact Publishers.

Barker, R.L. (1984). *Treating couples in crisis: Fundamentals and practice in marital therapy.* New York: The Free Press.

Barth, J.C. (1988). Family therapist dilemma: Systems therapy with divorcing couples. *Journal of Family Psychology, 1,* 469–475.

Baucom, D.H., Epstein, N., & LaTaillade, J.L. (2002). Cognitive-behavioral couple therapy. In A.S. Gurman & N.S. Jacobson (Eds.), *The clinical handbook of couple therapy* (3rd ed., pp. 26–58). New York: Guilford Press.

Bradbury, K. (1995). The longitudinal course of marital satisfaction: A review of theory, methods and research. *Psychological Bulletin, 118,* 3–34.

Emery, R.E. (1999). *Marriage, divorce and children's adjustment.* Thousand Oaks, CA: Sage Publications.

Emery, R.E. & Sbarra, D.A. (2002). Addressing separation and divorce during and after couples therapy. In A.S. Gurman & N.S. Jacobson (Eds.), *The clinical handbook of couple therapy* (3rd ed., pp. 508–530). New York: Guilford Press.

Evans, P. (1992). *The verbally abusive relationship.* Holbrook, MA: Bob Adams.

Fisher, B.L. & Calhoun, R.W. (1989). "I do and I don't": Treating systemic ambivalence. In J.F. Crosby (Ed.), *When one wants out and the other doesn't: Doing therapy with polarized couples* (pp. 22–44). New York: Brunner/Mazel.

Folberg, J., Milne, A.L., & Salem, P. (2004). *Divorce and family mediation.* New York: Guilford Press.

Glass, S.P. (2002). Couples therapy after the trauma of infidelity. In A.S. Gurman & N.S. Jacobson (Eds.), *The clinical handbook of couple therapy* (3rd ed., pp. 488–507). New York: Guilford Press.

Goldenberg, I. & Goldenberg, H. (1996). *Family therapy: An overview.* Pacific Grove, CA: Brooks/Cole.

Gottman, J. (1999). *The seven principles for making marriage work.* New York: The Three Rivers Press.

Gray, C. (1996). When therapy is not in the client's best interest: Adapting clinical interventions to the stages of divorce. *The Journal of Divorce and Remarriage, 5–6,* 117–127.

Hackney, H. & Bernard, J.M. (1990). Dyadic adjustment processes in divorce counseling. *Journal of Counseling and Development, 69,* 134–143.

Harway, M. (Ed.). (2004). *Handbook of couples therapy.* Hoboken, NJ: John Wiley & Sons.

Holtzworth-Munroe, A., Waltz, J., Jacobson, N., Monaco, V., Fehrenbach, P.A., & Gottman, J.M. (1992). Recruiting non-violent men as control subjects for research on marital violence: How easily can it be done? *Violence and Victims, 7,* 79–88.

Johnson, S.M. (2007). *The practice of emotionally focused couple therapy: Creating connection,* (2nd ed.). New York: Taylor & Francis.

Janus, S.S. & Janus, C.L. (1993). *The Janus Report on sexual behavior.* New York: John Wiley & Sons.

Johnston, J.R. & Campbell, L.E.G. (1988). *Impasses of divorce: The dynamics and resolution of family conflict.* New York: The Free Press.

Jurich, A.P. (1989). The art of depolarization. In J.F. Crosby (Ed.), *When one wants out and the other doesn't: Doing therapy with polarized couples* (pp. 45–66). New York: Brunner/Mazel.

Karpel, M.A. (1994). *Evaluating couples.* New York: W.W. Norton.

Kayser, K. & Rao, S.S. (2006). Process of disaffection in relationship breakdown. In M.A. Fine & J.H. Harvey (Eds.), *Handbook of divorce and relationship dissolution* (pp. 201–221). Mahwah, NJ: Lawrence Erlbaum Associates.

Keim, J. & Lappin, J. (2002). Structural-strategic marital therapy. In A.S. Gurman & N.S. Jacobson (Eds.), *The clinical handbook of couple therapy* (3rd ed., pp. 86–117). New York: Guilford Press.

Kraslow, F. (1987). *The dynamics of divorce: A life cycle perspective (frontiers in couples and family therapy).* New York: Routledge.

Lebow, J. (2008). Separation and divorce issues in divorce therapy. In A.S. Gurman (Ed.), *The clinical handbook of couple therapy* (4th ed., pp. 459–477). New York: Guilford Press.

Markman, H.J. Stanley, S.M., & Blumberg, S.L. (2001). *Fighting for your marriage.* San Francisco: Jossey-Bass.

Marvin, C. & Miller, D. (2000). Lesbian couples entering the 21st century. In P. Papp (Ed.), *Couples on the fault line* (pp. 259–283). New York: Guilford Press.

Mowatt, M.H. (1987). *Divorce counseling.* Lexington, MA: D.C. Heath.

O'Leary, K.D., Vivian, D., & Malone, J. (1992). Assessment of physical aggression against women in marriage: The need for multimodal assessment. *Behavioral Assessment, 14,* 5–14.

Papp, P. (Ed.). (2000). *Couples on the fault line.* New York: Guilford Press.

Portnoy, S. (2006). Divorce coaches: A new resource for matrimonial lawyers. *American Journal of Family Law, Winter,* 231–236.

Rice, J.K. & Rice, D.G. (1986). *Living through divorce: A developmental approach to divorce therapy.* New York: Guilford Press.

Roberts, L.J. & Linney, K.D. (2000). Alcohol problems and couples: Drinking in an intimate context. In K.B. Schmaling & Goldman Sher, T. (Eds.), *The psychology of couples and illness: Theory, research and practice* (pp. 269–310). Washington, DC: American Psychological Association.

Rollie, S.S. & Duck, S. (2006). Divorce and dissolution of romantic relationships: Stage models and their limitations. In M.A. Fine & J.H. Harvey (Eds.), *Handbook of divorce and relationship dissolution* (pp. 221–240). Mahwah, NJ: Lawrence Erlbaum Associates.

Schnarch, D. (1991). *Constructing the sexual crucible*. New York: W.W. Norton.

Spinelli, E. (1989). *The interpreted world: An introduction to phenomenological psychology*. London: Sage Publications.

Spring, J.A. (1997). *After the affair: Healing the pain and rebuilding trust when a partner has been unfaithful*. New York: Harper Collins.

Trafford, A. (1992). *Crazy times*. New York: Harper Perennial.

Wallerstein, J.S. (1990). Transference and countertransference in clinical interventions with divorcing families. Retrieved September 19, 2008 from http://search.ebscohost.com/login.aspx?direct=true&db=pdh&AN=ort-6

Wallerstein, J.S. (1997). Transference and countertransference in clinical interventions with divorcing families. In M.F. Solomon & J. Siegal (Eds.), *Countertransference in couples therapy* (pp.113-124). New York: W.W. Norton.

Walsh, F., Jacob, L., & Simons, V. (1995) Facilitating healthy divorce processes: Therapy and mediation approaches. In A.S. Gurman & N.S. Jacobson (Eds.), *The clinical handbook of couple therapy* (pp. 340–355). New York: Guilford Press.

Whitfield, K.E., Markman, H.J., Stanley, S.M., & Blumberg, S.L. (2001). *Fighting for your African American marriage*. San Francisco: Jossey-Bass.

Whisman, M.A., Dixon, A.E., & Johnson, B. (1997). Therapist's perceptions of couple problems and treatment issues. *Journal of Family Psychology, 11,* 361–366.

Index